Course	Introduction to Leadership Behaviors
Course Number	**LDRS 302**
	Fort Hays State University
	Leadership Studies

http://create.mheducation.com

ISBN-10: 0390163473   ISBN-13: 9780390163479

Contents

Credits

Chapter 10

Groups, Teams, and Their Leadership

Introduction

As we have already presented, leaders need to understand some things about themselves. Their skills, abilities, values, motives, and desires are important considerations in determining their leadership style and preferences. Leaders also need to understand, as much as possible, the same characteristics about their followers. But if you could know characteristics about yourself and characteristics about each of your followers, that would still not be enough. This is because groups and teams are different than solely the skills, abilities, values, and motives of those who comprise them. Groups and teams have their own special characteristics.

While much of the leadership literature today is about the individual who fills the leadership role, it is worthwhile noting that a survey of 35 texts on organizational behavior found that, in each one, the chapter on leadership is in the section on group behavior.[1] This should not be terribly surprising since groups (even as small as two people) are essential if leaders are to impact anything beyond their own behavior. What may be surprising is that the concept of groups is sometimes omitted entirely from books on leadership. The **group perspective** looks at how different group characteristics can affect relationships both with the leader and among the followers.

With *teams* and *teamwork* being the buzzwords of the new millennium, it is worth clarifying the difference between groups and teams, although the difference is mostly one of degree. We will begin the chapter with that clarification. The larger distinction, as noted above, is between the characteristics of groups and the characteristics of individuals. We will spend the first half of the chapter discussing some of these factors unique to groups. Given the high interest in organizational teamwork, the latter portion of this chapter will present a model developed to help leaders

We are born for coopera-tion, as are the feet, the hands, the eyelids, and the upper and lower jaws.
Marcus Aurelius

design, diagnose, and leverage high-impact factors to create the conditions that foster team effectiveness. This chapter will conclude with a section on virtual teams, which are becoming ever more present, if not popular.

Individuals versus Groups versus Teams

As noted previously, there is a significant difference between individual work and group work. But what is the difference between group work and teamwork?

You will learn, in the next section of this chapter, that two identifying characteristics of groups are mutual interaction and reciprocal influence. Members of teams also have mutual interaction and reciprocal influence, but we generally distinguish teams from groups in four other ways. First, team members usually have a stronger sense of identification among themselves than group members do. Often, both team members and outsiders can readily identify who is and who is not on the team (athletic uniforms are one obvious example); identifying members of a group may be more difficult. Second, teams have common goals or tasks; these may range from the development of a new product to an athletic league championship. Group members, on the other hand, may not have the same degree of consensus about goals as team members do. Group members may belong to the group for a variety of personal reasons, and these may clash with the group's stated objectives. (This phenomenon probably happens with teams, too, although perhaps not to the same extent.)

Third, task interdependence typically is greater with teams than with groups. For example, basketball players usually are unable to take a shot unless other team members set picks or pass the ball to them (see Profiles in Leadership 10.1 about Phil Jackson). On the other hand, group members often can contribute to goal accomplishment by working independently; the successful completion of their assigned tasks may not be contingent on other group members. Of course, task interdependence can vary greatly even across teams. Among athletic teams, for example, softball, football, soccer, and hockey teams have a high level of task interdependence, whereas swimming, cross-country, and track teams have substantially lower levels of task interdependence. Fourth, team members often have more differentiated and specialized roles than group members. In the preceding section, we noted that group members often play a variety of roles within the group; however, team members often play a single, or primary, role on a team. Finally, it is important to bear in mind that the distinctions we have been highlighting probably reflect only matters of degree. One might consider teams to be highly specialized groups.

Phil Jackson

PROFILES IN LEADERSHIP 10.1

In the previous section on individual leadership characteristics, it was fairly easy to come up with a leader who typified the particular aspect of leadership we were illustrating. Turns out, it's not quite so easy in this section on teams. If you consider Ginnett's definition of leadership ("The leader's job is to create the conditions for the team to be successful"), then the real team leader might be behind the scenes or, in this case, not even on the court.

Phil Jackson is a basketball coach, but not just any coach. Jackson was the coach of champion Michael Jordan, but ultimately of the championship Chicago Bulls. Certainly, basketball is a team sport and as Michael Jordan and other Bulls found out, having arguably the best player in the sport does not necessarily translate to the best team in the game. In many of the years when Jordan won the individual scoring championship, the Bulls didn't win the championship. Jackson's job as head coach was to transform spectacular individual players into a spectacular team.

Perhaps the best way to get a sense of this challenge and the teamwork Jackson built to win the championship is to extract a few lines from his book, *Sacred Hoops.*

"The most important part of the (coach's) job takes place on the practice floor, not during the game. After a certain point you have to trust the players to translate into action what they've learned in practice. Using a comprehensive system of basketball makes it easier for me to detach myself in that way. Once the players have mastered the system, a powerful group intelligence emerges that is greater than the coach's ideas or those of any individual on the team. When a team reaches that state, the coach can step back and let the game itself "motivate" the players. You don't have to give them any 'win one for the Gipper' pep talks, you just have to turn them loose and let them immerse themselves in the action."

"The sign of a great player was not how much *he* scored, but how much he lifted his teammate's performance."

"You can't beat a good defensive team with one man. It's got to be a team effort."

"It took a long time for Michael to realize he couldn't do it all by himself. Slowly, however, as the team began to master the nuances of the system, he learned that he could trust his teammates to come through in the clutch. It was the beginning of his transformation from a gifted solo artist into a selfless team player."

"What appealed to me about the system was that it empowered everybody on the team by making them more involved in the offense, and demanded that they put their individual needs second to those of the group. This is the struggle every leader faces: how to get members of the team who are driven by the quest for individual glory to give themselves over wholeheartedly to the group effort."

Source: P. Jackson, and H. Delehanty. *Sacred Hoops: Spiritual Lessons of a Hardwood Warrior.* New York. Hyperion, 1995.

The Nature of Groups

Perhaps we should begin by defining what a **group** is. A group can be thought of as "two or more persons who are interacting with one another in such a manner that each person influences and is influenced by each other person."[2] Three aspects of this definition are particularly important to the study of leadership. First, this definition incorporates the concept of reciprocal influence between leaders and followers, an idea considerably different from the one-way nature of influence implicit in the dictionary's definition of followers. Second, group members interact and influence each other. Thus, people waiting at a bus stop would not constitute a group, as there generally is neither interaction nor influence between the various individuals. On the other hand, eight people meeting to plan a school bond election would constitute a group, as there probably would be a high level of mutual interaction among the attendees. Third, the definition does not constrain individuals to only one group. Everyone belongs to a number of different groups; an individual could be a member of various service, production, sports, religious, parent, and volunteer groups simultaneously.

It is important to realize that though people belong to many groups, just as they do to many organizations, groups and organizations are not the same thing (groups, of course, can exist within organizations). Organizations can be so large that most members do not know most of the other people in the organization. In such cases there is relatively little inter-member interaction and reciprocal influence. Similarly, organizations typically are just too large and impersonal to have much effect on anyone's feelings, whereas groups are small and immediate enough to impact both feelings and self-image. People often tend to identify more with the groups they belong to than with the organizations they belong to; they are more psychologically "invested" in their groups. Also, certain important psychological needs (e.g., social contact) are better satisfied by groups than by organizations.

Perhaps an example will clarify the distinction between groups and organizations. Consider a church so large that it may fairly be described as an organization: so large that multiple services must be offered on Sunday mornings; so large that dozens of different study classes are offered each week; so large there are numerous different choirs and musical ensembles. In so large a church, the members hardly could be said to interact with or influence each other except on an occasional basis. Such size often presents both advantages and disadvantages to the membership. On the one hand, it makes possible a rich diversity of activities; on the other hand, such size can make the church itself (i.e., the overall organization) seem relatively impersonal. It may be difficult to identify with a large organization other than in name only (e.g., "I belong to First

Presbyterian Church"). In such cases many people identify more with particular groups within the church than with the church itself; it may be easier to *feel* a part of some smaller group such as the high school choir or a weekly study group.

Although groups play a pervasive role in society, in general people spend very little time thinking about the factors that affect group processes and intragroup relationships. Therefore, the rest of this section will describe some group characteristics that can affect both leaders and followers. Much of the research on groups goes well beyond the scope of this chapter (see Gibbard, Hartman, & Mann, 1978; Shaw, 1981; Hackman, 1990), but six concepts are so basic to the group perspective that they deserve our attention.[2,41] These six concepts are group size, stages of group development, roles, norms, communication, and cohesion. Five of them will be addressed in sections below. The sixth, communication, permeates them all.

Group Size

The size of any group has implications for both leaders and followers. First, leader emergence is partly a function of group size. The greater number of people in a large versus a small group will affect the probability that any individual is likely to emerge as leader. Second, as groups become larger, **cliques** are more likely to develop.[3] Cliques are subgroups of individuals who often share the same goals, values, and expectations. Because cliques generally wield more influence than individual members, they are likely to exert considerable influence—positively or negatively— on the larger group. Leaders need to identify and deal with cliques within their groups, as many intragroup conflicts are the results of cliques having different values, goals, and expectations.

Third, group size also can affect a leader's behavioral style. Leaders with a large **span of control** tend to be more directive, spend less time with individual subordinates, and use more impersonal approaches when influencing followers. Leaders with a small span of control tend to display more consideration and use more personal approaches when influencing followers.[4-7] Fourth, group size also affects group effectiveness. Whereas some researchers have suggested the optimal number of workers for any task is between five and seven,[8,9] it probably is wise to avoid such a simple generalization. The answer to the question of appropriate group size seems to be "just big enough to get the job done." Obviously, the larger the group, the more likely it is that it will involve differentiated skills, values, perceptions, and abilities among its members. Also, there certainly will be more "people power" available to do the work as group size increases.

There are, however, limits to the benefits of size. Consider the question, "If it takes 1 person two minutes to dig a 1-cubic-foot hole, how long will it take 20 people to dig the same size hole?" Actually, it probably will take

A committee is an animal with four back legs.
Jean le Carre

the larger group considerably *longer,* especially if they all participate at the same time. Beyond the purely physical limitations of certain tasks, there also may be decreasing returns (on a per capita basis) as group size increases. This is true even when the efforts of all group members are combined on what is called an **additive task.** An additive task is one where the group's output simply involves the combination of individual outputs.[10] Such a case may be illustrated by the number of individuals needed to push a stalled truck from an intersection. One individual probably would not be enough—maybe not even two or three. At some point, though, as group size increases in this additive task, there will be enough combined force to move the truck. However, as the group size increases beyond that needed to move the truck, the individual contribution of each member will appear to decrease. Steiner[11] suggested this may be due to **process loss** resulting from factors such as some members not pushing in the right direction. Process losses can be thought of as the inefficiencies created by more and more people working together.

Group size can affect group effectiveness in a number of other ways. As group size increases, the diminishing returns of larger work groups may be due to **social loafing.**[12] Social loafing refers to the phenomenon of reduced effort by people when they are not individually accountable for their work. Experiments across different sorts of tasks have tended to demonstrate greater effort when every individual's work is monitored than when many individuals' outputs are anonymously pooled into a collective product. Recent evidence, however, suggests the process may be considerably more complicated than initially thought.[13] The performance decrement may be affected more by the level of task complexity or the reward structure (e.g., cooperative versus competitive) than by outcome attribution.

Sometimes, working in the presence of others may actually increase effort or productivity through a phenomenon called **social facilitation.** Social facilitation was first documented in classic experiments at the Hawthorne plant of the Western Electric Company (see Highlight 10.1). However, social facilitation is not limited to research situations. It refers to any time people increase their level of work due to the presence of others. Typically this occurs when the presence of others increases individual accountability for work, in contrast to other occasions when being in a group reinforces individual anonymity and social loafing.[14]

Developmental Stages of Groups

Just as children go through different stages of development, so do groups. Tuckman's[15] review of over 60 studies involving leaderless training, experimental, or therapeutic groups revealed that groups generally went through four distinct stages of development. The first stage, **forming,** was characterized by polite conversation, the gathering of superficial information about fellow members, and low trust. The group's rejection of emerging potential leaders with negative characteristics also took place during the forming

Social Facilitation and the Hawthorne Effect

HIGHLIGHT 10.1

Social facilitation was first documented in experiments conducted at the Hawthorne plant of the Western Electric Company during the late 1920s and early 1930s. These classic studies were originally designed to evaluate the impact of different work environments.[17,18] Among other things, researchers varied the levels of illumination in areas where workers were assembling electrical components and found production increased when lighting was increased.

When lighting was subsequently decreased, however, production again increased. Faced with these rather confusing data, the researchers turned their attention from physical aspects of the work environment to its social aspects. As it turns out, one reason workers' production increased was simply because someone else (in this case, the researchers) had paid attention to them. The term *Hawthorne effect* is still used today to describe an artificial change in behavior due merely to the fact a person or group is being studied.

stage. The second stage, **storming,** usually was marked by intragroup conflict, heightened emotional levels, and status differentiation as remaining contenders struggled to build alliances and fulfill the group's leadership role. The clear emergence of a leader and the development of group norms and cohesiveness were the key indicators of the **norming** stage of group development. Finally, groups reached the **performing** stage when group members played functional, interdependent roles that were focused on the performance of group tasks.

The four stages of group development identified by Tuckman[16] are important for several reasons. First, people are in many more leaderless groups than they may realize. For example, many sports teams, committees, work groups, and clubs start out as leaderless teams. Team or club captains or committee spokespersons are likely to be the emergent leaders from their respective groups. On a larger scale, perhaps even many elected officials initially began their political careers as the emergent leaders of their cliques or groups, and were then able to convince the majority of the remaining members in their constituencies of their viability as candidates.

Another reason it is important to understand stages of group development is the potential relationships between leadership behaviors and group cohesiveness and productivity. Some experts have maintained that leaders need to focus on consideration or group maintenance behaviors during the norming stage to improve group cohesiveness, and on task behaviors during the performing stage in order to improve group productivity.[19,20] They also have suggested that leaders who reverse these behaviors during the norming and performing stages tend to have less cohesive and less productive groups. Thus, being able to recognize stages of group development may enhance the likelihood that one will emerge as a leader as well as increase the cohesiveness and productivity of the group being led.

If you start yelling and becoming obtrusive and beboppin' around, you give the impression of insecurity, and that becomes infectious. It bleeds down into the actors, and they become nervous; then it bleeds down into the crew, and they become nervous, and you don't get much accomplished that way. You have to set a tone and just demand a certain amount of tranquility.

Clint Eastwood, on being a film director

While Tuckman's model is widely known if for no other reason than its components rhyme with each other, it is not without criticism. Recall that the subjects for Tuckman's research were training, experimental, or therapy groups. None of these particularly represent teams forming to do work in an organizational context. For example, Ginnett observed many surgical teams and never once saw them engage in storming behaviors as they formed. You wouldn't want to be the patient if there was a formation argument between the surgeon, the anesthesiologist, and the scrub nurse about who was going to get to use the scalpel today.

Gersick[21] proposed a better model for teams in organizational settings. In studying **project teams,** she found that teams don't necessarily jump right in and get to work. Rather, they spend most of the first half of the team's life muddling through various ideas and strategies. Then, about midway into the project, the team seems to experience the equivalent of a midlife crisis where there is a flurry of activity and a reexamination of the strategy to see if it will allow them to complete their work. Gersick labeled this process **punctuated equilibrium,** which is obviously quite different from Tuckman's four-stage model.

Group Roles

Group roles are the sets of expected behaviors associated with particular jobs or positions. Most people have multiple roles stemming from the various groups with which they are associated. In addition, it is not uncommon for someone to occupy numerous roles within the same group as situations change. Ginnett[22] found that members of airline crews have varying roles over the course of a day. Although some behaviors were universally associated with certain roles, effective team members on these airline crews generally were more flexible in changing their behavior as other role demands changed. For example, whereas the captain of an airplane is responsible for the overall operation and decision making during a flight, flight attendants often take over responsibility for planning and carrying out the crew's social activities in the evening (i.e., when the flight is over). One captain in the study, however, continued to make *all* the crew's decisions, including their evening social plans; he was inflexible with regard to the role of decision maker. Not coincidentally, he was seen as a less-effective leader—even during the actual flights—than more flexible captains.

Some roles, like positions on athletic teams, have meaning only in relatively specific contexts. Generally speaking, for example, one only plays a lineman's role during football games (admittedly, one might argue that at many schools being an intercollegiate athlete is a role that extends to aspects of student life outside sports). Other roles are more general in nature, including certain common ones that play a part in making any group work—or not work—well. Highlight 10.2 presents a vivid example of how powerful roles can be as determinants of behavior.

The Stanford Prison Experiment

HIGHLIGHT 10.2

A fascinating demonstration of the power of roles occurred when social psychologist Philip Zimbardo and his colleagues[24] created a simulated prison environment at Stanford University. From a larger group of volunteers, two dozen male college students were randomly assigned to be either "prisoners" or "guards." The simulation was quite realistic, with actual cells constructed in the basement of one of the university buildings. The guards wore uniforms, and carried nightsticks and whistles; their eyes were covered by sunglasses. The prisoners were "arrested" at their homes by police cars replete with blazing sirens. They were handcuffed, frisked, blindfolded, and brought to the "jail." They were fingerprinted, given prisoner outfits, and assigned numbers by which they would henceforth be addressed.

It did not take long for the students' normal behavior to be overcome by the roles they were playing. The guards became more and more abusive with their power. They held prisoners accountable for strict adherence to arbitrary rules of prison life (which the guards themselves created), and seemed to enjoy punishing them for even minor infractions. They increasingly seemed to think of the prisoners—truly just other college students—as bad people. The emotional stress on the prisoners became profound, and just six days into the two-week episode the experiment was halted. This unexpected outcome basically occurred because participants' roles had become their reality. They were not just students role-playing guards and prisoners; to a disconcerting degree they became guards and prisoners.

What should people conclude from the Stanford prison study? At an abstract level, the study dramatically points out how behavior is partly determined by social role. Additionally, it is clear how just being in the role of leader, especially to the extent it is attended by tangible and symbolic manifestations of power, can affect how leaders think and act toward followers. Still another lesson people might draw involves remembering the volunteers all had many different roles in life than those assigned to them in the study, though being a guard or a prisoner was certainly the salient one for a period of time. Whereas everyone has many roles, the salience of one or another often depends on the situation, and a person's behavior changes as his or her role changes in a group.

Source: P. Zimbardo, C. Haney, W. Banks, and D. Jaffe, "The Mind Is a Formidable Jailer: A Pirandellian Prison." *New York Times Magazine,* April 8, 1973, pp. 38–60.

In Chapter 8, leader behavior was characterized initially in terms of two broad functions. One deals with getting the task done (**task role**), and the other with supporting relationships within the work group (**relationship role**). Similarly, roles in groups can be categorized in terms of task and relationship functions (see Highlight 10.3). Many of the roles in Highlight 10.3 are appropriate for followers, not just the official group leader; all of these different roles are part of the leadership process and all contribute to a group's overall effectiveness. Moreover, it is important to recognize that the very distinction between task and relationship roles is somewhat arbitrary. It is sensible enough when looking at the short-term impact of any given behavior, but in another sense relationship roles are task roles. After all, task-oriented behavior may be adequate for accomplishing short-term objectives, but an appropriately cohesive and supportive group increases the potential for long-term effectiveness at future

Task and Relationship Roles in Groups

HIGHLIGHT 10.3

Task Roles

Initiating: Defining the problem, suggesting activities, assigning tasks.

Information Seeking: Asking questions, seeking relevant data or views.

Information Sharing: Providing data, offering opinions.

Summarizing: Reviewing and integrating others' points, checking for common understanding and readiness for action.

Evaluating: Assessing validity of assumptions, quality of information, reasonableness of recommendations.

Guiding: Keeping group on track.

Relationship Roles

Harmonizing: Resolving interpersonal conflicts, reducing tension.

Encouraging: Supporting and praising others, showing appreciation for others' contributions, being warm and friendly.

Gatekeeping: Assuring even participation by all group members, making sure that everyone has a chance to be heard and that no individual dominates.

Source: Adapted from K. D. Benne and P. Sheats, "Functional Roles of Group Members." *Journal of Social Issues* 4 (1948), pp. 41–49.

Dysfunctional Roles

HIGHLIGHT 10.4

Dominating: Monopolizing group time, forcing views on others.

Blocking: Stubbornly obstructing and impeding group work, persistent negativism.

Attacking: Belittling others, creating a hostile or intimidating environment.

Distracting: Engaging in irrelevant behaviors, distracting others' attention.

Source: Adapted from K. D. Benne and P. Sheats, "Functional Roles of Group Members." *Journal of Social Issues* 4 (1948), pp. 41–49.

tasks as well as present tasks. Although the roles in Highlight 10.3 generally contribute to a group's overall effectiveness, several types of problems can occur with group roles that can impede group performance. One type of role problem concerns the **dysfunctional roles,** listed in Highlight 10.4. The common denominator among these roles is how the person's behavior primarily serves selfish or egocentric purposes rather than group purposes.

Another role problem is **role conflict.** Role conflict involves receiving contradictory messages about expected behavior and can in turn adversely affect a person's emotional well-being and performance.[23]

Role conflict can occur in several different ways. Perhaps most common is receiving inconsistent signals about expected behavior from the same person. When the same person sends mixed signals, it is called **intrasender role conflict** ("I need this report back in five minutes, and it had better be perfect"). **Intersender role conflict** occurs when someone receives inconsistent signals from several others about expected behavior. Still another kind of role conflict is based on inconsistencies between different roles a person may have. Professional and family demands, for example, often create role conflicts. **Interrole conflict** occurs when someone is unable to perform all of his roles as well as he would like. A final type occurs when role expectations violate a person's values. This is known as **person–role conflict.**

An example of person–role conflict might be when a store manager encourages a salesperson to mislead customers about the quality of the store's products when this behavior is inconsistent with the salesperson's values and beliefs.

A different sort of role problem is called **role ambiguity.** In role conflict, one receives clear messages about expectations, but the messages are not all congruent. With role ambiguity, the problem is lack of clarity about just what the expectations are.[25,26] There may have been no role expectations established at all, or they may not have been clearly communicated. A person is experiencing role ambiguity if she wonders, "Just what am I supposed to be doing?" It is important for leaders to be able to minimize the degree to which dysfunctional roles, role conflict, and role ambiguity occur in their groups, as these problems have been found to have a negative impact on organizational commitment, job involvement, absenteeism, and satisfaction with co-workers and supervisors.[27]

Group Norms

Norms are the informal rules groups adopt to regulate and regularize group members' behaviors. Although norms are only infrequently written down (see Highlight 10.5) or openly discussed, they nonetheless often have a powerful and consistent influence on behavior.[28] That is because most people are rather good at reading the social cues that inform them about existing norms. For example, most people easily discern the dress code in any new work environment without needing written guidance. People also are apt to notice when a norm is violated, even though they may have been unable to articulate the norm before its violation was apparent. For example, most students have expectations (norms) about creating extra work for other students. Imagine the reaction if a student in some class complained that not enough reading was being assigned each lesson or that the minimum length requirements for the term paper needed to be substantially raised.

Norms do not govern all behaviors, just those a group feels are important. Norms are more likely to be seen as important and apt to be

Putting It In Writing[29]

Rick Reilly

HIGHLIGHT 10.5

Why are sports' unwritten rules unwritten? Get a Xerox machine under these puppies and have a copy on everybody's desk in the morning

After we gave up a touchdown in our first Touch Football/Pulled Groinathon of the year, the guys on the other team sneered and said, "Suckers walk."

"Says who?" asked our left tackle, Cementhead.

"It's an unwritten rule," explained the other side's captain. "Oh, yeah?" said Cementhead. "Show me where." Which is exactly my point. Why are sport's unwritten rules unwritten? Get a Xerox machine under these puppies and have a copy on everybody's desk in the morning.

The coach always sits in the first row on the team bus. If he is out sick or dead, the seat remains empty.

Apologize for a point won on a net cord.

Take two or three pitches if your pitcher just made the second out of the inning.

Never, ever put your finger in someone else's bowling ball.

The starting goalie is always the first player on the ice.

If a line judge makes a bad call in your favor, purposely double-fault the next point.

A manager never drinks at the same bar as his players.

Never knock in the tying run in the ninth inning of an exhibition game. Far better to lose than go extra innings in spring training.

No NBA player attempting a layup in the fourth quarter of a tight game should go unfouled.

In a losing clubhouse you must act as if there has been a death in the family.

Hand the manager the ball when he comes to the mound to take you out.

Never shoot the puck into the net after a whistle blows.

Do not talk to or sit near a pitcher with a no-hitter going. And never bunt to break one up.

A first base coach never stands in the first base coaching box.

Never blow your nose before a fight. (It makes the eyes swell easier later on.)

Stand as far away as possible from a skeet shooter with a perfect score going.

Never walk on a player's putting line, including the two feet on the other side of the cup.

Always clear the inside lane for faster runners.

Never stand behind the pool table pocket your opponent is shooting for.

Never let the interviewee hold the mike.

A catcher may complain to the ump all he wants about balls and strikes, as long as he doesn't turn around and do it face-to-face.

Never hit the quarterback during practice.

Never start the 100 meters in a decathlon into a wind. Trade false starts until the breeze is favorable.

When a soccer player is hurt, the opponents must kick the ball out of play.

Except for Rocky Marciano, the challenger always enters the ring first—and always will.

Throw a handful of salt into the air before your sumo wrestling match begins.

It's true: Suckers walk.

The bus may be delayed by superstars only.

When the coach finally wraps up a long meeting with "Any questions?" nobody better ask one.

Rookies shag balls, whether they are millionaires or not.

Never shoot high on the goalie during warmups.

The back nine is always pressed.

You must admit it when you hit a forehand on the second bounce.

On the playground, offense calls the fouls.

Never write down the score of a bowler who is on a run of strikes.

continued

Continued

Never admit you trapped the ball while trying to make a catch.

No overhead smashes at women in mixed doubles.

The caddie of the last player to putt plants the flag.

NBA refs will take some trash from head coaches but not a word from an assistant.

Never steal with a five-run lead after the seventh inning.

You must alter your course to help a boat in distress.

Boxers never blink during a ref's prefight instructions.

When a receiver drops a pass, go back to him on the next play.

Card games are played in the back of the plane.

Scrubs stand during NBA timeouts.

Winners buy.

Got it, Cementhead?

enforced if they (*a*) facilitate group survival; (*b*) simplify, or make more predictable, what behavior is expected of group members; (*c*) help the group avoid embarrassing interpersonal problems; or (*d*) express the central values of the group and clarify what is distinctive about the group's identity.[30]

The norms that group members import, such as those listed above, are essentially inward looking. They help the team take care of itself and avoid embarrassing situations caused by inappropriate member behaviors. Hackman[31] recommends that the leader has a responsibility to focus the team outwardly to enhance performance. Specifically, he suggests two core norms be created to enhance performance:

1. Group members should actively scan the environment for opportunities that would require a change in operating strategy to capitalize upon them, and

2. The team should identify the few number of behaviors which team members must always do and those which they should never do to conform to the organization's objectives.

By actively implementing these two norms, the team is forced to examine not only its organizational context but the much larger industry and environmental shells in which it operates. One irony about norms is that an outsider to a group often is able to learn more about norms than an insider. An outsider, not necessarily subject to the norms himself, is more apt to notice them. In fact, the more "foreign" an observer is, the more likely it is the norms will be perceived. If a man is accustomed to wearing a tie to work, he is less likely to notice that men in another organization also wear ties to work, but is *more* likely to note that the men in a third organization typically wear sweaters and sweatshirts around the office.

Group Cohesion

Group cohesion is the glue that keeps a group together. It is the sum of forces that attracts members to a group, provides resistance to leaving it, and motivates them to be active in it. Highly cohesive groups interact with and influence each other more than do less cohesive groups. Furthermore, a highly cohesive group may have lower absenteeism and lower turnover than a less cohesive group, and low absenteeism and turnover often contribute to higher group performance; higher performance can, in turn, contribute to even higher cohesion, thus resulting in an increasingly positive spiral.

However, greater cohesiveness does not always lead to higher performance. A highly cohesive but unskilled team is still an unskilled team, and such teams will often lose to a less cohesive but more skilled one. Additionally, a highly cohesive group may sometimes develop goals that are contrary to the larger organization's goals. For example, members of a highly cohesive research team at a particular college committed themselves to working on a problem that seemed inherently interesting to them. Their nearly zealous commitment to the project, however, effectively kept them from asking, or even allowing others to ask, if the research aligned itself well with the college's stated objectives. Their quite narrow and basic research effort deviated significantly from the college's expressed commitment to emphasize applied research. As a result, the college lost some substantial outside financial support.

Other problems also can occur in highly cohesive groups. Researchers[32,33] have found that some groups can become so cohesive they erect what amount to fences or boundaries between themselves and others. Such **overbounding** can block the use of outside resources that could make them more effective. Competitive product development teams can become so overbounded (often rationalized by security concerns or inordinate fears of "idea thieves") that they will not ask for help from willing and able staff within their own organizations.

One example of this problem was the failed mission to rescue U.S. embassy personnel held hostage in Iran during the Carter presidency. The rescue itself was a rather complicated mission involving many different sorts of U.S. military forces. Some of these forces included sea-based helicopters. The helicopters and their crews were carried on regular naval vessels, though most sailors on the vessels knew nothing of the secret mission. Senior personnel were so concerned that some sailor might leak information, and thus compromise the mission's secrecy, that maintenance crews aboard the ships were not directed to perform increased levels of maintenance on the helicopters immediately before the critical mission. Even if a helicopter was scheduled for significant maintenance within the next 50 hours of flight time (which would be exceeded in the rescue mission), crews were not told to perform the maintenance. According to knowledgeable sources, this practice did impact the performance of at least one of the failed helicopters, and thus the overall mission.

Symptoms of Groupthink

HIGHLIGHT 10.6

An illusion of invulnerability, which leads to unwarranted optimism and excessive risk taking by the group.

Unquestioned assumption of the group's morality and therefore an absence of reflection on the ethical consequences of group action.

Collective rationalization to discount negative information or warnings.

Stereotypes of the opposition as evil, weak, or stupid.

Self-censorship by group members from expressing ideas that deviate from the group consensus due to doubts about their validity or importance.

An illusion of unanimity such that greater consensus is perceived than really exists.

Direct pressure on dissenting members, which reinforces the norm that disagreement represents disloyalty to the group.

Mindguards, who protect the group from adverse information.

Source: Adapted from I. L. Janis, *Groupthink,* 2nd ed. Boston: Houghton Mifflin, 1982.

Janis[34] discovered still another disadvantage of highly cohesive groups. He found that people in a highly cohesive group often become more concerned with striving for unanimity than in objectively appraising different courses of action. Janis labeled this phenomenon **groupthink** and believed it accounted for a number of historic fiascoes, including Pearl Harbor and the Bay of Pigs invasion. It may have played a role in the *Challenger* disaster, and it also occurs in other cohesive groups ranging from business meetings to air crews, and from therapy groups to school boards.

What is groupthink? Cohesive groups tend to evolve strong informal norms to preserve friendly internal relations. Preserving a comfortable, harmonious group environment becomes a hidden agenda that tends to suppress dissent, conflict, and critical thinking. Unwise decisions may result when concurrence seeking among members overrides their willingness to express or tolerate deviant points of view and think critically. Janis[35] identified a number of symptoms of groupthink, which can be found in Highlight 10.6.

A policy-making or decision-making group displaying most of the symptoms in Highlight 10.6 runs a big risk of being ineffective. It may do a poor job of clarifying objectives, searching for relevant information, evaluating alternatives, assessing risks, and anticipating the need for contingency plans. Janis[36] offered the following suggestions as ways of reducing groupthink and thus of improving the quality of a group's input to policies or decisions. First, leaders should encourage all group members to take on the role of critical evaluator. Everyone in the group needs to appreciate the importance of airing doubts and objections. This includes the leader's willingness to listen to criticisms of his or her own ideas. Second, leaders should create a climate of open inquiry through their own impartiality and objectivity. At the outset, leaders should refrain from stating personal preferences or expectations, which may bias group discussion. Third, the risk of group-think can be reduced if independent groups are established to make rec-ommendations on the same issue. Fourth, at least one member of the group should be assigned the role of devil's advocate, an assignment that should rotate from meeting to meeting.

One final problem with highly cohesive groups may be what Shephard[37] has called **ollieism.** Ollieism, a variation of groupthink, occurs when illegal actions are taken by overly zealous and loyal subordinates who believe that what they are doing will please their leaders. It derives its name from the actions of Lieutenant-Colonel Oliver North, who among other things admitted he lied to the U.S. Congress about his actions while working on the White House staff during the Iran-Contra affair. Shephard cited the slaying of Thomas à Becket by four of Henry II's knights and the Watergate break-in as other prime examples of ollieism. We will probably see similar examples in the Enron trials. Ollieism dif-fers from groupthink in that the subordinates' illegal actions usually occur without the explicit knowledge or consent of the leader. Never-theless, Shephard pointed out that, although the examples cited of ollieism were not officially sanctioned, the responsibility for them still falls squarely on the leader. It is the leader's responsibility to create an ethical climate within the group, and leaders who create highly cohe-sive yet unethical groups must bear the responsibility for the group's actions.

After reading about the uncertain relationships between group cohe-sion and performance, and the problems with overbounding, groupthink, and ollieism, one might think that cohesiveness should be something to avoid. Nothing, however, could be further from the truth. First of all, problems with overly cohesive groups occur relatively infrequently and, in general, leaders will be better off thinking of ways to create and main-tain highly cohesive teams than not developing these teams out of con-cern for potential groupthink or overbounding situations. Second, perhaps the biggest argument for developing cohesive groups is to con-sider the alternative—groups with little or no cohesiveness. In the latter groups, followers would generally be dissatisfied with each other and the leader, commitment to accomplishing group and organizational goals may be reduced, intragroup communication may occur less frequently, and interdependent task performance may suffer.[38] Because of the prob-lems associated with groups having low cohesiveness, leadership practi-tioners need to realize that developing functionally cohesive work groups is a goal they all should strive for.

In summary, the group perspective provides a complementary level of analysis to the individual perspective presented earlier in this chapter. A follower's behavior may be due to his or her values, traits, or experience (i.e., the individual perspective), or this behavior may be due to the fol-lowers' roles, the group norms, the group's stage of development, or the group's level of cohesiveness (i.e., the group perspective). Thus, the group perspective can also provide both leaders and followers with a number of explanations of why individuals in groups behave in certain ways. Moreover, the six group characteristics just described can give leaders and followers ideas about (*a*) factors that may be affecting their ability to influence other group members and (*b*) what to do to improve their level of influence in the group.

Teams

With so much attention devoted to teams and teamwork in today's organizations, it is appropriate to spend a fair amount of time examining teams and the factors that impact their effectiveness. After considering some differential measures of team effectiveness, we will look at a comprehensive model of team leadership.

Effective Team Characteristics and Team Building

And yes, teams do vary in their effectiveness. Virtually identical teams can be dramatically different in terms of success or failure (see Highlight 10.7). We must ask, therefore, what makes one team successful and another unsuccessful? Although this is an area only recently studied, exploratory work at the Center for Creative Leadership has tentatively identified several key characteristics for effective team performance (see Highlight 10.8 for an astronaut's perspective on teamwork).

Examples of Effective and Ineffective Teams

HIGHLIGHT 10.7

Most people can readily think up a number of examples of ineffective and effective teamwork. Consider the relative effectiveness of the teams depicted in the following two true stories:

Ineffective Teamwork: After an airline flight crew failed to get a "nose gear down and locked" indicator light to come on while making a landing approach into Miami, all three crew members became involved in trying to change the burned-out indicator bulb in the cockpit. Nobody was flying the airplane and none of them were monitoring the flight of the L-1011 as it descended into the Everglades and crashed.

Effective Teamwork: The crew of a DC-10, after having lost all capability to control the airplane through flight controls as a result of an engine explosion, realized they needed all the help they could get. Captain Al Haynes discovered another experienced captain was traveling in the passenger cabin and invited him to come up to the cabin to help the regular crew out. Miraculously, their combined abilities enabled the crew—using techniques developed on the spot—to control the plane to within a few feet of the ground. Even though there were fatalities, over 100 people survived a nearly hopeless situation.

Women in Leadership: Teamwork from an Astronaut's Perspective

HIGHLIGHT 10.8

Dr. Bonnie J. Dunbar is an American astronaut. She has flown on four space shuttle missions. We asked her to share a few personal reflections about the meaning of teamwork and followership to her as she was growing up, as well as presently in her role in the space program. She wrote this during preparation for her flight in June 1992. She was payload commander for that space shuttle mission.

Above all, the success of a space flight depends upon teamwork: within the crew and between the ground controllers and the crew. Teamwork is a valued attribute among currently selected astronauts.

I was very fortunate as a young girl to have been exposed to that concept by my family. With four children and a multitude of chores to be performed, my mother and father impressed upon us our responsibilities within the family unit. Success of the farm (and our future) depended upon our contribution. As the oldest, I was expected to participate in all chores, including driving the tractor and "round-up" by horseback. There were no distinctions in these responsibilities between my brothers and me. Group experiences within the 4-H organization (showing steers, etc.) and playing on baseball, volleyball, and basketball teams reinforced the pride of sharing success together and consoling each other in defeat.

When I attended college, some of that team experience was missed. By virtue of my gender, I was considered an unwelcome minority by many in the engineering college. Therefore, I was never invited to the study groups or participated in group solution of the homework problems. Still, I found an outlet in group activities by belonging to Angel Flight (co-ed auxiliary to Air Force ROTC—I was elected Commander of 50 my junior year) and by continuing to play co-ed baseball. Ironically, my engineering classmates needed my athletic ability as first baseman on the playing field.

I was also supported by three very important individuals during this time: my father, my mother, and the chairman of the Ceramic Engineering Department, Dr. James I. Mueller. My parents always encouraged me to pursue my "dreams" and to be the best person I could be. The fact that I was the first in the family to attend college was a source of pride for them. That I subscribed to their principles of hard work, human compassion, and honesty was probably a source of greater pride. They were proud of my selection as an astronaut but my father was more concerned that I not forget how to get manure on my boots.

In my professional life, the closest I have come to real group esprit de corps has come through my association with the Astronaut Office. Perhaps it was due to the concept of "class training," or the similarity of individuals involved, but I consider those I work with as also my closest friends. Our successes are really those of a family team that extends out to the engineers, managers, and administrative support in the Space Shuttle program.

I am now on my third NASA Space Shuttle crew. As Payload Commander I have tried to convey to the noncareer payload specialists on my next flight the importance of being part of the crew . . . that we will share both the successes and the failures of the flight. It has been an interesting experience to assess others' ability to become "part of the team." I have seen what not being part of the team can do, and in a flight environment that can be highly risky. Not being a team member does more than cause internal friction within the crew; it can be hazardous.

So, what does being "part of the team" mean? It doesn't always mean being the smartest or the fastest. It does mean recognizing the big picture goal and the contribution that each individual brings to the whole. It may not mean being the life of the party, but it does mean being able to get along with people and to tread a fine line . . . knowing when to compromise and knowing when to stand firm. And, in an organization such as ours with competitive individuals used to being on top of the hill, it means knowing when to be a Chief and when to be an Indian. In the Astronaut Office, mission specialists rotate through technical jobs and different responsibilities during flights. Sometimes they are Indians instead of Chiefs. Those that perform best and appear to be well-regarded can do each equally well.

He that would be a leader must be a bridge.
Welsh proverb

The Center for Creative Leadership's research with teams indicated that successful and unsuccessful teams could be differentiated on the basis of eight key characteristics, the first six of which are primarily concerned with task accomplishment.[39] First, effective teams had a *clear mission* and *high performance standards.* Everyone on the team knew what the team was trying to achieve and how well he or she had to perform in order to achieve the team's mission. Second, leaders of successful teams often *took stock* of their equipment, training facilities and opportunities, and outside resources available to help the team. Leaders of effective teams spent a considerable amount of time *assessing the technical skills* of the team members. After taking stock of available resources and skills, good leaders would work to *secure those resources and equipment* necessary for team effectiveness. Moreover, leaders of effective teams would spend a considerable amount of time *planning* and *organizing* in order to make optimal use of available resources, to select new members with needed technical skills, or to improve needed technical skills of existing members.

The last two characteristics of effective teams were concerned with the group maintenance or interpersonal aspects of teams. Hallam and Campbell's[40] research indicated that *high levels of communication* were often associated with effective teams. These authors believed this level of communication helped team members to stay focused on the mission and to take better advantage of the skills, knowledge, and resources available to the team. High levels of communication also helped to *minimize interpersonal conflicts* on the team, which often drained energy needed for team success and effectiveness. The characteristics of effective teams identified in this research provide leadership practitioners with a number of ideas about how they may be able to increase the effectiveness of their work units or teams.

A different avenue to group and team effectiveness has been to use a normative approach. One example of this technique is described in *Groups That Work (and Those That Don't).*[41] Ginnett[42,43] has developed an expanded model focusing specifically on team leadership, which we will examine in more detail later in this chapter. For now, our concern is with one of the three major leadership functions in Ginnett's model that focuses on team design. The model suggests four components of design of the team itself that help the team get off to a good start, whatever its task. This is important because it is not uncommon to find that a team's failure can be traced to its being set up inappropriately from the very beginning. If a team is to work effectively, the following four variables need to be in place from the beginning.

1. *Task structure:* Does the team know what its task is? Is the task reasonably unambiguous and consistent with the mission of the team? Does the team have a meaningful piece of work, sufficient autonomy to perform it, and access to knowledge of its results?

2. *Group boundaries:* Is the collective membership of the team appropriate for the task to be performed? Are there too few or too many members? Do the members collectively have sufficient knowledge and skills to

perform the work? In addition to task skills, does the team have sufficient maturity and interpersonal skills to be able to work together and resolve conflicts? Is there an appropriate amount of diversity on the team (e.g., members are not so similar that they do not have differing perspectives and experiences, and yet not so diverse that they cannot communicate or relate to one another)?

3. *Norms:* Does the team share an appropriate set of norms for working as a team? Norms can be acquired by the team in three ways: (*a*) They can be imported from the organization existing outside the team, (*b*) they can be instituted and reinforced by the leader or leaders of the team, or (*c*) they can be developed by the team itself as the situation demands. If the team is to have a strategy that works over time, then it must ensure that conflicting norms do not confuse team members. It also needs to regularly scan and review prevailing norms to ensure they support overall objectives.

4. *Authority:* Has the leader established a climate where her authority can be used in a flexible rather than a rigid manner? Has she, at one end of the authority continuum, established sufficient competence to allow the group to comply when conditions demand (such as in emergencies)? Has she also established a climate such that any member of the team feels empowered to provide expert assistance when appropriate? Do team members feel comfortable in questioning the leader on decisions where there are no clear right answers? In short, have conditions been created where authority can shift to appropriately match the demands of the situation?

Many of these team design components may be imported from preexisting conditions in the organization within which the team is forming, from the industry in which the organization operates, or even from the environment in which the industry exists. To help team leaders consider these various levels, Hackman and Ginnett[44,45] developed the concept of **organizational shells** (see Figure 10.1). Notice that the four critical factors for team design (task, boundary, norms, and authority) are necessary for the group to work effectively. In some cases, all the information about one of these critical factors may be input from the industry or organizational shell level. In these cases, the leader need do little else but affirm that condition. In other cases, there may be too little (or even inappropriate) input from the organizational level to allow the team to work effectively. In these cases, the leader needs to modify the factors for team design. Ideally this is done during the formation process—the final shell before the team actually begins work.

These ideas may require a new way of thinking about the relationship between a leader and followers. In many organizational settings, leaders are assigned. Sometimes, however, the people who create conditions for

(のトの)

(タトの)

FIGURE 10.1 Organizational shells.

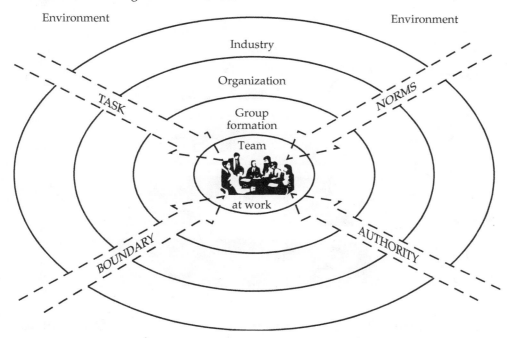

improved group effectiveness are not the designated leaders at all; they may emerge from the ranks of followers. This model has been used to differentiate between effective and ineffective "self-managing work groups"—teams where the followers and leaders were the same people. Moreover, because the model is prescriptive, it also provides a number of suggestions about what ineffective work groups can do to be successful. That same purpose underlies the following model as well.

Ginnett's Team Leadership Model

Since we have emphasized that leadership is a group or team function and have suggested that one measure of leadership effectiveness may be whether the team achieves its objectives, it is reasonable to examine a model specifically designed to help teams perform more effectively: the **Team Leadership Model,** or **TLM**[46–48] (shortened from earlier versions when it was referred to as the Team Effectiveness Leadership Model). Another way to think of this model is as a mechanism to first identify what a team needs to be effective, and then to point the leader either toward the roadblocks that are hindering the team or toward ways to make the team even more effective than it already is. This approach is similar to McGrath's[49] description of leadership, which suggested that the

FIGURE 10.2
Systems Theory
Applied to Teams.

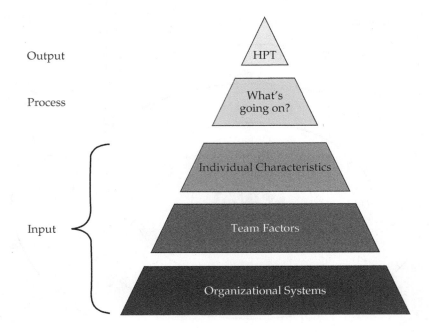

Output

Process

Input

HPT

What's
going on?

Individual Characteristics

Team Factors

Organizational Systems

leader's main job is to determine what needs the team is faced with and then take care of them. This approach also will require us to think about leadership not as a function of the leader and his or her characteristics but as a function of the team. As the title of the model suggests, team effectiveness is the underlying driver.

We have mentioned this model of group or team effectiveness briefly before, but now we will explore it in greater detail. The original model for examining the "engine of a group" was developed by Richard Hackman and has been the basis for much research on groups and teams over the last 30 years.[50] The model presented here includes major modifications by Ginnett and represents an example of a leadership model that has been developed primarily using field research. While there have been controlled experimental studies validating portions of the model,[51] the principal development and validation have been completed using actual high-performance teams operating in their own situational context. Examples of the teams studied in this process include commercial and military air crews in actual line flying operations, surgical teams in operating suites, executive teams, product development and manufacturing teams, and teams preparing the Space Shuttle fleet for launch. A complete illustration of the model will be shown later. Because of its complexity, it is easier to understand by starting with a few simpler illustrations.

At the most basic level, this model (see Figure 10.2) resembles a systems theory approach with inputs at the base (i.e., individual, team, and organizational factors), processes or throughputs in the center (i.e., what one can tell about the team by actually observing team members at work),

FIGURE 10.3

Basic TLM outputs: outcomes of High Performance Teams.

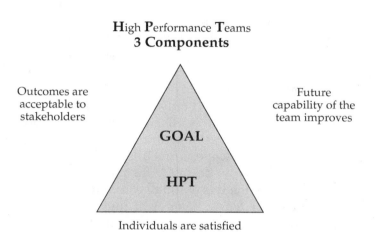

High Performance Teams
3 Components

Outcomes are acceptable to stakeholders

Future capability of the team improves

GOAL

HPT

Individuals are satisfied

and outputs at the top (i.e., how well the team did in accomplishing its objectives, ideally a High Performance Team). We will examine each of these stages. However, we will proceed through the model in reverse order—looking at outputs first, then the process stage, then inputs.

Outputs

What do we mean by outputs? Quite simply, **outputs** (see Figure 10.3) are the results of the team's work. For example, a football team scores 24 points. A production team produces 24 valves in a day. A tank crew hits 24 targets on an artillery range. Such raw data, however, are insufficient for assessing team effectiveness.

How do we know if a team's output is good? How do we know if a team is effective? Even though it was possible for the three different teams mentioned above to measure some aspect of their work, these measurements are not very helpful in determining their effectiveness, either in an absolute sense or in a relative sense. For comparison and research purposes, it is desirable to have some measures of team effectiveness that can be applied across teams and tasks. Hackman[52] argued that a group is effective if (*a*) the team's productive output (goods, services, decisions) meets the standards of quantity, quality, and timeliness of the people who use it; (*b*) the group process that occurs while the group is performing its task enhances the ability of the members to work as members of a team (either the one they were on or any new teams they may be assigned to) in the future; and (*c*) the group experience enhances the growth and personal well-being of the individuals who compose the team.

Process

It should be obvious why leaders should be concerned with the outputs listed in the preceding section. After all, if a team does not "produce" (output), then it could not be considered effective. But what is process?

And why should a leader care about it? Actually, there are several reasons a leader might want to pay attention to the team's process—how the team goes about its work. Some teams may have such a limited number of products that the leader can ill afford to wait until the product is delivered to assess its acceptability to the client. For example, a team whose task is to build one (and only one) satellite to be launched into orbit will have no second chances. There may be no opportunity to correct any problem once the satellite is launched (or, as was the case with the flawed Hubble Space Telescope, correction can be made only after great expense). Therefore, it may be desirable for the leader of such a team to assess his team's work while it is working rather than after the satellite is launched. Other kinds of teams have such high standards for routine work that there simply are not enough critical indicators in the end product to determine effectiveness from outcome measures. As an example of this situation, a team operating a nuclear power plant is surrounded by so many technical backup systems that it may be difficult to determine team effectiveness by looking at "safe operation" as a measurement criterion. But we have evidence that not all teams in nuclear power plants operate equally well (Chernobyl and Three Mile Island are but two examples). It would seem helpful to be able to assess real teams "in process" rather than learn of team problems only following disastrous outcomes. Even leaders of noncritical teams might like to be able to routinely monitor their teams for evidence of effective or ineffective processes. So it turns out that the way teams go about their work can provide some very useful information to the leader.

Since process assessment is so important, let us focus for a moment on the block containing the four process measures of effectiveness in Figure 10.4.

FIGURE 10.4
TLM diagnosis process: diagnose using the process variables.

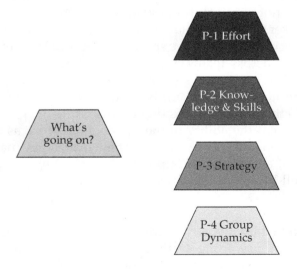

These four **process measures** of effectiveness provide criteria by which we can examine the ways in which teams work. If a team is to perform effectively, it must (*a*) work hard enough, (*b*) have sufficient knowledge and skills within the team to perform the task, (*c*) have an appropriate strategy to accomplish its work (or ways to approach the task at hand), and (*d*) have constructive and positive group dynamics among its members. The phrase *group dynamics* refers to interactions among team members, including such aspects as how they communicate with others, express feelings toward each other, and deal with conflict with each other, to name but a few of the characteristics. Assessing and improving group process is no trivial matter, as has been documented extensively in a comprehensive view of group process and its assessment by Wheelan.[53]

What should the leader do if she discovers a problem with one of these four process measures? Paradoxically, the answer is not to focus her attention on that process per se. While the four process measures are fairly good diagnostic measures for a team's ultimate effectiveness, they are, unfortunately, not particularly good leverage points for fixing the problem. An analogy from medicine would be a doctor who diagnoses the symptoms of an infection (a fever) but who then treats the symptoms rather than attacking the true underlying cause (a nail in the patient's foot). Similarly at the team level, rather than trying to correct a lack of effort being applied to the task at hand (perhaps a motivation problem), the team leader would be better advised to discover the underlying problem and fix that than to assume that a motivational speech to the team will do the job. This is not to imply that teams cannot benefit from process help. It merely suggests that the leader should ensure that there are no design problems (at the input level) that should be fixed first.

Inputs

In a manufacturing plant, **inputs** are the raw materials that are processed into products for sale. Similarly in team situations, inputs are what is available for teams as they go about their work. However, an important difference between an industrial plant and a team is that for a plant, the inputs are physical resources. Often for team design, we are considering psychological factors. There is a variety of levels of inputs, ranging from the individual level to the environmental level. Some of the inputs provide little opportunity for the leader to have an influence—they are merely givens. Leaders are often put in charge of teams with little or no control over the environment, the industry, or even the organizational conditions. There are other inputs, however, that the leader can directly impact to create the conditions for effective teamwork.

Figure 10.2 shows the multiple levels in the input stage of the model. Note that there are input factors at the individual and organizational levels and that these levels both surround and affect the team design level.

Ask not what your country can do for you. Ask what you can do for your country.
John F. Kennedy

Leadership Prescriptions of the Model

Creation

Following McGrath's[54] view of the leader's role (the leader's main job is to identify and help satisfy team needs), and using the TLM, it is possible to identify constructive approaches for the leader to pursue. As described earlier in this chapter, what leaders do depends on where a team is in its development. Ideally, we should build a team like we build a house or an automobile. We should start with a concept, create a design, engineer it to do what we want it to do, and then manufacture it to meet those specifications. The TLM provides the same linear flow for design of a team. The somewhat more complex version of the TLM model is shown in Figure 10.5 and the leader should, as noted above, begin on the left with the Dream, proceed through all of the Design variables and then pay attention to the Development needs of the team. In this way, she can implement the three critical functions for team leadership: **dream, design,** and **development.**

FIGURE 10.5   Three functions of leadership.

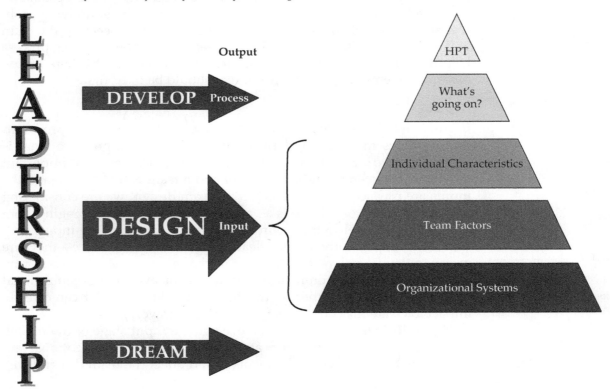

Dream

Obviously, the team needs to have clear vision. In their book *The Wisdom of Teams*[55] Katzenbach and Smith suggested that this may be the most important single step in teamwork. If the team has a challenging and demanding goal, teamwork may be necessary to accomplish the task. In highly effective work teams, the leader ensures that the team has a clear vision of where they are going. The communication of a vision frequently involves metaphorical language so that team members actually "paint their own picture" of where the team is headed.

Design

The importance of the design function of leadership cannot be overstated. Whether in the start-up of a team or in the midstream assignment of leaders, designing the team is critical. It is also often the most frequently omitted step. Managers have long been trained to detect deviations and correct them. But what if the deviations are not detectable until the output stage? At their best, managers often detect deviations at the process stage and attempt to fix them "right where they are seen." Far too often, little time or attention is focused at the input level. Senior-level leaders may resist changing the organizational systems for a number of reasons, including having a vested interest in maintaining the status quo (whatever it is, it has at least let them rise to their current position!). And while individual team leaders may have little control over the organizational context and systems, they always have the opportunity for making an impact in their own team's design.

Development

If the leader finds that the team has a clear sense of direction and vision, and the input variables at the individual, organizational, and team levels are contributing positively to team effectiveness (i.e., the design portion of the leader's job has been taken care of), then she can turn her attention to the development level. Development is the ongoing work done with the team at the process level to continue to find ways to improve an already well-designed team. Given our individualistic culture, we have identified many teams in organizations that are apparently well designed and supported at the input level, but that have had no training or experience in the concept of teamwork. There are times when effective teamwork is based on very different concepts than effective individual work. For example, for a team to do well, the individuals composing the team must sometimes not maximize their individual effort. Referred to as subsystem nonoptimization, this concept is at first not intuitively obvious to many newly assigned team members. Nevertheless, consider the example of a high school football team that has an extremely fast running back and some very good (but considerably slower) blocking linemen as members of the offense. Often, team members are told they all need to do their absolute best if the team is going to do well. If our running back does his absolute best on a sweep around the end, then he will run as fast as he can. By doing so, he will leave his blocking linemen behind. The team is not likely to gain much yardage on such a play, and the linemen and the running back, who have done their individual best, are apt to learn an important experiential lesson about teamwork. Most important, after several such disastrous plays, all of the team members may be inclined to demonstrate poor team process (lower effort, poor strategy, poor use of knowledge, and poor group dynamics represented by intrateam strife). If we assume that all the input stage variables are satisfactorily in place, ongoing coaching may now be appropriate. The coach would get better results if he worked out a better coordination plan between the running back and the linemen. In this case, the fast running back needs to slow down (i.e., not perform maximally) to give the slower but excellent blockers a chance to do their work. After they have been given a chance to contribute to the play, the running back will have a much better chance to then excel individually, and so will the team as a whole.

As straightforward as this seems, very few leaders get the opportunity to build a team from the ground up. More often the leader is placed into a team that already exists, has most, if not all, of its members assigned, and is in a preexisting organizational context that might not be team friendly. While this situation is more difficult, all is not lost. The TLM also provides a method for diagnosis and identification of key **leverage points** for change.

Diagnosis and Leverage Points

Let us assume that you, as a new leader, have been placed in charge of a poorly performing existing team. After a few days of observation, you have discovered that its members are just not working very hard. They seem to be uninterested in the task, frequently wandering off or not even showing up for scheduled teamwork. By focusing on the Process block of the TLM, (the core or "engine" of the TLM is shown in Figure 10.6, which can be thought of as a four-sided pyramid), we would diagnose this at the process level as a problem of Effort. Note that preceding the term *Effort at the process level* is the label (P-1). Rather than just encouraging them to work harder (or threatening them), we should first look at the Input level to see if there is some underlying problem. But you do not need to examine all 12 Input variables. Since we have already diagnosed a P-1 level process problem, the TLM is designed to focus your attention on the key leverage points to target change. Each face of the pyramid shows the input variables at the Individual, Team, and Organizational levels that most impact the Process variable that one might diagnose. These are referred to as the leverage points for impacting (P-1) Effort. (See the no. 1 face of the pyramid in Figure 10.6.) The individual level (I-1) suggests that we look at the interests and motivations of the individual team members. These are referred to as **individual factors** in the model. If we have built a team to perform a mechanical assembly task, but the individuals assigned

FIGURE 10.6   Team Leadership Model, Robert C. Ginnett, PhD: The four faces of the "engine" of the Team Leadership Model.

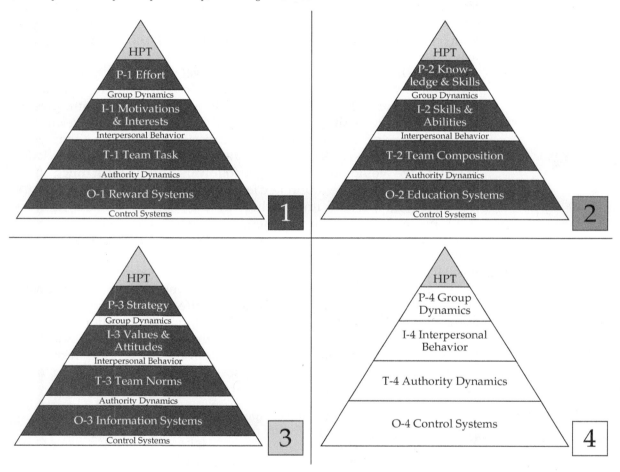

have little or no interest in mechanical work and instead prefer the performing arts, they may have little interest in contributing much effort to the team task. Here, using instruments such as the Campbell Interest and Skills Survey to select personnel may help our team's effort level from an individual perspective.[56]

While it may seem tempting to move to the team-level inputs next, it is important to remember that this model emphasizes the way teams are influenced by both individual and organizational level inputs. Therefore, we will look at the **organizational level** next. At the organizational level (O-1), the model suggests that we should examine the reward system that may be impacting the team. If the individuals have no incentive provided by the organization for putting forth effort, they might not be inclined to work very hard or, perhaps, at all. Similarly, the reward system may be solely structured to reward individual performance. Such a reward structure would be inconsistent with designs for a team task where interdependence and cooperation among members is often an underlying premise. If a professional basketball organization provides rewards for players based only on individual points scored, with no bonuses for team performance (games won or making the playoffs), you can expect little passing, setting picks for teammates, and so on.

Both the individual and organizational level variables contribute to the team's ability to perform the task. But there can also be problems at the **team design** level. Here (T-1), a poorly designed task is hypothesized to be unmotivating. (An approach for designing intrinsically rewarding work based on job characteristics will be discussed in the next chapter.) If a job is meaningless, lacks sufficient autonomy, or provides no knowledge of results, we would not expect to see followers putting forth much effort.

Using the model, we found key leverage points at various levels of the input stage that would impact the way the team went about its work (team process). In the example cited, we diagnosed a process-level problem with effort (P-1), so we examined the 1-level variables at the individual, organizational, and team levels as the most likely location for finding input stage problems. By the way, the concept of leverage point does not imply that only factors at corresponding "numbers" should be considered. For example, a team's effort might be affected by an oppressive and authoritarian leader. As we will discuss next, this "foundation-level variable" can have a tremendous impact on the other variables. Indeed, so powerful is this component, we should examine the process measure of group dynamics (P-4) and its corresponding leverage points in more detail. Consider the following two examples:

> *Surgical team.* A surgical team composed of highly experienced members is involved in a surgical procedure that each member has participated in numerous times before. During one portion of the procedure, the surgeon asks for a particular instrument. The scrub nurse looks across the table at the assistant with a questioning gaze and then hands the surgeon the instrument he requested. Recognizing the instrument he has been handed (and asked for) is not correct for the current procedure, he throws it down on the table and curses at the scrub nurse. All members of the surgical team take a half-step back from the table and all casual conversation stops. No one offers any further voluntary assistance to the surgeon.
>
> *Commercial airline crew.* A commercial airline crew is making a routine approach into an uncrowded airport on a clear day. The captain is flying and has declared a visual approach. His final approach to the runway is not good, which greatly complicates the plane's landing, and the landing is poor. After taxiing to the gate, the captain and his entire crew debrief (discuss) the poor approach, and the team members talk about what they could do individually and collectively to help the captain avoid or improve a poor approach in the future. The captain thanks the members for their help and encourages them to consider how they could implement their suggestions in other situations.

Obviously, the group dynamics are very different in these two cases. In the first example, the surgeon's behavior, coupled with his status, created a condition inappropriate for effective teamwork. The airline captain in the second example, even though not performing the task well, created a team environment where the team was much more likely to perform well in the future. In both of these cases, we would have observed unusual (one negative and one positive) group dynamics while the team was at work. These are examples of the group dynamics at the P-4 level.

Again returning to the model for determining points of leverage, we would check the I-4 variable at the individual level to determine if the team members involved had adequate interpersonal skills to interact appropriately. At the organizational level, the O-4 variable would suggest we check organizational components to determine if there are organizational control systems that inhibit or overly structure the way in which the team can make decisions or control its own fate. Such factors may include organizational design or structure limitations (a subject we will discuss in more detail in Chapter 11), or it may be a rigid computerized control system that specifies every minute detail of the tasks not only of the teams as a whole but of all the individuals composing the team. These excessive controls at the organizational level can inhibit effective teamwork. Finally, at the team design level, the T-4 variable would have us examine authority dynamics created between the leader and the followers. Authority dynamics describe the various ways the team members, including the leader, relate and respond to authority. It is at the team level that the followers have opportunities to relate directly with the team's authority figure, the team leader. The intricacies of how these various authority dynamics can play themselves out in a team's life are more complex than is warranted for this chapter. Suffice it to say that there is a range of authority relationships that can be created, from autocratic to laissez-faire. For a more detailed explanation of this concept, see Ginnett.[57] But even without further description, it should be no surprise that the varied group dynamics observed in the previous two examples were leveraged by the leaders' use of authority in very different ways.

It would be simple if leaders could identify and specify in advance the ideal type of authority for themselves and their teams, and then work toward that objective. However, teams seldom can operate effectively under one fixed type of authority over time. The leader might prefer to use his or her favorite style, and the followers might also have an inherent preference for one type of authority or another; but if the team is to be effective, then the authority dynamics they are operating with should complement the demands of the situation. Since situations often change over time, so should the authority dynamics of the team. This idea is very similar to a point made earlier in the book—that effective leaders tend to use all five sources of leader power.

In research on the behavior of leaders in forming their teams, Ginnett[58] found that highly effective leaders used a variety of authority dynamics in the first few minutes of the team's life. This does not mean that each highly effective leader used a single style that was different from the others' (i.e., other leaders'). It does mean that each one of the effective leaders used a variety of authority styles. At one point in the first meeting of the team, the leader would behave directively, which enabled him to establish his competence and hence his legitimate authority. At another time, he would engage the team in a very participative process and actively seek participation from each member of the team. By modeling a range of authority behaviors in the early stages of the team's life, the effective leaders laid the groundwork for continuing expectations of shifting authority as the situational demands changed.

Concluding Thoughts about Ginnett's Team Leadership Model

It is helpful to point out that not all components of the TLM have been discussed here because of its complexity. For example, we have not discussed **material resources.** Even if a team is well designed, has superior organizational systems supporting its work, and has access to superior-quality ongoing development, without adequate physical resources it is not likely to do well on the output level. Also note that background shells (discussed earlier in this chapter) representing the industry and the environment have *not* been included in this simplified depiction of the TLM. While the team leader may have little opportunity to influence these shells, the shells will certainly have an impact on the team.

Finally, there are several feedback loops which provide information to various levels of the organization. Usually, information is available to the organization as a whole (either formally or informally) about which teams are doing well and which are struggling. Whether leaders have access to this information is largely a function of whether they have created or stifled a safe climate. Feedback at the individual level can influence the perceived efficacy of the individual members of the team,[59,60] while the overall potency of the team is impacted even for tasks that the team has yet to attempt.[61]

Lastly, let us reinforce a limitation noted earlier. For ease of use and guidance, this model has been presented as if it were a machine (e.g., if P-2 breaks, check I-2, O-2, and T-2). As with other models of leadership or other human systems, however, nothing is that simple. There are obviously other variables that impact teams and team effectiveness. There are also complex interactions between the variables described even in this model. But we have considerable evidence that the model can be useful for understanding teams,[62] and, in light of the relationship between teams and leadership, we are now using it as an underlying framework in courses to help leaders more effectively lead their teams.

It has been shown that leaders can influence team effectiveness by (*a*) insuring the team has a clear sense of purpose and performance expectations; (*b*) designing or redesigning input stage variables at the individual, organizational, and team design levels; and (*c*) improving team performance through ongoing coaching at various stages, but particularly while the team is actually performing its task. These "midcourse corrections" should not

"Well, I guess I did it again, guys? Missed a field goal in the final seconds. But hey, we're a team, right? Right, guys? Guys?"

only improve the team outcomes but also help to avoid many of the team-generated problems that can cause less-than-optimal team performance.[63] Whether the leader gets the luxury of creation or is thrust into the leadership of an existing team, the TLM has been shown to be a useful tool in guiding their behavior. It also is a most effective tool if you believe that the leader's job is to create the conditions for the team to be effective.

Let us integrate the variables from this model into our L–F–S framework (see Figure 10.7). Clearly, there are variables of importance in each of the three arenas. However, in this model the characteristics of the leader play a lesser role because the leader's job is to work on what is not being provided for the team in order for it to perform its task. The focus thus has shifted from the leader to the followers and to the situation.

Virtual Teams

Just as teams and teamwork have become essential to the accomplishment of work in organizations in the present (and as far as we can foresee in the future), so too will be an understanding of teams that are not in a single location. With the movement toward the global marketplace and the result-ant globalization of organizations, it is appropriate to briefly consider the difficulties and recommended solutions for leading **geographically dis-persed teams (GDTs)** or, as they are more commonly referred to, virtual teams. There is considerable discussion about the labeling of such teams,[64] but for simplicity we will call them **virtual teams** here.

470 Part Three *Focus on the Followers*

FIGURE 10.7 Factors from the normative model of group effectiveness and the interactional framework.

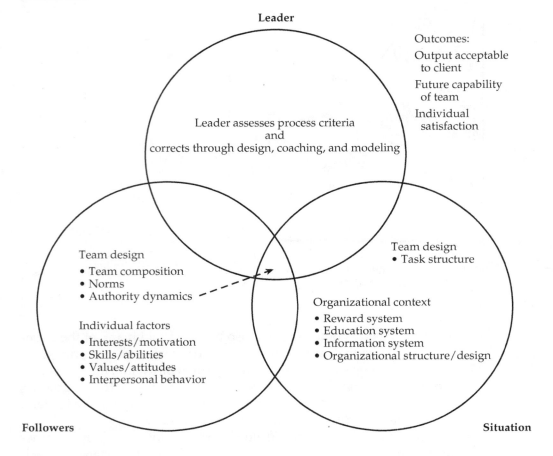

The marketplace is the globe (see Highlight 10.9). Western corporations are recognizing that growth and development opportunities are often much greater in Russia and other nations of the former Soviet Union, China, Latin America, and Africa than they are in their traditional markets of North America and Europe. But with this realization come new challenges for leading teams that are not only dispersed geographically but are often culturally different as well. Fortunately, information and communication technology is offering some new opportunities, if not solutions, for part of these problems. Early in this millennium, personal computer sales should top 100 million annually, which would be one PC for every 60 people on the planet; more than 60 million people will use cellular phones; and the Internet and World Wide Web are expanding at approximately 100 percent annually.[65] But is the mere opportunity to communicate electronically sufficient to ensure teamwork? Apparently not.

What Is the "Global Population" of Your Classroom?

HIGHLIGHT 10.9

Your authors attended a training session conducted by a major corporation intended for its newly appointed executives. One session was devoted to demonstrating the need for a global perspective in today's environment. To illustrate the key point, the instructor divided the room into unequal groups representing the geographical distribution of the world's population and had each group stand up in turn. As each group stood, she told them the proportion of the global population they represented.

The proportions she used are provided below. You might try it in your classroom—it makes the point dramatically.

Australia and New Zealand	2%
North America	5%
Former Soviet Union	5%
Latin America	7%
Western/Eastern Europe	10%
Africa	12%
Asia	56%

Researchers at the Conference Board[66] reported that there were five major areas that needed to change if global teams were to work. The five listed were senior management leadership, innovative use of communication technology, adoption of an organization design that enhances global operations, the prevalence of trust among team members, and the ability to capture the strengths of diverse cultures, languages, and people.

Armstrong and Cole[67] did in-depth studies of virtual teams and have reported three conclusions that should be considered by leaders of these teams. First, the distance between members of a virtual team is multidimensional. "Distance" includes not just geographical distance, but also organizational distance (e.g., different group or department cultures), temporal distance (e.g., different time zones), and differences in national culture. Second, the impact of such distances on the performance of a distributed work group is not directly proportional to objective measures of distance. In fact, Armstrong and Cole suggested that a new measure of distance between group members that reflects the degree of group cohesion and identity, a measure of psychological distance between members, would predict group performance better than geographical distance. Finally, the differences in the effects that distance seems to have on work groups are due at least partially to two intervening variables: (1) integrating practices *within* a virtual team, and (2) integrating practices *between* a virtual team and its larger host organization.

Finally, there are a number of frameworks under development to help leaders work with virtual teams, and there may be specific factors that these frameworks provide which can be useful. However, in our admittedly limited exposure to virtual teams in a pure research sense, a number of our clients have reported the TLM (discussed earlier) has been quite useful in considering the process problems that present themselves and in suggesting appropriate leverage points for intervention.

Leading Virtual Teams: Ten Principles

HIGHLIGHT 10.10

Terence Brake is the president of TMA-Americas and specializes in globalization. He suggests the following guidance for leaders of virtual teams.

Virtual when used in relation to teamwork is an unfortunate term. It implies there is almost teamwork, but not quite. *Virtual* has associations with *nearly, close to,* and *bordering on.* As one wit said, "If you want virtual results, create a virtual team." Alternatively, it is a fortunate term if taken it to imply that greater efforts are needed to achieve real teamwork in virtual teams. What principles can help you do this?

1. **Be proactive.** We often talk of "virtual" teams (VTs) as if they were all of a kind, but each one has its unique challenges. Some have a high level of cultural diversity. Others are more homogeneous. Some use one primary technology for collaboration, while others use a diverse mix. Some are short-lived, targeted on solving an immediate problem. Others are longer-term and strategic. Some cross time zones, and others none. By understanding the most likely challenges to occur, you can take proactive measures and increase team confidence. Confidence is a building block of virtual team performance.

2. **Focus on relationships before tasks.** Early on, team communications should have a significant "getting to know you" component. They should also demonstrate enthusiasm and optimism. Members need to feel valued for who they are, not just what they do. They need to feel engaged and connected. Trust is usually built early on virtual teams, or not at all. Some observers talk of the "virtual paradox"—virtual teams being highly dependent on trust, but not operating under conditions supportive of trust-building. Trust is often built on perceived similarities, but distance makes this process difficult. Chances for misunderstanding are also increased. Goodwill and engagement will solve most problems. Isolation and alienation create problems. Connect, and then collaborate.

3. **Seek clarity and focus early on.** Invest up-front time in clarifying the team's purpose and roles and responsibilities. There is enough uncertainty when working at a distance; it doesn't need to be added to by ambiguity and confusion. Clear purpose and accountabilities support cohesion. Translate purpose and overall accountabilities into specific objectives and tasks so that everyone knows what is expected, by whom, and by when. Virtual teams are highly susceptible to "focus drift" and fragmentation, so keep reminding the team of purpose, objectives, etc.

4. **Create a sense of order and predictability.** In a world wanting us to embrace chaos, "order" and "predictability" might appear unfashionable. But they are critical to the success of virtual teams. Uncertainty creates anxiety, fear, and withdrawal. The result is a demotivated and unproductive team. Use common team tools, templates, and processes; have predetermined times for communicating together; check in with team members regularly without trying to micro-manage; be accessible and an anchor point for the team. Shared expectations are psychological threads connecting separate minds.

5. **Be a cool-headed, objective problem solver.** Problems on virtual teams can appear larger than they actually are; people feeling isolated can lose perspective. Small issues, quickly resolved when working face-to-face, often fester and spread paranoia and distrust. You should establish yourself as someone who is totally fair; you don't play favorites, and you don't overburden some at the expense of others. You also need to be pragmatic. When there is a problem, you keep calm, you engage the team in finding practical solutions, and you communicate often. Panic is a virus that breeds exceptionally well in silent, isolated spaces.

6. **Develop shared operating agreements.** To reduce threats of uncertainty and ambiguity, common methods and processes—operating agreements—need to be established quickly. These agreements provide the team with shared mental models for working together. Typically, operating agreements need to be created in

continued

Continued

areas such as: planning, decision making, communicating, and coordination. A Team Charter acts as a common reference point, and can help orient new team members. Take time during team "meetings" to review how well the operating agreements are working.

7. **Give team members personal attention.** Just as you would on a face-to-face team, allocate time to "meet" with individuals. Find out how he or she is feeling about things. Give each person an opportunity to share personal successes, challenges, needs, and wants. It can be difficult to do this in team "meetings" where the emphasis is on shared tasks and problem solving. Empathize with that person who is on the road, working at home, or in a remote office. Listening, caring, sympathizing, recognizing—they cost little, but benefit everyone.

8. **Respect the challenges of the virtual environment.** I once lived on a boat, and I soon learned to respect the power of nature—the winds, tides, swells, rain, ice, and drought. I had to pay very close attention to these elements or they could sink me, swamp me, or ground me. There is always the temptation to carry over habits from one environment (e.g., land, face-to-face teamwork) into another (e.g., river, working at a distance). We must recognize the differences and adapt. Listening, empathizing, communicating, coordinating, engaging, energizing, and enabling all need to be enhanced.

9. **Recognize the limits of available technologies.** Unless you really have to, don't try and do everything via a virtual team. Sometimes teams are working on projects so complex that no matter how much video- or teleconferencing time they have, it will not be enough. Sometimes it pays dividends to bring people together for a few days. Never assume that because you have been designated a "virtual" team, you must always work in that mode. Focus on cost/benefit over the life of the project. Technology is a tool, and all tools are good for some tasks and not others.

10. **Stay people-focused.** Distance can make faceless abstractions of us all. Never lose sight of the fact that your virtual team members are people, with all that that entails—needs for belonging, meaning, accomplishment, and recognition; feelings of frustration, anger, excitement, boredom, and alienation; political pressures and personal pressures. Think about those features of your physical workplace that enable teams to work well together, e.g., formal meeting rooms, informal spaces, the coffee area, and see what you can do to humanize your virtual workplace, e.g., team pictures and bios, bulletin boards, chat areas.

Applying these virtual team leadership principles will help you avoid *almost* and *close to* teamwork. Virtual teamwork is only going to increase, so many of us need to re-skill ourselves for leading at a distance.

Summary

The group perspective showed that followers' behaviors can be the result of factors somewhat independent of the individual characteristics of followers. Group factors that can affect followers' behaviors include group size, stages of group development, roles, norms, and cohesion. Leadership practitioners should use these concepts to better understand followers' behaviors. Leaders should also use a team perspective for understanding follower behavior and group performance. Leadership practitioners need to bear in mind how a team's sense of identity, common goals or tasks, level of task interdependence, and differentiated roles affect functional and dysfunctional follower behavior. Additionally, because effective teams have several readily identifiable characteristics, leadership practitioners may want to use the suggestions provided by Hackman,[68] Ginnett,[69] or Hallam and Campbell[70] to develop more effective teams.

The Team Leadership Model posited that team effectiveness can best be understood in terms of inputs, processes, and outcomes. The input level consists of the individual characteristics of the followers; the design of the team itself; and various organizational systems that create the context in which the teams will operate. The process level concerns the way in which teams behave while going about their tasks, and the output level concerns whether customers and clients are satisfied with the team's product, whether the team improves and develops as a performing unit, and whether followers are satisfied to be members of the team. By identifying certain process problems in teams, leaders can use the model to diagnose appropriate leverage points for action at the individual, team design, or organizational levels, or for ongoing development at the process level. Leaders concerned with teamwork in organizational settings have found this framework useful in helping them conceptualize factors affecting team effectiveness and identifying targets for change.

Key Terms

group perspective, 437
group, 440
cliques, 441
span of control, 441
additive task, 442
process loss, 442
social loafing, 442
social facilitation, 442
forming, 442
storming, 443
norming, 443
performing, 443
project teams, 444
punctuated equilibrium, 444
group roles, 444
task role, 445

relationship role, 445
dysfunctional roles, 446
role conflict, 446
intrasender role conflict, 447
intersender role conflict, 447
interrole conflict, 447
person-role conflict, 447
role ambiguity, 447
norms, 447
group cohesion, 450
overbounding, 450
groupthink, 451
ollieism, 452
organizational shells, 456

Team Leadership Model (TLM), 457
outputs, 459
process measures, 461
inputs, 461
dream, 462
design, 462
development, 462
leverage point, 464
individual factors, 464
organizational level, 465
team design, 466
material resources, 468
geographically dispersed teams (GDTs), 469
virtual teams, 469

Questions

1. How do the tenets of Ginnett's Team Leadership Model compare with the components of team performance described earlier?

2. Not all group norms are positive or constructive from the leader's perspective. If a group holds counterproductive norms, what should the leader do?

3. On the basis of what you know about global cultures, would people from the U.S., Japan, or Chile be more comfortable with a group or team-based approach to work?

Activity

NASA Exercise: Lost on the Moon

Your spaceship has crash-landed on the dark side of the moon and you are scheduled to rendezvous with the mother ship, which is 200 miles away on the lighted side of the moon. The crash has ruined the ship and destroyed all the equipment except for the 15 items listed below. Your crew's survival depends on reaching the mother ship, so you must choose the most critical items available to take on the 200-mile trip. Your task is to rank-order the 15 items in the order of their importance for your survival. Place a "1" beside the most important item, a "2" beside the second most important item, and so on until you have ranked all 15 items.

_____ Box of matches
_____ Food concentrate
_____ 50 feet of nylon rope
_____ Parachute silk
_____ Solar-powered portable heating unit
_____ Two .45 caliber pistols
_____ One case of dehydrated milk
_____ Two 100-pound tanks of oxygen
_____ Stellar map
_____ Self-inflating life raft
_____ Magnetic compass
_____ Five gallons of water
_____ Signal flares
_____ First-aid kit with hypodermic syringes
_____ Solar-powered FM transmitter/receiver

Your instructor has the "NASA Expert" answers and the instructions for completing the exercise.

Minicase

"Integrating Teams at Hernandez & Associates"

Marco Hernandez is president of Hernandez & Associates Inc., a full-service advertising agency with clients across North America. The company provides a variety of marketing services to support its diverse group of clients. Whether called on to generate a strategic plan, create interactive Web sites, or put together a full-blown media campaign, the team at Hernandez & Associates prides itself on creative solutions to its clients' marketing challenges.

The firm was founded in 1990 with an emphasis in the real estate industry. It quickly expanded its client base to include health care, as well as food and consumer products. Like many small firms, the company grew quickly in the "high-flying" 1990s, but its administrative costs to obtain and service businesses also skyrocketed. And, as with many businesses, the agency's business was greatly affected by the terrorist attacks of September 11 and the economic downturn that followed. Clients' shrinking budgets forced them to scale back their business with Hernandez & Associates and cutbacks in staffing meant clients needed more marketing support services as opposed to full-scale campaigns.

Hernandez & Associates now faced a challenge—to adapt its business to focus on what the clients were asking for. Specifically, clients, with their reduced staffs, were looking for help responding to their customers' requests and looking for ways to make the most of their more limited marketing budgets. Its small, cohesive staff of 20 employees needed to make some changes, and quickly.

As president of Hernandez & Associates, Marco Hernandez knew his team was up for the challenge. He had worked hard to create an environment to support a successful team—he recruited people who had solid agency experience and he consistently communicated the firm's mission to his team. He made sure the team had all the resources it needed to succeed and constantly took stock of these resources. He had built his team as he built his business and knew the group would respond to his leadership. But where to start? Getting the team to understand that growth depended on a shift in how it serviced its clients was not difficult—each of the employees of the small firm had enough contact with the clients that they knew client needs were changing. But making significant changes to the status quo at Hernandez & Associates would be difficult. Group roles had to change—creative folks had to think about how to increase a client's phone inquiries and Web site visits; account people needed a better understanding of the client's desire for more agency leadership. And everyone had to have a better sense of the costs involved. The company as a whole needed a more integrated approach to servicing their clients if they hoped to survive. Marco needed a plan.

1. Like many leaders, Marco has a team in place and does not have the luxury of building a new team from the ground up to adapt to the changing business environment his firm is faced with. Use the TLM to help Marco diagnose the problems faced by the firm and identify leverage points for change.

   a. Consider the major functions of the TLM—input, process, and output. Where do most of the firm's challenges fall?

   b. What are the team's goals for outputs?

2. Identify potential resources for Marco and his team in implementing a strategy to change the way they do business at Hernandez & Associates.

Chapter Notes

1. Ginnett, R. C. "Effectiveness Begins Early: The Leadership Role in the Formation of Intra-Organizational Task Groups." Unpublished manuscript, 1992.

2. Shaw, M. *Group Dynamics: The Psychology of Small Group Dynamics.* 3rd ed. New York: McGraw-Hill, 1981.

3. Yukl, G. A. *Leadership in Organizations.* 1st ed. Englewood Cliffs, NJ: Prentice Hall, 1981.

4. Badin, I. J. "Some Moderator Influences on Relationships between Consideration, Initiating Structure, and Organizational Criteria." *Journal of Applied Psychology* 59 (1974), pp. 380–82.

5. Goodstadt, B. E., and D. Kipnis. "Situational Influences on the Use of Power." *Journal of Applied Psychology* 54 (1970), pp. 201–07.

6. Kipnis, D., S. M. Schmidt, and I. Wilkinson. "Intraorganizational Influence Tactics: Explorations in Getting One's Way." *Journal of Applied Psychology* 65 (1980), pp. 440–52.

7. Udell, J. G. "An Empirical Test of Hypotheses Relating to Span of Control." *Administrative Science Quarterly* 12 (1967), pp. 420–39.

8. Bass, B. M. *Leadership, Psychology, and Organizational Behavior.* New York: Harper, 1960.

9. Indik, B. P. "Organizational Size and Member Participation: Some Empirical Tests of Alternative Explanations." *Human Relations* 18 (1965), pp. 339–50.

10. Steiner, I. D. *Group Process and Productivity.* New York: Academic Press, 1972.

11. Steiner, I. D. *Group Process and Productivity.* New York: Academic Press, 1972.

12. Latane, B., K. Williams, and S. Harkins. "Social Loafing." *Psychology Today* (1979), p. 104.

13. Porter, D. B., M. Bird, and A. Wunder. "Competition, Cooperation, Satisfaction, and the Performance of Complex Tasks among Air Force Cadets." *Current Psychology Research and Reviews* 9, no. 4 (1991), pp. 347–54.

14. Zajonc, R. "Social Facilitation." *Science* 149 (1965), pp. 269–74.

15. Tuckman, B. W. "Developmental Sequence in Small Groups." *Psychological Bulletin* 63 (1965), pp. 384–99.

16. Tuckman, B. W. "Developmental Sequence in Small Groups." *Psychological Bulletin* 63 (1965), pp. 384–99.

17. Mayo, E. *The Human Problems of an Industrial Civilization.* New York: Macmillan, 1933.

18. Roethlisberger, F. J., and W. J. Dickson. *Management and the Worker: An Account of a Research Program Conducted by the Western Electric Company, Hawthorne Works, Chicago.* Cambridge: Harvard University Press, 1939.

19. Stogdill, R. M. "Group Productivity, Drive, and Cohesiveness." *Organizational Behavior and Human Performance* 8 (1972), pp. 26–43.

20. Terborg, J. R., C. H. Castore, and J. A. DeNinno. "A Longitudinal Field Investigation of the Impact of Group Composition on Group Performance and Cohesion." Paper presented at the annual meeting of the Midwestern Psychological Association, Chicago, 1975.

478 Part Three *Focus on the Followers*

21. Gersick, C. J. G. "Time and Transition in Work Teams: Toward a New Model of Group Development." *Academy of Management Journal* 31 (1988), pp. 9–41.

22. Ginnett, R. C. "Airline Cockpit Crew." In *Groups That Work (and Those That Don't)*. Ed. J. Richard Hackman. San Francisco: Jossey-Bass, 1990.

23. Jamal, M. "Job Stress and Job Performance Controversy: An Empirical Assessment." *Organizational Behavior and Human Performance* 33 (1984), pp. 1–21.

24. Zimbardo, P., C. Haney, W. Banks, and D. Jaffe. "The Mind Is a Formidable Jailer: A Pirandellian Prison." *New York Times Magazine*, April 8, 1973, pp. 38–60.

25. House, R. J., R. S. Schuler, and E. Levanoni. "Role Conflict and Ambiguity Scales: Reality or Artifact?" *Journal of Applied Psychology* 68 (1983), pp. 334–37.

26. Rizzo, J. R., R. J. House, and S. I. Lirtzman. "Role Conflict and Ambiguity in Complex Organizations." *Administrative Science Quarterly* 15 (1970), pp. 150–63.

27. Fisher, C. D., and R. Gitleson. "A Meta-analysis of the Correlates of Role Conflict and Ambiguity." *Journal of Applied Psychology* 68 (1983), pp. 320–33.

28. Hackman, J. R. "Group Influences on Individuals." In *Handbook of Industrial and Organizational Psychology*. Ed. M. D. Dunnette. Chicago: Rand McNally, 1976.

29. Reilly, Rick. *Sports Illustrated* 104 (15) (2006), p. 76.

30. Feldman, D. C. "The Development and Enforcement of Group Norms." *Academy of Management Review,* January 1984, pp. 47–53.

31. Hackman, J. Richard. *Leading Teams—Setting the Stage for Great Performances.* Boston, MA: Harvard Business School Press, 2002.

32. Alderfer, C. P. "Group and Intergroup Relations." In *Improving Life at Work.* Eds. J. R. Hackman and J. L. Suttle, Santa Monica, CA: Goodyear, 1977.

33. Ginnett, R. C. "The Formation Process of Airline Flight Crews." *Proceedings of the Fourth International Symposium on Aviation Psychology.* Columbus, OH, 1987.

34. Janis, I. L. *Groupthink.* 2nd ed. Boston: Houghton Mifflin, 1982.

35. Janis, I. L. *Groupthink.* 2nd ed. Boston: Houghton Mifflin, 1982.

36. Janis, I. L. *Groupthink.* 2nd ed. Boston: Houghton Mifflin, 1982.

37. Shephard, J. E. "Thomas Becket, Ollie North, and You." *Military Review* 71, no. 5 (1991), pp. 20–33.

38. Robbins, S. P. *Organizational Behavior: Concepts, Controversies, and Applications.* Englewood Cliffs, NJ: Prentice Hall, 1986.

39. Hallam, G. L., and D. P. Campbell. "Selecting Team Members? Start with a Theory of Team Effectiveness." Paper presented at the Seventh Annual Meeting of the Society of Industrial/Organizational Psychologists, Montreal, Canada, May 1992.

40. Hallam, G. L., and D. P. Campbell. "Selecting Team Members? Start with a Theory of Team Effectiveness." Paper presented at the Seventh Annual Meeting of the Society of Industrial/Organizational Psychologists, Montreal, Canada, May 1992.

41. Hackman, J. R. *Groups That Work (and Those That Don't)*. San Francisco: Jossey-Bass, 1990.

42. Ginnett, R. C. "Crews as Groups: Their Formation and Their Leadership." In *Cockpit Resource Management.* Eds. E. Wiener, B. Banki, and R. Helmreich. Orlando, FL: Academic Press, 1993.

43. Ginnett, R. C. "Team Effectiveness Leadership Model: Identifying Leverage Points for Change." *Proceedings of the 1996 National Leadership Institute Conference.* College Park, MD: National Leadership Institute, 1996.

44. Hackman, J. R. "Group Level Issues in the Design and Training of Cockpit Crews." In *Proceedings of the NASA/MAC Workshop on Cockpit Resource Management.* Eds. H. H. Orlady and H. C. Foushee. Moffett Field, CA: NASA Ames Research Center, 1986.

45. Ginnett, R. C. "Crews as Groups: Their Formation and Their Leadership." In *Cockpit Resource Management.* Eds. E. Wiener, B. Banki, and R. Helmreich. Orlando, FL: Academic Press, 1993.

46. Ginnett, R. C. "Crews as Groups: Their Formation and Their Leadership." In *Cockpit Resource Management.* Eds. E. Wiener, B. Banki, and R. Helmreich. Orlando, FL: Academic Press, 1993.

47. Ginnett, R. C. "Team Effectiveness Leadership Model: Identifying Leverage Points for Change." *Proceedings of the 1996 National Leadership Institute Conference.* College Park, MD: National Leadership Institute, 1996.

48. Ginnett, R. C. "Team Effectiveness Leadership Model: Design & Diagnosis." 12th Annual International Conference on Work Teams. Dallas, TX, 2001.

49. McGrath, J. E. *Leadership Behavior: Some Requirements for Leadership Training.* Washington, DC: Office of Career Development, U.S. Civil Service Commission, 1964.

50. Hackman, J. R. *Groups That Work (and Those That Don't).* San Francisco: Jossey-Bass, 1990.

51. Smith, K. W., E. Salas, and M. T. Brannick. "Leadership Style as a Predictor of Teamwork Behavior: Setting the Stage by Managing Team Climate." Paper presented at the Ninth Annual Conference of the Society for Industrial and Organizational Psychology, Nashville, TN, 1994.

52. Hackman, J. R. *Groups That Work (and Those That Don't).* San Francisco: Jossey-Bass, 1990.

53. Wheelan, S. A. *Group Processes.* Needham Heights, MA: Allyn & Bacon, 1994.

54. McGrath, J. E. *Leadership Behavior: Some Requirements for Leadership Training.* Washington, DC: Office of Career Development, U.S. Civil Service Commission, 1964.

55. Katzenbach, J. R., and B. K. Smith. *The Wisdom of Teams.* Boston: HarperBusiness, 1994.

56. Campbell, D. P., S. Hyne, and D. L. Nilsen. *Campbell Interests and Skill Survey Manual.* Minneapolis, MN: National Computer Systems, 1992.

57. Ginnett, R. C. "Crews as Groups: Their Formation and Their Leadership." In *Cockpit Resource Management.* Eds. E. Wiener, B. Banki, and R. Helmreich. Orlando, FL: Academic Press, 1993.

58. Ginnett, R. C. "Crews as Groups: Their Formation and Their Leadership." In *Cockpit Resource Management.* Eds. E. Wiener, B. Banki, and R. Helmreich. Orlando, FL: Academic Press, 1993.

59. Bandura, A. "Self-Efficacy: Toward a Unifying Theory of Behavioral Change." *Psychological Review* 84 (1977), pp. 191–215.

60. Lindsley, D. H., D. J. Brass., and J. B. Thomas. " Efficacy-Performance Spirals: A Multilevel Perspective." *Academy of Management Review* 20 (1995), pp. 645–78.

480   Part Three   *Focus on the Followers*

61. Guzzo, R. A., P. R. Yost, R. J. Campbell, and G. P. Shea. "Potency in Teams: Articulating a Construct." *British Journal of Social Psychology* 32 (1993), pp. 87–106.

62. Hackman, J. R. *Groups That Work (and Those That Don't)*. San Francisco: Jossey-Bass, 1990.

63. Steiner, I. D. *Group Process and Productivity*. New York: Academic Press, 1972.

64. Kossler, M., and S. Prestridge. "Geographically Dispersed Teams." *Issues and Observations* 16 (1996), pp. 2–3.

65. Lipnack, J., and J. Stamps. *Virtual Teams: Reaching across Space, Time and Organizations with Technology*. New York: John Wiley, 1997.

66. Conference Board. "Global Management Teams: A Perspective." *HR Executive Review* 4 (1996).

67. Armstrong, D. J., and P. Cole. "Managing Distances and Differences in Geographically Distributed Work Groups." In *Distributed Work*. Eds. P. Hinds and S. Kiesler, Cambridge, MA: MIT Press, 2002, pp. 167–89.

68. Hackman, J. R. *Groups That Work (and Those That Don't)*. San Francisco: Jossey-Bass, 1990.

69. Ginnett, R. C. "Effectiveness Begins Early: The Leadership Role in the Formation of Intra-Organizational Task Groups." Unpublished manuscript, 1992.

70. Hallam, G. L., and D. P. Campbell. "Selecting Team Members? Start with a Theory of Team Effectiveness." Paper presented at the Seventh Annual Meeting of the Society of Industrial/Organizational Psychologists, Montreal, Canada, May 1992.

A Newsletter from Harvard Business School Publishing

ARTICLE REPRINT NO. U0410E

The Case for Collaborative Leadership

by H. James Wilson

For a complete list of Harvard Business
School Publishing newsletters:
http://newsletters.harvardbusinessonline.org

For reprint and subscription information
for *Harvard Management Update*:
Call 800-988-0866 *or* 617-783-7500
http://hmu.harvardbusinessonline.org

For customized and quantity orders of reprints:
Call 617-783-7626   *Fax* 617-783-7658

For permission to copy or republish:
Call 617-783-7587

Guest Column

The Case for Collaborative Leadership

In spite of apparent hurdles to effectiveness, some prominent executives are mining the value of a democratic leadership style and delivering impressive financial results

by H. James Wilson

A T A TIME WHEN ORGANIZATIONS are struggling to find the right balance between the classic top-down hierarchy and the modern ideal of a leaner, flatter, and more participatory culture, leaders face a critical question: Is it possible to loosen my grip on power, while actually enhancing my ability to get things done through others?

There would appear to be a paradox: On the one hand, the ostensible activities of strategic leadership—top-down analysis, decisiveness, and so on—often seem at odds with a management approach that seeks broad support.

On the other hand, psychologist Daniel Goleman and others have shown that collaborative or "democratic" style leadership—marked by building consensus, seeking broad input, creating vision collaboratively, and sharing responsibility for results—correlates positively with company performance.

Develop practices to make your strategy reverberate at the grass roots.

What's the secret? My interviews with dozens of leaders and executive coaches revealed two common themes in the successful deployment of democratic leadership styles. First, "democratic style" is really an umbrella term. There are as many permutations of this approach as there are businesses. The key is to modify the style to meet the strategic challenge at hand as well as your firm's idiosyncratic habits, preferences, and strengths. Second, because you need to sustain broad support and input, it's essential to develop practices that make your strategy reverberate at the grass roots. Below I discuss how three business leaders—the first two facing a crisis, the third a less dire challenge—used these principles to deliver extraordinary execution and bottom-line results.

Become a man of the people

When Peter Michel took the reins as CEO, Brinks Home Security (Irving, Texas) was in crisis. "The company was hemorrhaging cash and out of control," Michel says. Management and employees reveled in teamwork and collaboration, but in the absence of disciplined leadership, this potential asset had devolved into "ad hoc decision-making

and an inability to implement the decisions."

Michel, a former White House staffer, used three approaches to address the problem: First, he assembled town meeting–style Q&A forums to learn what employees were thinking; second, he worked at the grass-roots level to see what was working and what wasn't; and third, he developed political campaign–like slogans that applied to everyone but could be implemented in individual ways.

Researchers have long noted the importance of a new leader's first three months on the job, when employees are most open to new direction. But Michel chose to ask questions rather than deliver mandates. "I gave presentations; I took all the public statements made by the parent company from the previous four to five years and said, 'This is who the parent company says we are… Is that accurate? What do you really think?'"

The result of tapping into the culture's bias toward collaboration? Michel demonstrated that he was one of them—a leader inclined toward consensus building. But the approach also signaled his intention to add discipline; for instance, he asked questions in a purposeful, directed way. He also made clear that the forums were not merely open-ended discussions but a way to gather practical information.

Next, Michel became a corporate citizen of the people—a variation of "Management by Wandering Around." He worked the front lines to understand how employees interacted with customers, how decisions were made, and how processes operated in reality—unearthing several insights that couldn't have been gleaned by studying balance sheets. For instance, in the call center, "everybody was focused on making the customer happy, but there was no process or system to answer customer questions." Because an employee could spend all day trying to get to the bottom of a single query, the unit was extremely inefficient—an opportunity for Michel to add discipline. Working with call center managers, Michel developed a set of simple guidelines for serving customers: "If there is a question about pricing or opening a new market or adding a new piece of equipment, the guidelines have the right answer."

Finally, Michel used rhetoric to improve decision-making processes throughout each stage of the company's turnaround, during which its customer base and revenues grew

Collaborative Leadership *(continued)*

more than tenfold, and the company moved from 22 markets to more than 100. One slogan—"Make every decision as if we had 1 million customers"—became a template for managers to think about scale each time the firm upgraded its IT infrastructure. During one period of rapid growth—a time when most companies lose strategic discipline—the slogan "reinforced an effective behavior pattern, one that workers could recycle with increasing confidence to solve many different operational challenges."

Assemble a cabinet

When Dave Lemmon became CEO of Colonial Pipeline, the largest mover of refined petroleum in the world, the company was also in a strategic predicament. Oil leaks and other accidents had hurt the company's bottom line and, more important, its good name.

Colonial was a capital-intensive firm with a small number of employees. But Lemmon knew he needed to distribute leadership widely enough to put his safety-focused strategy into practice across the organization, which included the frontline staff that monitors the thousands of miles of oil pipeline. To that end, the CEO built a cabinet-style team by enlisting his business-unit managers, who previously focused more on function than on strategy.

Lemmon's approach transmuted an apparent structural limitation—that Colonial lacked a leadership team that focused exclusively on C-level matters and strategy—into an asset. The close links between the cabinet members and their respective unit workers improved the CEO's ability to bring strategy directly to the grass roots. For example, Lemmon and his team now benchmark companies that have best-in-class safety cultures. "We take off-sites, immersing ourselves in safety training, looking to where we could be top in safety," he says. "It requires us to do a lot of due diligence; if there's a cut finger, we'll first make sure employees are safe, receiving any medical treatment they need, then pull people off their jobs and do a root-cause analysis." The feedback loop between the leader, his cabinet, and workers promotes continual discovery of practices to improve safety across the firm. The result? "It took us five years, but in the last four years, we have been judged the safest pipeline company in the industry," he says.

Make your cause a popular cause

The late Malcolm Pennington once faced circumstances that were not as calamitous but every bit as strategically important. When Pennington was a senior manager and director of Japanese global food manufacturer Kikkoman, he had to find new ways to boost productivity to stay competitive. Although the firm had a long tradition of ongoing improvement, good ideas had become increasingly elusive. As he once noted, "The Wisconsin factory gave us about a 10% increase in operational efficiency every year for its first 25 years. But improving efficiency got harder and harder as we moved up the S curve."

Pennington, however, had a trick up his sleeve: his line workforce was exceptionally talented. The company had built a base human capital with an immense amount of knowledge and a quirky streak of Emersonian self-reliance when facing the kind of business problems that top management or consultants generally take on.

To capitalize on this cultural asset, Pennington used a few specific incentives and tools to inform workers and distribute responsibility. First, he educated them about the options senior management was considering to tackle the problem. At the top of this list was the possibility of hiring more workers, but he pointed out that more employees meant lower wages for everyone. Pennington sensed this option might be unacceptable to a workforce that was deeply proud of being the highest paid in the state and in the industry. The information was an invitation to participate in solving the strategic problem and also triggered workers' can-do mindset. People "felt empowered enough to say, 'Don't hire more workers. Let us try to improve the operation. If we succeed, pay us more.'"

Pennington used a simple approach to arm staff with the right tools. He subscribed to journals focused on innovation and emerging industry practices, and made them accessible to employees, "many of whom read them in their free time in the canteen."

The plant quickly realized a productivity bump. "One afternoon, a few of the bottling workers came to management and said, 'We think we have an answer: switch from electric controls to air-pressure actuated controls,'" Pennington recalled, "So we gave them the money, and they did it. They upgraded these fancy German filling machines, which were designed to run at 360 bottles a minute. They now have them running at 420 bottles a minute."

Most senior managers understand that they create the most value when they can get things done through others yet stop short of enlisting employees to tackle distinctively strategic problems. By creating organization-wide responsibility for your top challenges, you may have to give up a bit of turf, but you'll often get a solid result. ◆

H. James Wilson is coauthor of What's the Big Idea?: Creating and Capitalizing on the Best Management Thinking *(Harvard Business School Press, 2003). He can be reached at MUOpinion@hbsp.harvard.edu.*

Advanced Leadership Skills

Delegating

Why Delegating Is Important

Common Reasons for Avoiding Delegation

Principles of Effective Delegation

Although delegation is a relatively simple way for leaders to free themselves of time-consuming chores; provide followers with developmental opportunities; and increase the number of tasks accomplished by the work group, team, or committee, delegation is often an overlooked and underused management option (Bass, 1990; Leana, 1986). Delegation implies that one has been empowered by one's leader, boss, or coach to take responsibility for completing certain tasks or engaging in certain activities (Bass, 1990). Delegation gives the responsibility for decisions to those individuals most likely to be affected by or to implement the decision, and delegation is more concerned with autonomy, responsibility, and follower development than with participation (Leana, 1987).

Research has shown that leaders who delegate authority more frequently often have higher-performing businesses (Miller & Toulouse, 1986), but followers are not necessarily happier when their leaders frequently delegate tasks (Stogdill & Shartle, 1955). Bass (1990) maintained that the latter findings were due to subordinates who felt they were (*a*) not delegated the authority needed to accomplish delegated tasks, (*b*) monitored too closely, or (*c*) only delegated tasks leaders did not want to do. Nevertheless, Wilcox (1982) showed that leaders who delegated skillfully had more satisfied followers than leaders who did not delegate well. Because leaders who delegate skillfully often have more satisfied and higher-performing work groups, teams, or committees, the following suggestions from Taylor (1989) are provided to help leadership practitioners delegate more effectively and successfully. Taylor provided useful ideas about why delegating is important, common reasons for avoiding delegation, and principles of effective delegation.

Why Delegating Is Important

Delegation Frees Time for Other Activities

The essence of leadership is achieving goals through others, not trying to accomplish them by oneself. Learning to think like a leader partly involves developing a frame of mind wherein one thinks in terms of the whole group's or organization's capabilities and not just one's own. This requires a new frame of reference for many individuals, especially those whose past successes resulted primarily from personal achievement in interpersonally competitive situations. Still, leaders typically have so many different responsibilities they invariably must delegate some of them to others.

It is not just the mere quantity of work that makes delegation necessary. There is a qualitative aspect, too. Because leaders determine what responsibilities will be delegated, the process is one by which leaders can ensure that their time is allocated most judiciously to meet group needs. The leader's time is a precious commodity that should be invested wisely in those activities for which the leader is uniquely suited or situated to accomplish and that will provide the greatest long-term benefits to the group. What the leader *can* delegate, the leader *should* delegate.

Delegation Develops Followers

Developing subordinates is one of the most important responsibilities any leader has, and delegating significant tasks to them is one of the best ways to support their growth. It does so by providing opportunities for initiative, problem solving, innovation, administration, and decision making. By providing practical experience in a controlled fashion, delegation allows subordinates the best training experience of all: learning by doing.

Delegation Strengthens the Organization

Delegation is an important way to develop individual subordinates, but doing so also strengthens the entire organization. For one thing, an organization that uses delegation skillfully will be a motivating one to work in. Delegation sends an organizational signal that subordinates are trusted and their development is important. Moreover, skillful delegation inherently tends to increase the significance and satisfaction levels of most jobs, thus making subordinates' jobs better. Delegation also can be seen as a way of developing the entire organization, not just the individuals within it. To the extent that a whole organization systematically develops its personnel using delegation, its overall experience level, capability, and vitality increase. Finally, delegation stimulates innovation and generates fresh ideas and new approaches throughout the whole organization.

Common Reasons for Avoiding Delegation

Delegation Takes Too Much Time

Delegation saves time for the leader in the long run, but it costs time for the leader in the short run. It takes time to train a subordinate to perform any new task, so it often really does take less time for a leader to do the task herself than to put in the effort to train someone else to do it. When a task is a recurring or repetitive one, however, the long-term savings will make the additional effort in initial training worth it—both for the leader and for the subordinate.

Delegation Is Risky

It can feel threatening to delegate a significant responsibility to another person because doing so reduces direct personal control over the work one will be judged by (Dewhirst, Metts, & Ladd, 1987). Delegation may be perceived as a career risk by staking one's own reputation on the motivation, skill, and performance of others. It is the essence of leadership, though, that the leader will be evaluated in part by the success of the entire team. Furthermore, delegation need not and should not involve a complete loss of control by the leader over work delegated to others. The leader has a responsibility to set performance expectations, ensure that the task is understood and accepted, provide training, and regularly monitor the status of all delegated tasks and responsibilities (Bass, 1990).

The Job Will Not Be Done as Well

Often the leader can do many specific tasks or jobs better than anyone else. That is not surprising, as the leader is often the most experienced person in the group. This fact, however, can become an obstacle to delegation. The leader may rationalize not delegating a task to someone else because the follower lacks technical competence and the job would subsequently suffer (Dewhirst, Metts, & Ladd, 1987). However, this may be true only in the short term, and letting subordinates make a few mistakes is a necessary part of their development, just as it was for the leader at an earlier stage in her own development. Few things are likely to be so stifling to an organization as a leader's perfectionistic fear of mistakes. When thinking about delegating tasks to others, leaders should remember what their own skill levels used to be, not what they are now. Leaders should assess subordinates' readiness to handle new responsibilities in terms of the former, not the latter.

The Task Is a Desirable One

A leader may resist delegating tasks that are a source of power or prestige. He may be quite willing to delegate relatively unimportant responsibilities but may balk at the prospect of delegating a significant one having high visibility (Bass, 1990; Dewhirst, Metts, & Ladd, 1987). The greater the importance and visibility of the delegated task, though, the greater will be the potential developmental gains for the subordinate. Furthermore, actions always speak louder than words, and nothing conveys trust more genuinely than a leader's willingness to delegate major responsibilities to subordinates.

Others Are Already Too Busy

A leader may feel guilty about increasing a subordinate's already full workload. It is the leader's responsibility, though, to continually review the relative priority of all the tasks performed across the organization. Such a review might identify existing activities that could be eliminated, modified, or reassigned. A discussion with the subordinate about her workload and career goals would be a better basis for a decision than an arbitrary and unilateral determination by the leader that the subordinate could not handle more work. The new responsibility could well be something the subordinate wants and needs, and she might also have some helpful ideas about alternative ways to manage her present duties.

Principles of Effective Delegation

Decide What to Delegate

The first step leaders should take when deciding what to delegate is to identify all of their present activities. This should include those functions regularly performed and decisions regularly made. Next, leaders should estimate the actual time spent on these activities. This can be done fairly easily by developing and maintaining a temporary log. After collecting this information, leaders need to assess whether each activity justifies the time they are spending on it. In all likelihood, at least some of the most time-consuming recurring activities should be delegated to others. This process will probably also identify some activities that could be done more efficiently (either by the leader or someone else) and other activities that provide so little benefit they could be eliminated completely.

Decide Whom to Delegate To

There might be one individual whose talent and experience makes her the logical best choice for any assignment. However, leaders must be careful not to overburden someone merely because that individual always happens to be the best worker. Additionally, leaders have a responsibility to balance developmental opportunities among all their followers. Leaders should look for ways to optimize, over a series of assignments, the growth of all subordinates by matching particular opportunities to their respective individual needs, skills, and goals.

Make the Assignment Clear and Specific

As with setting goals, leaders delegating an assignment must be sure the subordinate understands just what the task involves and what is expected of him. Nevertheless, at times leaders provide too brief an explanation of the task to be delegated. A common communication error is overestimating one's own clarity, and in the case of delegation this can happen when the leader already knows the ins and outs of the particular task. Some of the essential steps or potential pitfalls in an assignment that seem self-evident to the leader may not be as obvious to someone who has never done the assignment before. Leaders should welcome questions and provide a complete explanation of the task. The time leaders invest during this initial training will pay dividends later on. When giving an assignment, leaders should ensure that they cover all of the points listed in Highlight D.1.

Points to Cover When Delegating a Task

Highlight D.1

How does the task relate to organizational goals?

When does the subordinate's responsibility for the task begin?

How has the task been accomplished in the past?

What problems were encountered with the task in the past?

What sources of help are available?

What unusual situations might arise in the future?

What are the limits of the subordinate's authority?

How will the leader monitor the task (e.g., provide feedback)?

Finally, in covering the above points, always convey high confidence and expectations.

Assign an Objective, Not a Procedure

Indicate what is to be accomplished, not *how* the task is to be accomplished. End results are usually more important than the methods. It is helpful to demonstrate procedures that have worked before, but not to specify rigid methods to follow in the future. Leaders should not assume their ways always were and always will be best. Leaders need to be clear about the criteria by which success will be measured, but allowing subordinates to achieve it in their own ways will increase their satisfaction and encourage fresh ideas.

Allow Autonomy, but Monitor Performance

Effective delegation is neither micromanagement of everything the subordinate does nor laissez-faire indifference toward the subordinate's performance. Leaders need to give subordinates a degree of autonomy (as well as time, resources, and authority) in carrying out their new responsibilities, and this includes the freedom to make certain kinds of mistakes. An organizational climate where mistakes are punished suppresses initiative and innovation. Furthermore, mistakes are important sources of development. Knowing this, one wise executive reassured a subordinate who expected to be fired for a gigantic mistake by saying, "Why should I fire you when I've just invested $100,000 in your development?" (McCall, Lombardo, & Morrison, 1988, p. 154).

Once a task has been delegated, even though the subordinate's training and development are continuing, the leader should be cautious about providing too much unsolicited advice or engaging in "rescue" activities. An exception would be when a subordinate's mistake would put significant organizational assets at risk. On the other hand, the leader needs to establish specific procedures for periodically reviewing the subordinate's performance of the delegated task. Leaders need to maintain good records of all the assignments they have delegated, including appropriate milestone and completion dates for each one.

Give Credit, Not Blame

Whenever leaders delegate, they must give subordinates *authority* along with responsibility. In the final analysis, however, leaders always remain fully responsible and accountable for any delegated task. If things should go wrong, then *leaders* should accept responsibility for failure fully and completely and never try to pass blame on to subordinates. On the other hand, if things go well, as they usually will, then leaders should give all the public credit to the subordinates. Also, when providing performance feedback privately to a subordinate, emphasize what went right rather than what went wrong. Leaders should not ignore errors in judgment or implementation, but they need not dwell on them, either. One helpful approach to performance feedback is called the sandwich technique. With this technique, negative feedback is placed in between two "pieces" of positive feedback. It affirms the subordinate's good work, puts the subordinate at least somewhat at ease, and keeps the ratio of positive and negative comments in balance. The idea of a sandwich, however, should not be taken too literally. There is nothing magical about two pieces of positive feedback for one piece of negative feedback. In fact, from the receiver's point of view the balance between positive and negative feedback may seem "about right" when the ratio is considerably higher than 2:1.

In summary, Taylor (1989) has provided useful insight about the importance of delegation as well as specific and helpful suggestions for delegating more effectively.

Managing Conflict

> What Is Conflict?
>
> Is Conflict Always Bad?
>
> Conflict Resolution Strategies

We read or hear every day in the news about various types of negotiations. Nations often negotiate with each other over land or fishing rights, trade agreements, or diplomatic relations. Land developers often negotiate with city councils for variances on local zoning laws for their projects. Businesses often spend considerable time negotiating employee salaries and fringe benefits with labor unions. In a similar fashion, negotiations go on every day about matters ranging from high school athletic schedules to where a new office copying machine will be located. In one sense, all these negotiations, big or small, are similar. In every case, representatives from different groups meet to resolve some sort of conflict. Conflict is an inevitable fact of life and an inevitable fact of leadership. Researchers have found that first-line supervisors and middle-level managers can spend more than 25 percent of their time dealing with conflict (Thomas & Schmidt, 1976), and resolving conflicts has been found to be an important factor in leadership effectiveness (Morse & Wagner, 1978). In fact, successfully resolving conflicts is so important that it is a central theme in some of the literature about organizations (Brown, 1983; Ouchi, 1981; Peters & Waterman, 1982). Moreover, successfully resolving conflicts will become an increasingly important skill as leadership and management practice moves away from authoritarian directives and toward cooperative approaches emphasizing rational persuasion, collaboration, compromise, and solutions of mutual gain.

What Is Conflict?

Conflict occurs when two opposing parties have interests or goals that appear to be incompatible (Robbins, 1986). There are a variety of sources of conflict in team, committee, work-group, and organizational settings. For example, conflict can occur when group or team members (*a*) have strong differences in values, beliefs, or goals; (*b*) have high levels of task or lateral interdependence; (*c*) are competing for scarce resources or rewards; (*d*) are under high levels of stress; or (*e*) face uncertain or incompatible demands—that is, role ambiguity and role conflict (Yukl, 1989). Conflict can also occur when leaders act in a manner inconsistent with the vision and goals they have articulated for the organization (Kets de Vries & Miller, 1984). Of these factors contributing to the level of conflict within or between groups, teams, or committees, probably the most important source of conflict is the lack of communication between parties (Thomas & Schmidt, 1976). Because many conflicts are the result of misunderstandings and communication breakdowns, leaders can minimize the level of conflict within and between groups by improving their communication and listening skills, as well as spending time networking with others (Yukl, 1989).

Before reviewing specific negotiation tips and conflict resolution strategies, it is necessary to describe several aspects of conflict that can have an impact on the resolution process. First, the size of an issue (bigger issues are more difficult to resolve), the extent to which parties define the problem egocentrically (how much they have personally invested in the problem), and the existence of hidden agendas (unstated but important concerns or objectives) can all affect the conflict resolution process. Second, seeing a conflict situation in win–lose or either/or terms restricts the (perceived) possible outcomes to either total satisfaction or total frustration. A similar but less-extreme variant is to see a situation in zero-sum terms. A zero-sum situation is one in which intermediate degrees of satisfaction are possible (i.e., not either/or), but increases in one party's satisfaction inherently decrease the other party's satisfaction, and vice versa. Still another variant can be when parties perceive a conflict as unresolvable. In such cases neither party gains at the expense of the other, but each continues to perceive the other as an obstacle to satisfaction (Thomas, 1976).

Is Conflict Always Bad?

So far, we have described conflict as an inherently negative aspect of any group, team, committee, or organization. This certainly was the prevailing view of conflict among researchers during the 1930s and 1940s, and it probably also represents the way many people are raised today (i.e., most people have a strong value of minimizing or avoiding conflict). Today, researchers studying group effectiveness have come to a different conclusion. Some level of conflict may be helpful in order to bolster innovation and performance (Robbins, 1986). Conflict that enhances group productivity is viewed as useful, and conflict that hinders group performance is viewed as counterproductive (Robbins, 1986). Various possible positive and negative effects of conflict are listed in Highlight MC.1.

Possible Effects of Conflict

Highlight MC.1

Possible Positive Effects of Conflict	**Possible Negative Effects of Conflict**
Increased effort	Reduced productivity
Feelings get aired	Decreased communication
Better understanding of others	Negative feelings
Impetus for change	Stress
Better decision making	Poorer decision making
Key issues surfaced	Decreased cooperation
Critical thinking stimulated	Political backstabbing

Along these lines, researchers have found that conflict can cause a radical change in political power (Bass, 1985; Weber, 1947; Willner, 1984), as well as dramatic changes in organizational structure and design, group cohesiveness, and group or organizational effectiveness (Roberts & Bradley, 1988; Kanter, 1983). Nevertheless, it is important to realize that this current conceptualization of conflict is still somewhat limited in scope. For example, increasing the level of conflict within a group or team may enhance immediate performance but may also have a disastrous effect on organizational climate and turnover. As we noted in Chapter 4, however, leaders may be evaluated in terms of many criteria, only one of which is group performance. Thus, leaders should probably use criteria such as turnover and absenteeism rates and followers' satisfaction or organizational climate ratings in addition to measures of group performance when trying to determine whether conflict is good or bad. Leaders are cautioned against using group performance alone, as these indices may not reveal the overall effects of conflict on the group or team.

Conflict Resolution Strategies

In addition to spending time understanding and clarifying positions, separating people from the problem, and focusing on interests, there are five strategies or approaches leaders can use to resolve conflicts. Perhaps the best way to differentiate between these five strategies is to think of conflict resolution in terms of two independent dimensions: cooperativeness/uncooperativeness and assertiveness/unassertiveness (see Figure MC.1). Parties in conflict do vary in their commitment to satisfy the other's concerns, but they also vary in the extent to which they assertively stand up for their own concerns (Thomas, 1976). Thus, conflict resolution can be understood in terms of how cooperative or uncooperative the parties are and how assertive or unassertive they are.

Using this two-dimension scheme, Thomas (1976) described five general approaches to managing conflict:

1. **Competition** reflects a desire to achieve one's own ends at the expense of someone else. This is domination, also known as a win–lose orientation.
2. **Accommodation** reflects a mirror image of competition, entirely giving in to someone else's concerns without making any effort to achieve one's own ends. This is a tactic of appeasement.
3. **Sharing** is an approach that represents a compromise between domination and appeasement. Both parties give up something, yet both parties get something. Both parties are moderately, but incompletely, satisfied.
4. **Collaboration** reflects an effort to fully satisfy both parties. This is a problem-solving approach that requires the integration of each party's concerns.
5. **Avoidance** involves indifference to the concerns of both parties. It reflects a withdrawal from or neglect of any party's interests.

Does one of these approaches seem clearly a better method than the other to you? Each of them does, at least, reflect certain culturally valued modes of behavior (Thomas, 1977). For example, the esteem many people hold for athletic, business, and military heroes reflects our cultural valuation of competition. Valuation of a pragmatic approach to settling problems is reflected in the compromising ap-

Advanced Leadership Skills   **489**

FIGURE MC.1

Five conflict-handling orientations, plotted according to party's desire to satisfy own and other's concerns.

Source: K. W. Thomas, "Conflict and Conflict Management," in *Handbook of Industrial and Organizational Psychology*, ed. M. D. Dunnette (Chicago: Rand McNally, 1976). Used by permission of Marvin D. Dunnette.

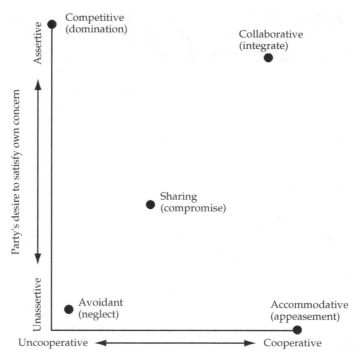

proach. Cultural values of unselfishness, kindness, and generosity are reflected in accommodation, and even avoidance has roots in philosophies that emphasize caution, diplomacy, and turning away from worldly concerns. These cultural roots to each of the approaches to managing conflict suggest that no single one is likely to be the right one all the time. There probably are circumstances when each of the modes of conflict resolution can be appropriate. Rather than seeking to find some single best approach to managing conflict, it may be wisest to appreciate the relative advantages and disadvantages of all approaches, and the circumstances when each may be most appropriate. A summary of experienced leaders' recommendations for when to use each strategy is presented in Highlight MC.2 (Thomas, 1977).

Negotiation

Prepare for the Negotiation
Separate the People from the Problem
Focus on Interests, Not Positions

Negotiation is an approach that may help resolve some conflicts. The following negotiating tips, from Fisher and Ury (1981), include taking the time to prepare for a negotiating session; keeping the people and problems separate; focusing on issues, not positions; and seeking win–win outcomes.

Situations in Which to Use the Five Approaches to Conflict Management

Highlight MC.2

COMPETING

1. When quick, decisive action is vital—e.g., emergencies.
2. On important issues where unpopular actions need implementing—e.g., cost cutting, enforcing unpopular rules, discipline.
3. On issues vital to company welfare when you know you're right.
4. Against people who take advantage of noncompetitive behavior.

COLLABORATING

1. To find an integrative solution when both sets of concerns are too important to be compromised.
2. When your objective is to learn.
3. To merge insights from people with different perspectives.
4. To gain commitment by incorporating concerns into a consensus.
5. To work through feelings which have interfered with a relationship.

COMPROMISING

1. When goals are important, but not worth the effort or potential disruption of more assertive modes.
2. When opponents with equal power are committed to mutually exclusive goals.
3. To achieve temporary settlements of complex issues.
4. To arrive at expedient solutions under time pressure.
5. As a backup when collaboration or competition is unsuccessful.

AVOIDING

1. When an issue is trivial or more important issues are pressing.
2. When you perceive no chance of satisfying your concerns.
3. When potential disruption outweighs the benefits of resolution.
4. To let people cool down and regain perspective.
5. When gathering information supersedes immediate decision.
6. When others can resolve the conflict more effectively.
7. When issues seem tangential to or symptomatic of other issues.

ACCOMMODATING

1. When you find you are wrong—to allow a better position to be heard, to learn, and to show your reasonableness.
2. When issues are more important to others than yourself—to satisfy others and maintain cooperation.
3. To build social credits for later issues.
4. To minimize loss when you are outmatched and losing.
5. When harmony and stability are especially important.
6. To allow subordinates to develop by learning from mistakes.

Source: K. W. Thomas, "Toward Multidimensional Values in Teaching: The Example of Conflict Management," *Academy of Management Review* 2, no. 3 (1977), pp. 484–90. Used with permission.

Prepare for the Negotiation

To successfully resolve conflicts, leaders may need to *spend considerable time preparing for a negotiating session.* Leaders should anticipate each side's key concerns and issues, attitudes, possible negotiating strategies, and goals.

Separate the People from the Problem

Fisher and Ury (1981) also advised negotiators to *separate the people from the problem.* Because all negotiations involve substantive issues and relationships between negotiators, it is easy for these parts to become entangled. When that happens, parties may inadvertently treat the people *and* the problem as though they were the same. For example, a group of teachers angry that their salary has not been raised for the fourth year in a row may direct their personal bitterness toward the school board president. However, reactions such as these are usually a mistake, as the decision may be out of the other party's hands, and personally attacking the other party often only serves to make the conflict even more difficult to resolve.

There are several things leaders can do to separate the people from the problem. First, leaders should not let their fears color their perceptions of each side's intentions. It is easy to attribute negative qualities to others when one feels threatened. Similarly, it does no good to blame the other side for one's own problems (Blake, Shepard, & Mouton, 1964). Even if it is justified, it is still usually counterproductive. Another thing leaders can do to separate the people from the problem is to communicate clearly. Earlier in this text, we suggested techniques for active listening. Those guidelines are especially helpful in negotiating and resolving conflicts.

Focus on Interests, Not Positions

Another of Fisher and Ury's (1981) main points is to *focus on interests, not positions.* Focusing on interests depends on understanding the difference between interests and positions. Here is one example. Say Raoul has had the same reserved seats to the local symphony every season for several years and he was just notified he will no longer get his usual tickets. Feeling irate, he goes to the ticket office to complain. One approach he could take would be to demand the same seats he has always had; this would be his *position.* A different approach would be to find alternative seats that are just as satisfactory as his old seats had been; this would be his *interest.* In negotiating, it is much more constructive to satisfy interests than to fight over positions. Furthermore, it is important to focus both on your counterpart's interests (not position) and on your own interests (not position).

Finally, winning a negotiation at your counterpart's expense is likely to be only a short-term gain. Leaders should attempt to work out a resolution by looking at long-term rather than short-term goals, and they should try to build a working relationship that will endure and be mutually trusting and beneficial beyond the present negotiation. Along these lines, leaders should always seek win–win outcomes, which try to satisfy both sides' needs and continuing interests. It often takes creative problem solving to find new options that provide gains for both sides. Realistically, however, not all situations may be conducive to seeking win–win outcomes (see Highlight N.1).

Problem Solving

Identifying Problems or Opportunities for Improvement

Analyzing the Causes

Developing Alternative Solutions

Selecting and Implementing the Best Solution

Assessing the Impact of the Solution

How to Swim with Sharks

Highlight N.1

It is dangerous to swim with sharks, but not all sharks are found in the water. Some people may behave like sharks, and a best-selling book for executives written a few years ago took its title from that theme. However, an article appeared in the journal *Perspectives in Biology and Medicine* nearly three decades ago claiming to be a translated version of an essay written in France more than a century earlier for sponge divers (Cousteau, 1973). The essay notes that while no one wants to swim with sharks, it is an occupational hazard for certain people. For those who must swim with sharks, it can be essential to follow certain rules. See if you think the following rules for interacting with the sharks of the sea serve as useful analogies for interacting with the sharks of everyday life.

Rule 1: Assume any unidentified fish is a shark. Just because a fish may be acting in a docile manner does not mean it is not a shark. The real test is how it will act when blood is in the water.

Rule 2: Don't bleed. Bleeding will prompt even more aggressive behavior and the involvement of even more sharks. Of course, it is not easy to keep from bleeding when injured. Those who cannot do so are advised not to swim with sharks at all.

Rule 3: Confront aggression quickly. Sharks usually give warning before attacking a swimmer. Swimmers should watch for indications an attack is imminent and take prompt counteraction. A blow to the nose is often appropriate since it shows you understand the shark's intentions and will respond in kind. It is particularly dangerous to behave in an ingratiating manner toward sharks. People who once held this erroneous view often can be identified by a missing limb.

Rule 4: Get out of the water if anyone starts bleeding. Previously docile sharks may begin attacking if blood is in the water. Their behavior can become so irrational, even including attacking themselves, that it is safest to remove yourself entirely from the situation.

Rule 5: Create dissension among the attackers. Sharks are self-centered and rarely act in an organized fashion with other sharks. This significantly reduces the risk of swimming with sharks. Every now and then, however, sharks may launch a coordinated attack. The best strategy then is to create internal dissension among them since they already are quite prone to it; often sharks will fight among themselves over trivial or minor things. By the time their internal conflict is settled, sharks often have forgotten about their organized attack.

Rule 6: Never divert a shark attack toward another swimmer. Please observe this final item of swimming etiquette.

Identifying Problems or Opportunities for Improvement

The first step in problem solving is to state the problem so that everyone involved in developing a solution has an informed and common appreciation and understanding of the task. This is a critical stage in problem solving and will take time and probably group discussion. It is dangerous to assume that everyone (or anyone!) knows at the outset what the problem is. A hurried or premature definition of the problem (e.g., as a result of groupthink) may lead to considerable frustration and wasted effort. In counseling and advising, for example, a significant portion of the work with a client is devoted to clarifying the problem. A student may seek help at the school counseling center to improve his study skills because he is spending what seems to be plenty of time studying yet is still doing poorly on examinations. A little discussion, however, may reveal that he is having difficulty concentrating on schoolwork because of problems at home. If the counselor had moved immediately to develop the client's study skills, the real cause of his difficulties would have gone untreated, and the client might have become even more pessimistic about his abilities and the possibility that others can help him. Or consider the case of a police chief who is concerned about the few volunteers willing to serve on a citizen's advisory committee to her department. There are many problems she might identify here, such as citizen apathy or poor publicity concerning the need and importance of the committee. The real problem, however, might be her own reputation for rarely listening to or heeding recommendations made by similar advisory committees in the past. If the chief were to take the time to explore and clarify the problem at the outset, then she *could* discover this important fact and take steps to solve the *real* problem (her own behavior). If, on the other hand, she pressed ahead aggressively, trusting her own appraisal of the problem, then nothing likely would change.

The reason it helps to take time to define a problem carefully is that sometimes people mistake symptoms for causes. In the case of the student, his poor studying was a symptom of another cause (family difficulties), not the cause of his poor grades. In the case of the police chief, lack of citizen participation on the advisory committee was a symptom of a problem, not the problem itself. If a plan addresses a symptom rather than the causes of a problem, the desired results will not be attained. It also is important during this stage to avoid scapegoating or blaming individuals or groups for the problem, which may just engender defensiveness and reduce creative thinking. This is a stage where conflict resolution techniques and negotiating skills can be very important. Finally, the statement of a problem should not imply that any particular solution is the correct one.

As an application of these considerations, let us consider two pairs of problem statements that a teacher might present to his class as a first step in addressing what he considers to be an unsatisfactory situation. These samples of dialogue touch on many aspects of communication, listening, and feedback skills addressed earlier in this book. Here, however, our focus is on differences in defining problems. In each case, the second statement is the one more likely to lead to constructive problem solving.

> **A:** I don't think you care enough about this course. No one is ever prepared. What do I have to do to get you to put in more time on your homework?
>
> **B:** What things are interfering with your doing well in this course?
>
> **A:** Your test grades are too low. I'm going to cancel the field trip unless they improve. Do you have any questions?
>
> **B:** I'm concerned about your test scores. They're lower than I expected them to be, and I'm not sure what's going on. What do you think the problem is?

Another aspect of this first stage of problem solving involves identifying those factors that, when corrected, are likely to have the greatest impact on improving an unsatisfactory situation. Since there are almost always more problems or opportunities for improvement than time or energy to devote to them all, it is crucial to identify those whose solutions offer the greatest potential payoff. A useful concept here is known as the Pareto principle. It states that about 80 percent of the

FIGURE PS.1
A cause-and-effect diagram.

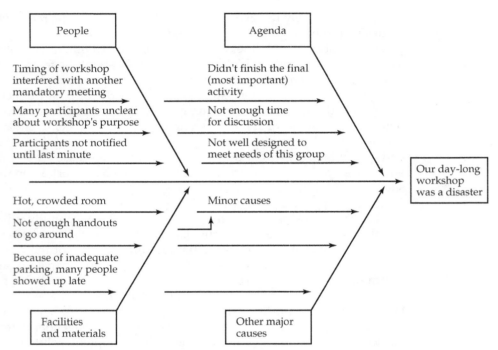

problems in any system are the result of about 20 percent of the causes. In school, for example, most of the discipline problems are caused by a minority of the students. Of all the errors people make on income tax returns, just a few kinds of errors (e.g., forgetting to sign them) account for a disproportionately high percentage of returned forms. We would expect about 20 percent of the total mechanical problems in a city bus fleet to account for about 80 percent of the fleet's downtime. The Pareto principle can be used to focus problem-solving efforts on those causes that have the greatest overall impact.

Analyzing the Causes

Once a problem is identified, the next step is to analyze its causes. Analysis of a problem's causes should precede a search for its solutions. Two helpful tools for identifying the key elements affecting a problem situation are the cause-and-effect diagram (also called the "fishbone" diagram because of its shape, or the Ishikawa diagram after the person who developed it) and force field analysis. The cause-and-effect diagram uses a graphic approach to depict systematically the root causes of a problem, the relationships between different causes, and potentially a prioritization of which causes are most important (see Figure PS.1).

Force field analysis (see Figure PS.2) also uses a graphic approach, this time to depict the opposing forces that tend to perpetuate a present state of affairs. It is a way of depicting any stable situation in terms of dynamic balance, or equilibrium,

FIGURE PS.2
Force field analysis example: Starting personal exercise program.

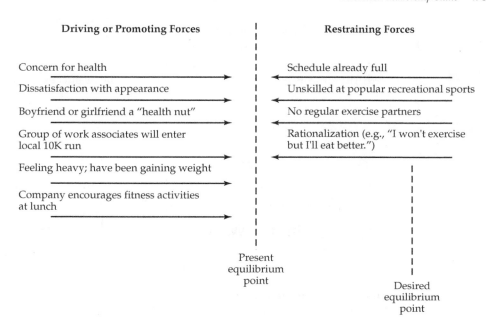

Driving or Promoting Forces	Restraining Forces

Concern for health → ← Schedule already full

Dissatisfaction with appearance → ← Unskilled at popular recreational sports

Boyfriend or girlfriend a "health nut" → ← No regular exercise partners

Group of work associates will enter local 10K run → ← Rationalization (e.g., "I won't exercise but I'll eat better.")

Feeling heavy; have been gaining weight →

Company encourages fitness activities at lunch →

Present equilibrium point

Desired equilibrium point

between those forces that tend to press toward movement in one direction and those other forces that tend to restrain movement in that direction. So long as the net sum of all those forces is zero, no movement occurs. When a change is desirable, force field analysis can be used to identify the best way to upset the balance between positive and negative forces so that a different equilibrium can be reached.

Developing Alternative Solutions

Several ideas we've examined previously are relevant here (e.g., brainstorming), as is the importance of solutions meeting criteria for quality and acceptance. A procedure called Nominal Group Technique (NGT) is another way to generate a lot of ideas pertinent to a problem (Delbecq, Van de Ven, & Gustafson, 1975). This procedure is similar to brainstorming in that it is an idea-generating activity conducted in a group setting. With NGT, however, group members write down ideas on individual slips of paper, which are later transferred to a blackboard or flipchart for the entire group to work with.

Selecting and Implementing the Best Solution

The first solution one thinks of is not necessarily the best solution, even if everyone involved finds it acceptable. It is better to select a solution on the basis of established criteria. These include such questions as the following: Have the advantages and disadvantages of all possible solutions been considered? Have all the possible solutions been evaluated in terms of their respective impacts on the whole organization, not just a particular team or department? Is the information needed to make a good decision among the alternatives available?

Assessing the Impact of the Solution

One should not assume that just by going through the preceding steps the actions implemented will solve the problem. The solution's continuing impact must be assessed, preferably in terms of measurable criteria of success that all parties involved can agree on.

Improving Creativity

> Seeing Things in New Ways
> Using Power Constructively
> Forming Diverse Problem-Solving Groups

Seeing Things in New Ways

There are several things leaders can do to increase their own and their followers' creativity. Some of these facilitating factors have already been discussed and include assuring adequate levels of technical expertise, delaying and minimizing the evaluation or judgment of solutions, focusing on the intrinsic motivation of the task, removing unnecessary constraints on followers, and giving followers more latitude in making decisions. One popular technique for stimulating creative thinking in groups is called brainstorming (see Highlight IC.1).

An additional thing leaders can do to enhance creativity is to *see things in new ways,* or to look at problems from as many perspectives as possible. This is, though, easier said than done. It can be difficult to see novel uses for things we are very familiar with, or to see such in novel ways. Psychologists call this kind of mental block functional fixedness (Duncker, 1945). Creative thinking depends on overcoming the functional fixedness associated with the rigid and stereotyped perceptions we have of the things around us.

One way to see things differently is to think in terms of analogies. Thinking in terms of analogies is a practical extension of Cronbach's (1984) definition of creativity—making fresh observations, or seeing one thing as something else. In this case, the active search for analogies is the essence of the problem-solving method. In fact, finding analogies is the foundation of a commercial creative-problem-solving approach called Synectics (W. J. J. Gordon, 1961). An actual example of use of analogies in a Synectics problem-solving group concerned designing a new roofing material that would adjust its color to the season, turning white in the summer to reflect heat and black in the winter to absorb heat. The group's first task was to find an analogy in nature, and it thought of fishes whose colors change to match their surroundings. The mechanism for such changes in fish is the movement of tiny compartments of pigments closer to or farther away from the skin's surface, thus changing its color. After some discussion, the group designed a black roof impregnated with little white plastic balls which would expand when it is hot, making the roof lighter, and contract when it is cold, making the roof darker (W. J. J. Gordon, 1961).

Another way to see things differently is to try putting an idea or problem into a picture rather than into words. Feelings or relationships that have eluded verbal description may come out in a drawing, bringing fresh insights to an issue.

Steps for Enhancing Creativity through Brainstorming

Highlight IC.1

Brainstorming is a technique designed to enhance the creative potential of any group trying to solve a problem. Leaders should use the following rules when conducting a brainstorming session:

1. Groups should consist of five to seven people: Fewer than five limits the number of ideas generated, but more than seven often can make the session unwieldy. It may be more important to carefully decide who should attend a session than how many people should attend.

2. Everybody should be given the chance to contribute. The first phase of brainstorming is idea generation, and members should be encouraged to spontaneously contribute ideas as soon as they get them. The objective in the first phase is quantity, not quality.

3. No criticism is allowed during the idea generation phase. This helps to clearly separate the activities of imaginative thinking and idea production from idea evaluation.

4. Freewheeling and outlandish ideas should be encouraged. With some modification, these ideas may be eventually adopted.

5. "Piggybacking" off others' ideas should be encouraged. Combining ideas or extending others' ideas often results in better solutions.

6. The greater the quantity and variety of ideas, the better. The more ideas generated, the greater the probability a good solution will be found.

7. Ideas should be recorded. Ideally, ideas should be recorded on a blackboard or butcher paper so that members can review all of the ideas generated.

8. After all of the ideas have been generated, each idea should be evaluated in terms of pros and cons, costs and benefits, feasibility, and so on. Choosing the final solution often depends on the results of these analyses.

Source: A. F. Osborn, *Applied Imagination* (New York: Scribner's, 1963).

Using Power Constructively

In addition to getting followers to see problems from as many perspectives as possible, a leader can also *use her power constructively to enhance creativity*. As noted earlier, groups may suppress creative thinking by being overly critical or by passing judgment during the solution generation stage. This effect may be even more pronounced when strong authority relationships and status differences are present. Group members may be reluctant to take the risk of raising a "crazy" idea when superiors are present, especially if the leader is generally perceived as unreceptive to new ideas, or they may be reluctant to offer the idea if they believe others in the group will take potshots at it in front of the leader. Leaders who wish to create a favorable climate for fostering creativity need to use their power to encourage the open expression of ideas and to suppress uncooperative or aggressive reactions (overt or covert) between group members. Further, leaders can use their power to encourage creativity by rewarding successes and by not punishing mistakes. Leaders can also use their power to delegate authority and responsibility, relax followers' constraints, and empower followers to take risks. By taking these steps, leaders can help followers to build idiosyncratic credits, which in turn will encourage them to take risks and to be more creative. Along these same lines, the entire climate of an organization can be either more or less conducive to creative thinking, differences that may be due to the use of power within the organization. In an insightful turn of the familiar adage, "Power corrupts," Kanter (1982) noted how powerlessness also corrupts. She pointed out how managers who feel powerless in an organization may spend more energy guarding their territory than collaborating with others in productive action. The need to actively support followers' creativity may be especially important for leaders in bureaucratic organizations, as such organizations tend to be so inflexible, formalized, and centralized as to make many people in them feel relatively powerless.

Forming Diverse Problem-Solving Groups

Leaders can enhance creativity by *forming diverse problem-solving groups.* Group members with similar experiences, values, and preferences will be less likely to create a wide variety of solutions and more apt to agree on a solution prematurely than more diverse groups. Thus, selecting people for a group or committee with a variety of experiences, values, and preferences should increase the creativity of the group, although these differences may also increase the level of conflict within the group and make it more difficult for the leader to get consensus on a final solution. One technique for increasing group diversity and, in turn, creativity in problem-solving groups involves the use of the four preference dimensions of the Myers-Briggs Type Indicator (MBTI). Actual evidence to support this specific approach appears scanty (Thayer, 1988), but perhaps preferences only assume significance after certain other conditions for group creativity already have been met. For example, diversity cannot make up for an absence of technical expertise. Although the MBTI dimensions may be useful in selecting diverse groups, this instrument should only be used after ensuring that all potential members have high levels of technical expertise. Choosing members based solely on MBTI preferences ignores the crucial role that technical expertise and intrinsic motivation play in creativity. Another aspect of the relationship between creativity and leadership is described in Highlight IC.2.

Diagnosing Performance Problems in Individuals, Groups, and Organizations

Expectations
Capabilities
Opportunities
Motivation

In many ways leaders will only be as effective as the followers and teams they lead. Along these lines, one of the more difficult issues leaders must deal with is managing individuals or teams that are not performing up to expectations. What makes this issue even more difficult is that although the lack of performance may be obvious, the reasons for it may not. Leaders who correctly determine why a follower or team is exhibiting suboptimal performance are much more likely to implement an appropriate intervention to fix the problem. Unfortunately, many leaders do not have a model or framework for diagnosing performance problems at work, and as

Managing Creativity

Highlight IC.2

T. Hogan and Morrison (1993) maintained that people who are seen as more creative tend to have several distinguishing personality characteristics. In general, creative people are open to information and experience, have high energy, can be personally assertive and even domineering, react emotionally to events, are impulsive, are more interested in music and art than in hunting and sports, and finally are very motivated to prove themselves (i.e., are concerned with personal adequacy). Thus, creative people tend to be independent, willful, impractical, unconcerned with money, idealistic, and nonconforming. Given that these tendencies may not make them ideal followers, the interesting question raised by Hogan and Morrison is: How does one lead or manage creative individuals? This question becomes even more interesting when considering the qualities of successful leaders or managers. As discussed earlier, successful leaders tend to be intelligent, dominant, conscientious, stable, calm, goal-oriented, outgoing, and somewhat conventional. Thus, one might think that the personalities of creative followers and successful leaders might be the source of considerable conflict and make them natural enemies in organizational settings. Because many organizations depend on creativity to grow and prosper, being able to successfully lead creative individuals may be a crucial aspect of success for these organizations. Given that creative people already possess technical expertise, imaginative thinking skills, and intrinsic motivation, Hogan and Morrison suggested that leaders take the following steps to successfully lead creative followers:

1. Set goals. Because creative people value freedom and independence, this step will be best accomplished if leaders use a high level of participation in the goal-setting process. Leaders should ask followers what they can accomplish in a particular time frame.

2. Provide adequate resources. Followers will be much more creative if they have the proper equipment to work with, as they can devote their time to resolving the problem rather than spending time finding the equipment to get the job done.

3. Reduce time pressures, but keep followers on track. Try to set realistic milestones when setting goals, and make organizational rewards contingent on reaching these milestones. Moreover, leaders need to be well organized to acquire necessary resources and to keep the project on track.

4. Consider nonmonetary as well as monetary rewards. Creative people often gain satisfaction from resolving the problem at hand, not from monetary rewards. Thus, feedback should be aimed at enhancing their feelings of personal adequacy. Monetary rewards perceived to be controlling may decrease rather than increase motivation toward the task.

5. Recognize that creativity is evolutionary, not revolutionary. Although followers can create truly novel products (such as the Xerox machine), often the key to creativity is continuous product improvement. Making next year's product faster, lighter, cheaper, or more efficient requires minor modifications that can, over time, culminate in major revolutions. Thus, it may be helpful if leaders think of creativity more in terms of small innovations than major breakthroughs.

Source: R. T. Hogan and J. Morrison, "Managing Creativity," in *Create & Be Free: Essays in Honor of Frank Barron,* ed. A. Montouri (Amsterdam: J. C. Gieben, 1993).

a result many do a poor job of dealing with problem performers. The model in Figure DPP.1 provides leaders with a pragmatic framework for understanding why a follower or team may not be performing up to expectations and what the leader can do to improve the situation. This model maintains that performance is a function of expectations, capabilities, opportunities, and motivation and integrates concepts discussed in more detail earlier in this book.

500   **Part Five**   *Leadership Skills*

FIGURE DPP.1
A model of performance.

Performance = f (Expectations $\times$ Capabilities $\times$ Opportunities $\times$ Motivation)

The model is also a modification of earlier models developed by J. P. Campbell (1977), Campbell, McCloy, Oppler, and Sager (1993), and Ramstad and Boudreau (2000). As a multiplicative rather than a compensatory model, a deficit in any one component should result in a substantial decrement in performance that cannot be easily made up by increasing the other components. An example might help to illuminate this point. Recently one of the authors was asked to help the manager of a nuclear power plant fix several safety and operational issues affecting the plant. Apparently many plant personnel did not feel they had to comply with governmental regulations regarding the proper use of safety equipment. An investigation into the problem revealed that the expectations for compliance were clear, everyone had been trained on the proper use of safety equipment, and the equipment was readily available. However, many personnel felt the equipment and procedures were a nuisance and unnecessary. The plant manager's initial attempt to rectify this problem was to run all plant personnel through a three-day nuclear safety training program. Much to the manager's surprise, the training program actually appeared to have a negative impact on safety compliance! This was due to the fact that the underlying issue was not expectations, capabilities, or opportunities but rather motivation. Even if the staff had 30 days of training it still would not have positively affected motivation, which was the underlying barrier to performance. Because there were few if any positive or negative consequences for the staff for properly using the equipment, the problem did not improve until the manager implemented a system of rewards and punishments for safety compliance. A more thorough explanation of the components of the model and what leaders can do to improve performance can be found below.

Expectations

Performance problems often occur because individuals or groups do not understand what they are supposed to do. There are many instances where talented, skilled groups accomplished the wrong objective because of miscommunication or sat idly by while waiting for instructions that never arrived. It is the leader's responsibility for ensuring that followers understand their roles, goals, performance standards, and the key metrics for determining success. More information about goal setting and clarifying team goals and roles can be found in the "Setting Goals" and "The Building Blocks of Team Building" sections in Part V of this text.

Capabilities

Just because followers understand what they are supposed to do does not necessarily mean they can do it. Sometimes followers and teams lack the capabilities needed to achieve a goal or perform above expectations. Abilities and skills are the two components that make up capabilities. Ability is really another name for raw talent, and includes such individual difference variables as athleticism, intelligence, creativity, and personality traits. As such, abilities are characteristics that are relatively difficult to change with training. Because abilities are relatively insensitive to training interventions, sending people who lack the required abilities to more training or motivating them to work harder will have relatively little impact on performance. Instead, the best remedy for this situation is to select those individuals with the abilities needed for performance.

Although followers may have the raw talent needed to perform a task, they still may lack the skills needed to perform at a high level. Such is the case with many athletic teams or musical groups at the beginning of the season or when a work group gets a new set of equipment or responsibility for tasks they have no previous experience with. As discussed in the "Leadership Behavior" chapter (8), skills consist of a well-defined body of knowledge and a set of related behaviors. Unlike abilities, skills are very amenable to training, and leaders with high levels of relevant expertise may coach others in the development of skills, see that they are obtained in other ways on the job, or send their followers to training programs in order to improve followers' skill levels. More information about selecting people with the right abilities can be found in Chapter 4. See Chapters 3 and 9 and the sections on "Building Technical Competence," "Coaching," and "Development Planning" in Part V for more information on building skills.

Opportunities

Performance can also be limited when followers lack the resources needed to get the job done. At other times followers may lack the opportunity to demonstrate acquired skills. Such is the case when passengers are hungry but flight attendants do not have any meals to pass out during the flight. In this situation the flight attendants could have very high levels of customer service goals, capabilities, and motivation but will still not be able to satisfy customer needs. Leaders must ensure that followers and teams have the needed equipment, financial resources, and the opportunities to exhibit their skills if they want to eliminate this constraint on performance. More about opportunities can be found in "The Building Blocks of Team Building" section in Part V of this text.

Motivation

Many performance problems can be attributed to a lack of motivation. The two critical issues here are whether followers or groups choose to perform or exhibit the level of effort necessary to accomplish a task. If this does not occur, then the leader should first try to learn why people are unmotivated. Sometimes the task may involve risks the leader is not aware of. At other times individuals or groups may simply run out of steam to perform the task or there are few consequences for superior or unsatisfactory performance. Leaders have several options to resolve motivation problems in followers and teams. First, they can select followers who have higher levels of achievement or intrinsic motivation for the task. Second, they can set clear goals or do a better job providing feedback about performance. Third, they can reallocate work across the team or redesign the task to improve skill variety, task significance, and task identity. Fourth, they can restructure rewards and punishments so they are more closely linked to performance levels. See the "Motivation, Satisfaction, and Performance" chapter (9) for more information about motivating followers.

Concluding Comments on the Diagnostic Model

In summary, this model provides an integrative framework for many of the topics affecting performance previously reviewed in this text. It reviews some of the factors that affect performance and suggests ideas for rectifying performance problems. It should be emphasized, however, that this model only addresses follower, group, and organizational performance. Leaders need to be mindful that there are other desirable outcomes, too, such as organizational climate and job satisfaction, and that actions to increase performance (especially just in the short term) may adversely impact these other desirable outcomes.

Team Building for Work Teams

Team-Building Interventions
What Does a Team-Building Workshop Involve?
Examples of Interventions

Few activities have become more commonplace in organizations these days than "team-building workshops." One reason for this level of activity is the powerful shift that has occurred in the workplace from a focus primarily on individual work to team-centered work. Unfortunately, however, they do not always achieve their objectives. As noted earlier in this text, it doesn't make sense to hold teams responsible for work if nothing else in the organizational environment changes. Team-building interventions, at the team level, may help team members understand why they are having so much difficulty in achieving team objectives, and even suggest coping strategies for an intolerable situation. They are not, however, very likely to remove root causes of the problem. In order to better understand the importance of looking at teams this way, let's use an example of this kind of erroneous thinking from a quite different context.

Team-Building Interventions

Suppose you have decided that the next car you drive must have outstanding ride and handling characteristics. Some cars you test, such as some huge American-made automobiles, have outstanding ride characteristics, but you are not happy with their handling. They sway and "float" in tight slalom courses. Other cars you test have just the opposite characteristics. They are as tight and as stable as you could hope for in turns and stops, but their ride is so hard that your dental work is in serious jeopardy. But you do find one car that seems to meet your requirements. In fact, a Mercedes-Benz does provide both an extremely comfortable ride and tremendous road handling characteristics in high-performance situations. There is, however, one small problem. The Mercedes costs a lot of money up front—more than you are willing to put into this project. So you arrive at an alternative solution. You find a used Yugo, a little car built in Yugoslavia and no longer imported into the United States, largely because of inferior quality. But it is really cheap, and after purchasing it, you know you will have lots of money left over to beef up the suspension, steering, and braking systems to provide you with the Mercedes-Benz ride you really want.

FIGURE TW.1

A rationale for individual, interpersonal, team, and organizational training.

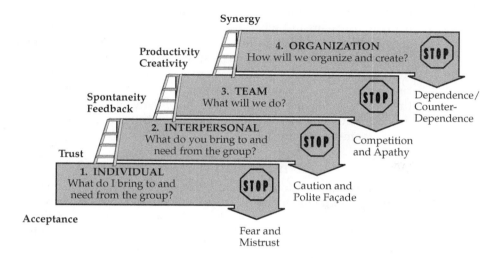

Ludicrous! Obviously, you are never going to get a Mercedes-Benz ride unless you are willing to put in considerable money and effort *up front* rather than doing little up front and putting all your money into repair work. But that is precisely what many organizations are attempting to do with teams. They do not seem willing to create the conditions necessary for teamwork to occur naturally (a point we will discuss in the section "Team Building at the Top"), but when the teams struggle in a hostile environment, as they invariably will, the leaders seem more than willing to pour tremendous amounts of money into team-building interventions to fix the problem. (And there are lots of team-building consultants out there willing to take their money.) These types of team-building problems are those we would categorize as "top-down."

An equally vexing problem occurs when organizations are committed to teamwork, are willing to change structures and systems to support it, but are not committed to the "bottom-up" work that will be required. This is best illustrated in the rationale for team training shown in Figure TW.1. In our work with organizations, we are frequently asked to help teams that are struggling. In Figure TW.1 we would place these requests at the "TEAM" level, which is the third platform up from the bottom. We believe this type of intervention will work only if the team members have achieved a stable platform from which to work. In this case, that would include the two previous platforms in Figure TW.1. If the foundation is not well established, the solely team-based intervention often leads to intrateam competition or apathy and withdrawal.

As a basis for any work at the team level, individual team members must first be comfortable with themselves. They must be able to answer the questions, "What do I bring to the team?" and "What do *I* need from the team?" Not to answer these questions breeds inherent fear and mistrust. When these questions have been answered, team members are then in a position to begin dealing at the interpersonal level, where they may now comfortably ask, "What do *you* bring to the team and what do *you* need from the team?" Not to resolve these issues results in caution in dealing with other members, and interactions at the "polite-façade" level rather than at the level of truth and understanding. If the first- and second-level platforms are in place, a true team-building intervention can be useful. (Incidentally, just because team members have not stabilized themselves at levels 1 and 2 does not mean an intervention can not be conducted. Rather, it means a more extensive intervention will be required than a solely team-based effort.)

What Does a Team-Building Workshop Involve?

There are literally hundreds, if not thousands, of team-building interventions that are being conducted today. There are many good sources, such as the *Team and Organization Development Sourcebook*, which contain team-based activities such as conflict resolution, problem solving, development of norms, building trust, or goal setting, to name but a few. Rather than trying to describe all of these suggestions, however, we will give you a few recommendations that we have found to be useful and then share a few examples of interventions we have used.

At the Center for Creative Leadership, staff are frequently asked to design custom team interventions for mid- to upper-level teams. While we enter these design meetings with no agenda of activities, neither do we enter with a completely blank slate. We believe an intervention at the team level must meet three general requirements to be successful, and at least one activity must be included in the intervention pertaining to each of those three requirements.

The first requirement involves awareness raising. As we noted in our previous chapters, not all cultures are equally prepared or nurtured in the concepts of teamwork. In fact, many of the lessons we think we have learned about teams are incorrect. So we believe we need to dispel such myths and include a healthy dose of team-based research findings about how teams *really* work as a critical element of a workshop. Second, we need some diagnostic, instrument-based feedback so team members can have a reasonably valid map of where they and their teammates now are located. Finally, each intervention must include a practice field, to use Senge's (1990) term. Practice is necessary for athletic success, and it is necessary in organizations too. It would be foolish to design a whole new series of plays for a hockey team to implement, talk about them in the locker room, but never actually practice any of them before expecting the team to implement them in a game. Similarly, if you are asking people to change their behaviors in the way they interact to improve teamwork, then it is only fair to provide them with a practice field upon which they can test their new behaviors in a reasonably risk-free, protected environment. This is where experiential exercises can be extremely useful. And it is here that the quality of the team-building facilitator is most critical. Conducting a pencil-and-paper exercise in the classroom does not require the same facilitator skill set as that required to conduct, say, a team-rappelling exercise off the face of a cliff—few facilitators get those requirements wrong and we have seldom discovered problems here. Where we have seen a significant breakdown in facilitator skills is in being able to make the link between the exercise that is conducted and the real world in which the team will be asked to perform. Here facilitators must have not only a good sense of real-time team dynamics, but also a sense of the business in which the team operates. They must help the participants make the links back to team dynamics that occur on the manufacturing floor or in the boardroom, and this seems to be the skill that separates highly effective facilitators from the pack.

Examples of Interventions

Now let us provide a few examples of the range of interventions that can be included in team building. Ginnett (1984) conducted an intervention with three interdependent teams from a state youth psychiatric hospital. The teams included members of the administrative services, the professional staff, and the direct care providers. The members of each team were dedicated to their roles in providing high-quality service to the youths under their care, but the three groups experienced great difficulty in working with each other. Extensive diagnosis of the groups revealed two underlying problems. First, each group had a very different vision of what the hospital was or should be. Second, each of the groups defined themselves as "care givers," thus making it very difficult for them to ask others for help since, in their minds, asking for help tended to put them in the role of their patients. We conducted a series of workshops to arrive at a common vision for the hospital, but the second problem required considerably more work. Since the staff members needed to experientially understand that asking for help did not place them in an inherently inferior position, a "Wilderness Experience" was designed where the entire staff was asked to spend four days together in a primitive wilderness environment with difficult hiking, climbing, and mountaineering requirements. By the end of the experience, everyone had found an occasion to ask someone else for help. Even more important, everyone found that actually asking others for help—something they had previously resisted—moved the overall team much higher in its ability to perform. Considerable time was spent each evening linking the lessons of the day with the work in the hospital.

In one of the more interesting programs we've conducted, a team of senior executives spent a week together at a ranch in Colorado. Each morning, the team met for a series of awareness sessions and data feedback sessions. Afternoons were reserved by the chief operating officer for fun and relaxation, with the only requirement being that attendees participate in them as a team or subteams. As facilitators, we actively participated with the teams, and related their team experiences each day to the lessons of the next morning, and to challenges facing the team in its normal work. In interventions like this we have learned that team building can be fun, and that the venues for it are almost limitless. Second, we have learned that being able to observe and process team activity in a real-time mode is critical for team-building facilitators. There is no substitute for first-hand observation as a basis for discerning group dynamics and noting the variety of revealing behaviors that emerge in unstructured team activities.

Building High Performance Teams: The Rocket Model

Mission
Talent
Norms
Buy-In
Power
Morale
Results
Implications of the Rocket Model

As stated throughout this text, leadership is not an individual process. Rather, it involves influencing a group to pursue some type of overarching goal. From Chapter 10 we know that teams vary on a number of important factors, such as group size, norms, development stages, and cohesion. We also know that leaders need to take these factors into consideration when creating and leading teams. The Team Effectiveness Leadership Model in Chapter 10 provides a very comprehensive description of team dynamics and what leaders must do if they want to create high performing teams. What follows is a much simpler and more pragmatic model of team effectiveness. **The Rocket Model of Team Effectiveness** (Curphy, 1999, 2000, 2004a, b, c; Curphy & Hogan, 2004; Krile, Curphy, & Lund, in press) is both a prescriptive and diagnostic model of team building. The model is prescriptive in that it tells leaders what steps to take and when to take them when building new teams. The model can also be used as a diagnostic tool for understanding where existing teams are falling short and what leaders need to do to get them back on track.

The Rocket Model is based on extensive research on and experience with teams in the health care, education, retail, manufacturing, service, software, telecommunications, energy, and financial service industries. The model has been used with executive teams at The Home Depot, Waste Management, and the Strategic Health Authority in the United Kingdom; midmanagement teams at Waste Management, Pfizer, and a number of rural hospitals and school districts; and project teams at Qwest Communications and Hewlett-Packard. The model seems to work equally well with different types of teams at different organizational levels in different industries. Leaders in particular like the Rocket Model because of its straightforward and practical approach to team building.

A graphic of the Rocket Model can be found in Figure BHPT.1. As depicted in the graphic, building a team can be analogous to building a house. Just as the booster stage is critical for getting a rocket off the ground, so are the Mission and Talent stages critical for starting a team. Once the Mission and Talent issues have been addressed, leaders will then need to work with team members to sort out team Norms and Buy-In, and so on. Research shows that the teams with the best Results are usually those who report a high level of team functioning on the six other components of the Rocket Model. Teams reporting a high level of functioning in only some of the components usually report mediocre Results, and those with low functioning on all six components usually achieve few if any Results. The following is a more in-depth description of the seven components of the Rocket Model.

**FIGURE
BHPT.1**
The Rocket
Model.

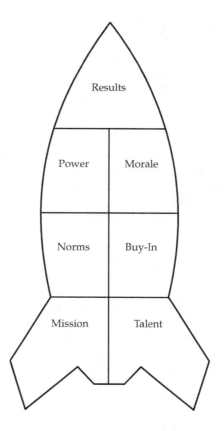

Mission

When building a new team, the first thing a leader must do is clarify the team's purpose and goals, set team performance standards, and ensure individual team member goals are aligned with the team's goals. Thus, the **Mission** component of the Rocket Model is concerned with setting a common direction for the team. In some cases the leader works closely with team members to sort out these issues; in other cases the leader makes these determinations; and in other cases the organization may make these decisions. For this component of the model, who makes these decisions is not as important as ensuring that everyone on the team understands what the team is trying to accomplish and how they personally contribute to team success. Teams with this common understanding often experience much lower levels of role ambiguity and conflict.

Of all the components in the Rocket Model, Mission may be the most important component. This is the case because it drives all the other components of the model. The Mission of the team will play a big role in determining the number and skills of people needed to achieve results (Talent), the rules by which the team operates (Norms), and the equipment and budget needed (Power). Because Mission plays such a critical role in team building, leaders of underperforming teams often find it worthwhile to first review the team's purpose, goals, and performance standards when striving to improve team performance.

If we were to apply the Rocket Model to a learning team in a college Leadership course, then the first thing the team should do is clarify what the team wants to accomplish. This might include such things as everyone on the team getting an A on the midterm, final exam, and overall course. Once the overall Mission and team goals are determined, the learning team would then need to decide who would do what and what the performance standards would be for each team member.

Talent

Teams with too many or too few people or with team members lacking the skills needed to achieve team goals often will report lower Talent scores than teams having the right number of people with the right skills. Selecting the right kind of people and continuously developing those skills needed to achieve team goals are two key leadership activities in this component of the Rocket Model. And the selection and development of Talent is precisely where many teams fall short. Professional athletic and elite military combat teams obsess over hiring decisions and spend countless hours practicing; they actually spend very little time performing. Most other teams seem to do just the opposite in that they do nothing more than throw a group of available people together and expect them to produce. These latter teams do not think through who needs to be on the team, spend little if any time developing needed skills, and never practice.

In the learning team example, Talent would come into play if team leaders selected their teammates on the basis of GPA and how well potential team members got along with others. Once the team was assembled, team leaders would then determine what skills they still needed to develop and work to ensure the team improved in these areas. Team skills could be developed through coaching, training programs, practice test sessions, and so on. Of course, this scenario assumes the leader gets to pick team members. Many times leaders do not have this luxury. If leaders do not get to pick team members, then it is imperative that they assess and develop those skills needed to accomplish team goals.

Norms

Once team members are selected and have a clear understanding of the team's purpose and goals, leaders then need to address the Norms component of the Rocket Model. Norms are the rules that govern how teams make decisions, conduct meetings, get work done, hold team members accountable for results, and share information. There are several important aspects of norms that are worth noting. First, the decisions the team makes, the way in which it makes decisions, how often and how long the team meets, and so forth, should all be driven by the team's purpose and goals. Second, Norms happen. If the team or team leader is not explicit about setting the rules that govern team behavior, they will simply evolve over time. And when they are not explicitly set, these rules may run counter to the team's purpose and goals. For example, one of the authors was working with a software development team that was responsible for delivering several new products in a six-month time period. The time frame was very aggressive, but one of the team Norms that had evolved was that it was okay for team members to show up late to team meetings, if they even bothered to show up. But the team meetings were very important to the success of the team, as they were the only time the team could discuss problems and coordinate its software development efforts. Team member behavior did not change until an explicit norm was set for team-meeting participation.

Third, there are many team Norms. These Norms might include where people sit in meetings, what time team members come in to work, what team members wear, the acronyms and terms they use, and so on. But of domain of possible Norms, those involving decision making, communication, meetings, and accountability seem to be the most important to team functioning. High performance teams are very explicit about what decisions the team makes and how it makes those decisions. These teams have also set rules about the confidentiality of team meetings, when team members speak for themselves or speak for the team, and how difficult or controversial topics get raised in team meetings. High performance teams also have explicit rules about team meetings and team member accountability. In our learning team example, the team would need to decide how it would prepare for the midterm exam, what the format and quality of the prep material would be, how often and where they would meet to prepare for the exam, what they would do both in and outside of the preparation meetings, and how they would use the results of the midterm exams to adjust their preparations for the final exam. Corporate teams often fail because they do not explicitly set decision-making, communication, meeting, and accountability Norms or ask themselves if the rules they have adopted are still working or need to be improved.

Buy-In

Just because team members understand the team's purpose and goals and the rules by which the team operates does not necessarily mean they will automatically be committed to them. Many times team members will do north to south head nods on the team's goals, rules, and action steps in team meetings, but then turn around and do something entirely different after the meetings. This is an example of a team that lacks Buy-In. Teams with high levels of Buy-In have team members who believe in what the team is trying to accomplish and will enthusiastically put forth the effort needed to make the team successful.

There are three basic ways team leaders can build Buy-In. One way to build Buy-In is to develop a compelling team vision or purpose. Many times team members want to be part of something bigger than themselves, and a team can be one venue for fulfilling this need. Whether or not team members will perceive the team to have a compelling vision will depend to a large extent on the degree to which the team's purpose and goals matches up to their personal values. Charismatic or transformational leaders (Chapter 13) are particularly adept at creating visions aligned with followers' personal values. A second way to create Buy-In is for the team leader to have a high level of credibility. Leaders with high levels of relevant expertise who share trusting relationships with team members often enjoy high levels of Buy-In. Team members often question the judgment of team leaders who lack relevant expertise, and they question the agendas of team leaders they do not trust. And because people prefer to make choices as opposed to being told what to do, a third way to enhance team Buy-In is to involve team members in the goal, standard, and rule-setting process.

In our learning team example, team Buy-In would likely be enhanced if the team got together and jointly determined their purpose, goals, roles, and rules. Alternatively, the team leader could assemble a group of students who wanted to achieve the same means and believed being part of a team would be the best way to make an A in the class. Team Buy-In might be somewhat lower if the instructor determined the learning team's Mission and Norms. Many teams in the public and private sector world fail because team members do not trust the team leader, believe the team leader to be incompetent, do not see how they personally benefit for being on the team, or were not involved with setting the team's goals.

Power

The Power component of the Rocket Model concerns the decision-making latitude and resources the team has in order to accomplish its goals. Teams reporting high levels of Power have considerable decision-making authority and all of the equipment, time, facilities, and funds needed to accomplish team goals. Teams with low Power often lack the necessary decision-making authority or resources needed to get things done. One of the authors was working with a group of public school administrators who felt they had very little Power to make decisions affecting the school district. The district had had three Superintendents over the past four years, and as a result the school board had stepped in to take over the day-to-day operation of the school district.

To improve the Power component of the Rocket Model, team leaders will first need to determine if they have all the decision-making latitude and resources they need to accomplish group goals. If they do not have enough Power, then they will either need to lobby higher ups to get what they need, devise ways to get team goals accomplished with limited resources, or revise team goals in light of the resource shortfalls. Most teams do not believe they have all the time, resources, or decision-making latitude they need to succeed, but more often than not they have enough of these things to successfully accomplish their goals. Good teams figure out ways to make do with what they have or devise ways to get what they need; dysfunctional teams spend all their time and energy complaining about a perceived lack of resources rather than figuring out ways to achieve team goals. Along these lines, many poor performing teams often make false assumptions or erect barriers that do not really exist. Team leaders will need to challenge these assumptions and break barriers if they are to help the team succeed.

Team Power will play a role in our learning team. In this case, the team leader may need to secure a room or facility to conduct the study sessions, obtain computer resources for team members, or even work with the instructor to see if the members could take group rather than individual exams. They will also need to determine how much time will be needed to adequately prepare for the examinations and whether all the team members can devote the time needed for the team to succeed. If the team does not have all the resources or time it believes it needs, then the team will either have to find ways to make do with what it has or make a downward revision of the team's goals.

Morale

Just because individual team members understand what the team is trying to accomplish, are committed to achieving team objectives, and understand the rules by which the team gets work done does not necessarily mean team members will all get along with each other. Teams that report high levels of Morale tend to effectively deal with interpersonal conflict and have high levels of morale and cohesion. This does not mean that highly cohesive teams do not experience interpersonal conflict. Instead, teams with high Morale scores have learned how to get conflict out in the open and deal with it in an effective manner. One way leaders can improve Morale is to work with team members to determine the rules for addressing team conflict. On the other hand, some of the best techniques for destroying team Morale are for leaders to either ignore interpersonal conflict or to tell team members to "quit fighting and just get along."

Because of values differences, work load inequities, miscommunication, and differing levels of commitment, it is likely that our learning team will experience some level of interpersonal conflict. If the learning team wanted to improve cohesiveness, then it would have to discuss how members were going to address conflict in the group. These discussions should happen relatively early in the group's formation and team conflict should be a regular topic in team meetings. Interestingly enough, many public and private sector teams report low Morale scores and often take some kind of action to improve team cohesiveness. Usually these actions include sending the team to some sort of team-building program, such as an outdoor learning or high ropes course. In almost all these cases, these interventions have little if any long-term effect on team cohesiveness, the reason being the Morale component of the Rocket Model is often a symptom of a deeper team problem. More often than not, the reason team members are not getting along is due to unclear goals and roles, ill-defined performance standards or accountability norms, a lack of commitment or resources, and so forth. In other words, the reason why team members are fighting has to do with a problem in one or more of the other components of the Rocket Model. Successfully addressing these problem components will not only improve results; they will also have a positive impact on team Morale.

Results

The Mission through Morale components of the Rocket Model describe the "how" of team building. In other words, these components tell team leaders what they specifically need to do if they need to improve team Mission, Norms, and so forth. The Results component of the Rocket model describes the "what" of team building—what did the team actually accomplish? Like Morale, Results are a symptom or an outcome of the other components of the Rocket Model. High performing teams get superior results because they have attended to the other six components of the Rocket Model. Those teams achieving less than optimal results can improve team performance by focusing on those problematic components of the Rocket Model. In our learning team example, if the team received a B on the midterm exam, the team could reexamine its purpose and goals, determine if it had some talent gaps, review its rules to see if they were spending enough time practicing the right things, find another venue or time to study, and so on.

FIGURE BHPT.2
Team assessment results for a dysfunctional health care team.

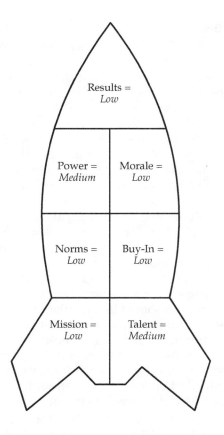

Results = *Low*

Power = *Medium*

Morale = *Low*

Norms = *Low*

Buy-In = *Low*

Mission = *Low*

Talent = *Medium*

One thing we do know about high performing teams is that they often build executable action plans with clear timelines and accountable parties in order to achieve results. These plans include key milestones and metrics, and good teams regularly review team progress and revise their plans accordingly. Many times these plans include specific action steps to improve team functioning as well as the actions specific team members need to take for the team to achieve results.

Implications of the Rocket Model

As stated at the beginning of this section, the Rocket Model is both prescriptive and diagnostic, and the model works equally well with student- through executive-level teams. When building a new team or determining where an existing team is falling short, leaders should always start with the Mission and Talent components before moving to other parts of the model. Just as a rocket needs a large booster to get off the ground, so do teams need a clear purpose and the right players in order to be successful. Along these lines, the Team Assessment Survey (Curphy, 2004c) was designed to provide teams with feedback on where they stand with respect to the seven components of the Rocket Model. Figures BHPT.2 and BHPT.3 show the

FIGURE BHPT.3

Team assessment results for a high performing retail team.

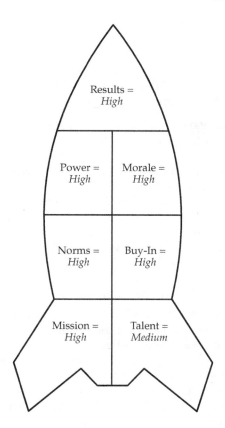

results of two executive level teams. Figure BHPT.2 is a highly dysfunctional group of executives who led a billion dollar health care organization. Because these executives never learned how to work together as a team, many were let go less than six months after their Team Assessment Survey was completed. Figure BHPT.3 shows the results for a top executive running a six billion dollar retail organization. This team was more or less hitting on all cylinders; its only real issue was grooming a successor for the soon to retire Division President.

Second, the components of the Rocket Model roughly correspond to Tuckman's (1965) four development stages of groups. According to Tuckman, forming is the first stage teams go through. Team leaders can help teams to successfully work through this stage by focusing on the Mission and Talent components of the Rocket Model. Tuckman maintained that teams then go into the storming stage, during which team leaders should concentrate on the Norms and Buy-In components of the model. Team leaders should focus on Power and Morale in Tuckman's norming phase and the Results component of the Rocket Model in Tuckman's performing stage.

Team Building at the Top

Executive Teams Are Different

Applying Individual Skills and Team Skills

Tripwise Lessons

In certain ways, executive teams are similar to any other teams. For example, just about any group of senior executives that has faced a dire crisis and survived will note that teamwork was essential for their survival. In a nutshell, then, *when teamwork is critical,* all the lessons of the previous section apply. More specifically, to really be able to benefit from a team-building intervention, individual members must be comfortable with their own strengths and weaknesses and the strengths and weaknesses of their peers. But this raises a question: If all this is true, why do we include a separate section on team building for top teams? Because there are two critical differences between most teams and "teams at the top" that should be addressed.

Executive Teams Are Different

As opposed to other kinds of work teams, not all the work at the executive level requires all (or even any) of the team to be present. An example might help. In our research on teams we studied the air crews who fly the B-1 bomber. These are four-person teams comprising an aircraft commander, a copilot, an offensive systems officer, and a defensive systems officer. While each has individual responsibilities, in every single bombing run we observed, it was absolutely essential that the team work together to accomplish the mission. They had all of the components of a true team (complex and common goal, differentiated skills, interdependence), and no individual acting alone could have achieved success. But this is not always the case for executive teams.

As Katzenbach (1998) has observed, many top leadership challenges do not really require teamwork at all. Furthermore, many top leadership challenges that do constitute real team opportunities do not require or warrant full involvement by everyone who is officially on the team. In fact, an official "team at the top" rarely functions as a collective whole involving all the formal members. Thus, the real trick for executive teams is to be able to apply both the technical individual skills that probably got the individuals to the team in the first place and the skills required for high-performance teamwork when a team situation presents itself.

Applying Individual Skills and Team Skills

There are two critical requirements if this is to work. First, one must have the diagnostic skills to discern whether the challenge presenting itself involves an individual situation or a team situation. Then, it requires that leaders "stay the course" when a team situation is present. This means, for example, when pressure for results intensifies, not slipping back into the traditional modes of assigning work to an individual (e.g., one member of that top team), but rather allowing the team to complete the work *as a team.* Again, Katzenbach (1998) stated this clearly:

Some leadership groups, of course, err in the opposite way, by attempting to forge a team around performance opportunities that do not call for a team approach. In fact, the increasing emphasis that team proponents place on "team-based organizations" creates real frustrations as top leadership groups try to rationalize good executive leadership instincts into time-consuming team building that has no performance purpose. Catalyzing real team performances at the top does not mean replacing executive leadership with executive teams; it means being rigorous about the distinction between opportunities that require single-leader efforts and those that require team efforts—and applying the discipline that fits.

To summarize this point, executives do not always need to perform as a team to be effective. But when they do need to perform as a team, the same lessons of team building discussed earlier can be very useful in helping them to enhance their team performance.

The second difference with executive teams is that they have an opportunity to enhance teamwork throughout their organization that few others have. It is our experience that *only the executive team can change organizational systems.* Recall from a chapter earlier in the book that we described the Team Effectiveness Leadership Model and mentioned there were four system issues critical to team performance. These systems were all located at the organizational level and consisted of reward systems, education systems, information systems, and control systems. The impact of these systems can be so pervasive across the entire organization that a small change in a system can have monumental impact in the organization. In a sense, then, the executive team has within its control the power to do widespread "team building" in a very different manner than we have discussed to this point. Just consider the impact of changing a compensation system (one element of a reward system) from an individual-based bonus plan to a team-based bonus plan!

Tripwire Lessons

Finally, our experience in working with executives has taught us that leaders at this level have some important lessons to learn about team building at the top. Richard Hackman, in preparing the huge editorial task of having many people produce one coherent book (by his own admission, not necessarily the best of team tasks), assembled the various authors at a conference center. As one of the contributors, one of this text's authors (RCG) recalls a most frustrating task of attempting to put together the simple checklist of steps to ensure a team developed properly. As this arduous process dragged on and tempers flared, it became obvious that "Teamwork for Dummies" was never going to emerge. But something else did start to emerge. It became clear *that some behaviors leaders engaged in could virtually guarantee failure for their teams.* While not our intent, this experience yielded a worthwhile set of lessons. A condensed version of those lessons, labeled "tripwires" by Hackman (1990), concludes our discussion of team building at the top.

Trip Wire 1: Call the Performing Unit a Team but Really Manage Members as Individuals

One way to set up work is to assign specific responsibilities to specific individuals and then choreograph individuals' activities so their products coalesce into a team product. A contrasting strategy is to assign a team responsibility and accountability for an entire piece of work and let members decide among themselves how they will proceed to accomplish the work. While either of these strategies can be effective, a choice must be made between them. A mixed model, in which people are told they are a team but are treated as individual performers with their own specific jobs to do, sends mixed signals to members, is likely to confuse everyone, and in the long run is probably untenable.

To reap the benefits of teamwork, one must actually build a team. Calling a set of people a team or exhorting them to work together is insufficient. Instead, explicit action must be taken to establish the team's boundaries, to define the task as one for which members are collectively responsible and accountable, and to give members the authority to manage both their internal processes and the team's relations with external entities such as clients and co-workers. Once this is done, management behavior and organizational systems gradually can be changed as necessary to support teamwork.

Trip Wire 2: Create an Inappropriate Authority Balance

The exercise of authority creates anxiety, especially when one must balance between assigning a team authority for some parts of the work and withholding it for other parts. Because both managers and team members tend to be uncomfortable in such situations, they may collude to "clarify" them. Sometimes the result is the assignment of virtually all authority to the team—which can result in anarchy or a team that heads off in an inappropriate direction. At other times, managers retain virtually all authority, dictating work procedures in detail to team members and, in the process, losing many of the advantages that can accrue from teamwork. In both cases, the anxieties that accompany a mixed model are reduced, but at significant cost to team effectiveness.

To achieve a good balance of managerial and team authority is difficult. Moreover, merely deciding how much authority will be assigned to the group and how much will be retained by management are insufficient. Equally important are the domains of authority that are assigned and retained. Our findings suggest that managers should be unapologetic and insistent about exercising their authority about *direction*—the end states the team is to pursue—and about *outer-limit constraints* on team behavior—the things the team must always do or never do. At the same time, managers should assign to the team full authority for the means by which it accomplishes its work—and then do whatever they can to ensure that team members understand and accept their responsibility and accountability for deciding how they will execute the work.

Few managerial behaviors are more consequential for the long-term being of teams than those that address the partitioning of authority between managers and teams. It takes skill to accomplish this well, and it is a skill that has emotional and behavioral as well as cognitive components. Just knowing the rules for partitioning authority is insufficient; one also needs some practice in applying those rules in situations where anxieties, including one's own, are likely to be high. Especially challenging for managers are the early stages in the life of a team (when managers often are tempted to give away too much authority) and when the going gets rough (when the temptation is to take authority back too soon). The management of authority relations with task-performing teams is indeed much like walking a balance beam, and our evidence suggests that it takes a good measure of knowledge, skill, and perseverance to keep from falling off.

Trip Wire 3: Assemble a Large Group of People, Tell Them in General Terms What Needs to Be Accomplished, and Let Them "Work Out the Details"

Traditionally, individually focused designs for work are plagued by constraining structures that have built up over the years to monitor and control employee behavior. When groups are used to perform work, such structures tend to be viewed as unnecessary bureaucratic impediments to team functioning. Thus, just as managers sometimes (and mistakenly) attempt to empower teams by relinquishing all authority to them, so do some attempt to get rid of the dysfunctional features of existing organizational structures simply by taking down all the structures they can. Apparently, the hope is that removing structures will release teams and enable members to work together creatively and effectively.

Managers who hold this view often wind up providing teams with less structure than they actually need. Tasks are defined only in vague, general terms. Group composition is unclear or fluid. The limits of the team's authority are kept deliberately fuzzy. The unstated assumption is that there is some magic in the group interaction process and that, by working together, members will evolve any structures that the team actually needs.

It is a false hope; there is no such magic. Indeed, our findings suggest the opposite: groups that have appropriate structures tend to develop healthy internal processes, whereas groups with insufficient or inappropriate structures tend to have process problems. Worse, coaching and process consultation are unlikely to resolve these problems, precisely because they are rooted in the team structure. For members to learn how to interact well within a flawed or underspecified structure is to swim upstream against a very strong current.

Trip Wire 4: Specify Challenging Team Objectives, but Skimp on Organizational Supports

Even if a work team has clear, engaging direction and an enabling structure, its performance can go sour—or, at least, it can fall below the group's potential—if the team is not well supported. Teams in high-commitment organizations (Walton, 1985) fall victim to this trip wire when given "stretch" objectives but not the wherewithal to accomplish them; high initial enthusiasm soon changes into disillusionment.

It is no small undertaking to provide these supports to teams, especially in organizations designed to support work by individuals. Corporate compensation policy, for example, may make no provision for team bonuses and, indeed, may explicitly prohibit them. Human resource departments may be primed to identify individuals' training needs and provide first-rate courses to fill those needs, but training in team skills may not be available at all. Existing performance appraisal systems, which may be state-of-the-art for measuring individual contributions, are likely to be wholly inappropriate for assessing and rewarding work done by teams. Information systems and control systems may provide managers with the data they need to monitor and control work processes, but they may be neither available nor appropriate for use by work teams. Finally, the material resources required for the work may have been prespecified by those who originally designed it, and there may be no procedure in place for a team to secure the special configuration of resources it needs to execute the particular performance strategy it has developed.

To align existing organizational systems with the needs of teams often requires managers to exercise power and influence upward and laterally in the organization.

An organization set up to provide teams with full support for their work is noticeably different from one whose systems and policies are intended to support and control individual work, and many managers may find the prospect of changing to a group-oriented organization both unsettling and perhaps even vaguely revolutionary.

It is hard to provide good organizational support for task-performing teams, but generally it is worth the trouble. The potential of a well-directed, well-structured, well-supported team is tremendous. Moreover, to stumble over the organizational support trip wire is, perhaps, the saddest of all team failures. When a group is both excited about its work and all set up to execute it superbly, it is especially shattering to fail merely because the organizational supports required cannot be obtained. It is like being all dressed up and ready to go to the prom only to have the car break down en route.

Trip Wire 5: Assume That Members Already Have All the Competence They Need to Work Well as a Team

Once a team is launched and operating under its own steam, managers sometimes assume their work is done. As we have seen, there are indeed some good reasons for giving a team ample room to go about its business in its own way: inappropriate or poorly timed managerial interventions impaired the work of more than one group in our research. However, a strict, hands-off managerial stance also can limit a team's effectiveness, particularly when members are not already skilled and experienced in teamwork.

Development Planning

Conducting a GAPS Analysis

Identifying and Prioritizing Development Needs: Gaps of GAPS

Bridging the Gaps: Building a Development Plan

Reflecting on Learnings: Modifying Development Plans

Transfer Learnings to New Environments

Change before you have to.

Jack Welch, General Electric CEO

Development planning is the systematic process of building knowledge and experience or changing behavior. Two people who have done a considerable amount of cutting-edge research in the development-planning process are Peterson and

Hicks (1995). These two researchers believe development planning consists of five interrelated phases. The first phase of development planning is identifying development needs. Here leadership practitioners identify career goals, assess their abilities in light of career goals, seek feedback about how their behaviors are affecting others, and review the organizational standards pertaining to their career goals. Once this information has been gathered, the second phase consists of analyzing this data to identify and prioritize development needs. The prioritized development needs in turn are used to create a highly focused and achievable development plan, the third phase of this process. To help ensure permanent behavioral change takes place, the plan itself must utilize many of the best-practices techniques described in Chapter 8. Some of these best practices include having a plan that is limited to no more than two or three objectives, that capitalizes on on-the-job activities, and that incorporates multiple sources of feedback. The fourth phase in development planning is periodically reviewing the plan, reflecting on learnings, and modifying or updating the plan as appropriate. As you might expect, the Action-Observation-Reflection (AOR) model, described in Chapter 3, is a key component during this phase of the development planning process. The last phase in development planning is transferring learnings to new environments. Just because a leadership practitioner can successfully delegate activities to his 3-person team may not mean he will effectively delegate tasks or utilize his staff efficiently when he is leading a group of 25 people. In that case, the leader will need to build and expand on the delegation skills he learned when leading a much smaller team. These five phases are well grounded in research—Hazucha, Hezlett, and Schneider (1993), Peterson (1993b), and Hezlett and Koonce (1995) show that approximately 75 percent of the leadership practitioners adopting these phases were successful in either changing their behaviors permanently or developing new skills. Because these five phases are so important to the development planning process, the remainder of this section will describe each phase in more detail.

Conducting a GAPS Analysis

The first phase in the development-planning process is to conduct a GAPS (Goals, Abilities, Perceptions, Standards) analysis. A GAPS analysis helps leadership practitioners to gather and categorize all pertinent development planning information. A sample GAPS analysis for an engineer working in a manufacturing company can be found in Figure DP.1. This individual wants to get promoted to a first-line supervisor position within the next year, and all of the information pertinent to this promotion can be found in her GAPS analysis. The specific steps for conducting a GAPS analysis are as follows:

- *Step 1: Goals.* The first step in a GAPS analysis is to clearly identify what you want to do or where you want to go with your career over the next year or so. This does not necessarily mean moving up or getting promoted to the next level. An alternative career objective might be to master one's current job, as you may have just gotten promoted and advancing to the next level is not as important at the moment. Other career objectives might include taking on more responsibilities in your current position, taking a

FIGURE DP.1

A sample GAPS analysis.

Sources: D. B. Peterson and M. D. Hicks, *Leader as Coach* (Minneapolis: Personnel Decisions International, 1996); and G. J. Curphy, *Career and Development Planning Workshop: Planning for Individual Development* (Minneapolis: Personnel Decisions International, 1998).

Goals: Where do you want to go?	Abilities: What can you do now?
Step 1: Career objectives: Career strategies:	*Step 2:* What strengths do you have for your career objectives? *Step 3:* What development needs will you have to overcome?
Standards: What does your boss or the organization expect?	Perceptions: How do others see you?
Step 5: Expectations:	*Step 4:* 360 and Performance Review Results, and feedback from others: • *Boss* • *Peers* • *Direct Reports*

lateral assignment in another part of the company, taking an overseas assignment, or even cutting back on job responsibilities to gain more work-life balance. This latter career objective may be very appropriate for leaders who are just starting a family or are taking care of loved ones who are suffering from poor health. The two most important aspects of this step in the GAPS analysis are that leadership practitioners will have a lot more energy to work on development needs that are aligned with career goals, and in many cases advancing to the next level may not be a viable or particularly energizing career goal. This latter point may be especially true with organizations that have been recently downsized. Management positions often bear the brunt of downsizing initiatives, resulting in fewer available positions for those wishing to advance.

- *Step 2: Abilities.* People bring a number of strengths and development needs to their career goals. Over the years, you may have developed specialized knowledge or a number of skills that have helped you to be successful in your current and previous jobs. Similarly, you may also have received feedback over the years that there are certain skills you need to develop or behaviors you need to change. Good leaders know themselves—over the years they know which strengths they need to leverage and which skills they need to develop.
- *Step 3: Perceptions.* The perceptions component of the GAPS model concerns how your abilities, skills, and behaviors impact others. What are others saying about your various attributes? What are their reactions to both your strengths and your development needs? A great way of obtaining this information is by asking others for feedback or through performance reviews or 360-degree feedback instruments.
- *Step 4: Standards.* The last step in a GAPS analysis concerns the standards your boss or the organization has for your career objectives. For example, your boss may say that you may need to develop better public speaking, delegation, or coaching skills before you can get promoted. Similarly, the organization may have policies stating that people in certain overseas positions must be proficient in the country's native language, or it may have educational or experience requirements for various jobs.

When completing a GAPS analysis you may discover that you do not have all the information you need. If you do not, then you need to get it before you complete the next step of the development-planning process. Only you can decide upon your career objectives, but you can solicit advice from others on whether these objectives are realistic given your abilities, the perceptions of others, and organizational standards. You may find that your one-year objectives are unrealistic given your development needs, organizational standards, or job opportunities. In this case, you may need to either reassess your career goals or consider taking a number of smaller career steps that will ultimately help you achieve your career goal. If you are lacking information about the other quadrants, then you can ask your boss or others whose opinions you value about your abilities, perceptions, or organizational standards. Getting as much up-to-date and pertinent information for your GAPS analysis will help ensure that your development plan is focusing on high-priority objectives.

Identifying and Prioritizing Development Needs: Gaps of GAPS

As seen in Figure DP.2, the Goals and Standards quadrants are future oriented; these quadrants ask where you want to go and what your boss or your organization expects of people in these positions. The Abilities and Perceptions quadrants are focused on the present; what strengths and development needs do you currently have and how are these attributes affecting others? Given what you currently have and where you want to go, what are the gaps in your GAPS? In other words, after looking at all of the information in your GAPS analysis, what are your biggest development needs? And how should these development needs be prioritized? You need to

FIGURE DP.2

A gaps-of-the-GAPS analysis.

Sources: D. B. Peterson and M. D. Hicks, *Leader as Coach* (Minneapolis, Personnel Decisions International, 1996); and G. J. Curphy, *The Leadership Development Process Manual* (Minneapolis, Personnel Decisions International, 1998).

Where you want to go

Goals

Where you are now

Abilities

←— Gaps? —→

Standards

Perceptions

Developmental Objectives

Current Position: _____

_____

_____

_____

_____

_____

_____

Next Proposed Position:_____

_____

_____

_____

_____

_____

review the information from the GAPS model, look for underlying themes and patterns, and determine what behaviors, knowledge, experiences, or skills will be the most important to change or develop if you are to accomplish your career goals.

Bridging the Gaps: Building a Development Plan

A gaps-of-the-GAPS analysis helps leadership practitioners identify high-priority development needs, but does not spell out what leaders need to do to overcome these needs. A good development plan is like a road map; it clearly describes the final destination, lays out the steps or interim checkpoints, builds in regular feedback to keep people on track, identifies where additional resources are needed, and builds in reflection time so that people can periodically review progress and determine whether an alternative route is needed. (See page 000 for a sample development plan.) The specific steps for creating a high-impact development plan are as follows:

- *Step 1: Career and Development Objectives.* Your career objective comes directly from the Goals quadrant of the GAPS analysis; it is where you want to be or what you want to be doing in your career a year or so in the future. The development objective comes from your gaps-of-the-GAPS analysis; it should be a high-priority development need pertaining to your career objective. People should be working on no more than two to three development needs at any one time.

- *Step 2: Criteria for Success.* What would it look like if you developed a particular skill, acquired technical expertise, or changed the behavior outlined in your development objective? This can be a difficult step in development planning, particularly with "softer" skills, such as listening, managing conflict, or building relationships with others.

- *Step 3: Action Steps.* The focus in the development plan should be on the specific, on-the-job action steps leadership practitioners will take in order to overcome their development need. However, sometimes it is difficult for leaders to think of the on-the-job action steps to overcome their development needs. Three excellent resources that provide on-the-job action steps for overcoming a variety of development needs are two books, *The Successful Manager's Handbook* (Davis, Skube, Hellervik, Gebelein, & Sheard, 1996) and *For Your Improvement* (Lombardo & Eichinger, 1996), and the development planning and coaching software *DevelopMentor* (PDI, 1995). These three resources can be likened to restaurant menus in that they provide leadership practitioners with a wide variety of action steps to overcome just about any development need.

- *Step 4: Whom to Involve and Reassess Dates.* This step in a development plan involves feedback—whom do you need to get it from and how often do you need to get it? This step in the development plan is important as it helps to keep you on track. Are your efforts being noticed? Do people see any improvement? Are there things you need to do differently? Do you need to refocus your efforts?

- *Step 5: Stretch Assignments.* When people reflect on when they have learned the most, they often talk about situations where they felt they were in over their heads. These situations stretched their knowledge and skills and often are seen as extremely beneficial to learning. If you know of a potential assignment, such as a task force, a project management team, or a rotational assignment, that would emphasize the knowledge and skills you need to develop and accelerate your learning, you should include it in your development plan.

- *Step 6: Resources.* Oftentimes people find it useful to read a book, attend a course, or watch a videotaped program to gain foundational knowledge about a particular development need. These methods generally describe the how-to steps for a particular skill or behavior.

- *Step 7: Reflect with a Partner.* In accordance with the Action-Observation-Reflection model of Chapter 3, people should periodically review their learnings and progress with a partner. The identity of the partner is not particularly important, as long as you trust his or her opinion and the partner is familiar with your work situation and development plan.

Reflecting on Learnings: Modifying Development Plans

Just as the development plan is a road map, this phase of development planning helps leaders to see whether the final destination is still the right one, if an alternative route might be better, and whether there is need for more resources or equipment. Reflecting on your learnings with a partner is also a form of public commitment, and people who make public commitments are much more likely to fulfill them. All things considered, in most cases it is probably better to periodically review your progress with your boss. Your boss should not be left in the dark with respect to your development, and periodically reviewing progress with your boss will help ensure there are no surprises at your performance appraisal.

Transfer Learnings to New Environments

The last phase in development planning concerns ongoing development. Your development plan should be a "live" document; it should be changed, modified, or updated as you learn from your experiences, receive feedback, acquire new skills, and overcome targeted development needs. There are basically three ways to transfer learnings to new environments. The first way is to constantly update your development plan. Another way to enhance your learning is to practice your newly acquired skills to a new environment. A final way to hone and refine your skills is to coach others in the development of your newly acquired skills. Moving from the student role to that of a master is an excellent way to reinforce your learnings.

Credibility

The Two Components of Credibility
Building Expertise
Building Trust
Expertise × Trust

Leaders know that while their position may give them authority, their behavior earns them respect. Leaders go first. They set an example and build commitment through simple, daily acts that create progress and momentum.

Jim Kouzes and Barry Posner

Interviews with thousands of followers as well as the results of over half a million 360-degree feedback reports indicate that credibility may be one of the most important components of leadership success and effectiveness (Kouzes & Posner, 1987, 1996; PDI, 1992). Employees working for leaders they thought were credible were willing to work longer hours, felt more of a sense of ownership in the company, felt more personally involved in work, and were less likely to leave the company over the next two years (Kouzes & Posner, 1996). Given the difficulties companies are having finding and retaining talented leaders and workers and the role intellectual capital and bench strength play in organizational success, it would appear that credibility could have a strong bottom-line impact on many organizations. Credibility is a little like leadership in that many people have ideas of what credibility is (or is not), but there may not be a lot of consensus on one "true" definition of credibility. This section will define what we believe credibility is, present the two components of credibility, and explore what leadership practitioners can do (and avoid doing) if they want to build their credibility.

The Two Components of Credibility

Credibility can be defined as the ability to engender trust in others. Leaders with high levels of credibility are seen as trustworthy; they have a strong sense of right and wrong, stand up and speak up for what they believe in, protect confidential information, encourage ethical discussions of business or work issues, and follow through with commitments. Sometimes dishonest leaders, personalized charismatic leaders, or power wielders can initially be seen by followers to be credible, but their selfish and self-serving interests usually come to light over time. Credibility is made up of two components, which include expertise and trust. Followers will not trust leaders if they feel their leaders do not know what they are talking about. Similarly, followers will not trust leaders if they feel confidential information will be leaked, if their leaders are unwilling to take stands on moral issues, or if their leaders do not follow through with their promises. Much about these two components of credibility have already been discussed in the sections on "Building Technical Competence," "Building Effective Relationships with Superiors," and "Building Effective Relationships with Peers." What follows is a brief overview of these three skills as well as some additional considerations that can help leadership practitioners build their credibility.

Building Expertise

Expertise consists of technical competence as well as organizational and industry knowledge, so building expertise means increasing your knowledge and skills in these three areas. Building technical competence, described earlier in Part V, concerns increasing the knowledge and repertoire of behaviors one can bring to bear to successfully complete a task. To build technical competence, leadership practitioners must determine how their job contributes to the overall mission of the company or organization, become an expert in the job through formal training or teaching others, and seek opportunities to broaden their technical expertise.

Nonetheless, building expertise takes more than just technical competence. Leaders also need to understand the company and the industry they are in. Many followers are not only looking for leaders to coach them on their skills, they are also looking to their leaders to provide some context for organizational, industry, and market events. Building one's organizational or industry knowledge may be just as important as building technical competence. However, the ways in which leadership practitioners build these two knowledge bases is somewhat different from building technical competence. Building technical competence often takes more of a hands-on approach to development, but it is hard to do this when building organizational or industry knowledge. One way to build your organizational or industry knowledge is by regularly reading industry-related journals, annual reports, *The Wall Street Journal, Fortune, Inc.,* or various websites. Many leaders spend 5–10 hours a week building their industry and organizational knowledge bases using this approach. Getting a mentor or being coached by your boss is another way to build these knowledge bases. Other leadership practitioners have taken stretch assignments where they work on special projects with senior executives. Often these assignments allow them to work closely with executives, and through this contact they better understand the competitive landscape, the organization's history and business strategies, and organizational politics. The bottom line is that your learning is not over once you have obtained your degree. In many ways, it will have just started.

Finally, it is important to remember that expertise is more than experience. As noted previously, some leaders get one year's worth of experience out of five years' work, whereas others get five years' worth of experience after one year's work. Leaders who get the most from their experience regularly discuss what they have been learning with a partner, and they frequently update their development plans as a result of these discussions.

Building Trust

The second component of credibility is building trust, which can be broken down into clarifying and communicating your values, and building relationships with others. In many ways leadership is a moral exercise. For example, one of the key differences between charismatic and transformational leaders is that the latter base their vision on their own and their followers' values, whereas the former base their vision on their own possibly selfish needs. Having a strong values system is an important component both in the Building Blocks Model of Skills and in leadership success. Because of the importance of values and relationships in building trust, the remainder of this section explores these two topics in more depth.

Chapter 6 defined values as generalized behaviors or states of affairs that an individual considers to be important. Provided that leaders make ethical decisions and abide by organizational rules, however, differences in values among leaders and followers may be difficult to discern. Since people do not come to work with their values tattooed to their foreheads, others typically make inferences about a leader's values based on their day-to-day behaviors (or just as importantly, their absence of certain day-to-day behaviors). Unfortunately, in many cases leaders' day-to-day behaviors are misaligned with their personal values; they are not living their life (at work, at least) in a manner consistent with their values.

An example of a leader not living life according to his values might be illustrative. An executive with an oil and gas firm was responsible for all exploration (i.e., drilling) operations in western Canada. Because he felt the discovery of new oil and gas fields was the key to the company's long-term success, he worked up to 18 hours a day, pushed his followers to work similar sorts of hours, had little patience for and would publicly disparage those oil rig operators who were behind schedule, and almost fired a manager who gave one of his followers a week off to see the birth of his son back in the United States. As these behaviors continued over time, more and more of his followers either requested transfers or quit to join other companies. Because of these problems with turnover and morale, he was asked to participate in a formal coaching program. Not surprisingly, his 360-degree feedback showed that his boss, peers, and followers found him very difficult to work with or for. These results indicated that he put a premium on getting results, getting ahead, and economic rewards, yet when he was asked to name the things he felt were most important to him as a leader, his priorities were his family, his religion, getting along with others, and developing his followers (altruism). Obviously, there was a huge gap between what he truly believed in and how he behaved. He felt the company expected him to hold people's feet to the fire and get results no matter what the cost, yet neither the boss nor his peers felt that this was the case. The executive had misconstrued the situation and was exhibiting behaviors that were misaligned with his values.

Although the case above was somewhat extreme, it is not unusual to find leaders acting in ways that are misaligned with their personal values. One way to assess the degree to which leaders are living their lives according to their personal values is by asking what they truly believe in and what they spend their time and money on. For example, you could write down the five things you believe most strongly in (i.e., your top five values), and then review your calendar, daytimer, checkbook, and credit card statements to determine where you spend your time and money. If the two lists are aligned, then you are likely to be living your life according to your values. If not, then you may be living your life according to how others think you should act. And if there is some level of discrepancy between the two lists, what should you do? Of course, some level of discrepancy is likely to occur, as situational demands and constraints can often influence the way leaders behave. On the other hand, large discrepancies between the lists may indicate that you are not living life consistently with your values, and those you interact with may infer that you have a very different set of values than those you personally believe in. A good first step in clarifying this discrepancy is to craft a personal mission statement or a leadership credo, a statement that describes what you truly believe in as a leader.

Examples of different leadership credos for managers across corporate America can be found in Highlight CR.1. There are several aspects of leadership credos worth additional comment. First, leadership credos are personal and are closely linked with a leader's values—a credo should describe what the leader believes in and will (or will not) stand for. Second, it should also describe an ideal state. A leader's behavior may never be perfectly aligned with his or her personal mission statement, but it should be a set of day-to-day behaviors that he or she will strive to achieve. Third, leadership credos should be motivating; leaders should be passionate and enthusiastic about the kind of leader they aspire to be. If the leader does not find his or her personal mission statement to be particularly inspiring, then it is hard to see how followers will be motivated by it. Much of the inspiration of a leadership credo stems from its being personal and values-based. Fourth, personal mission statements should be made public. Leaders need

Sample Leadership Credos

Highlight CR.1

As a leader, I . . .

. . . believe in the concept of whole persons and will seek to use the full range of talents and abilities of colleagues whenever possible.

. . . will seek to keep people fully informed.

. . . will more consistently express appreciation to others for a job well done.

. . . will take risks in challenging policies or protocol when they do not permit us to effectively serve our customers.

. . . will selectively choose battles to fight—rather than trying to fight all of the possible battles.

. . . will actively support those providing the most effective direction for our company.

. . . will seek to change the things I can in a positive direction and accept those things I have no chance or opportunity to change.

Source: *Impact Leadership* (Minneapolis: Personnel Decisions International, 1995).

to communicate their values to others, and a good way to do this is to display their leadership credos prominently in their offices. This not only lets others know what you as a leader think is important, it also is a form of public commitment to your leadership credo.

Another key way to build trust is to form strong relationships with others. There is apt to be a high level of mutual trust if leaders and followers share strong relationships; if these relationships are weak, then the level of mutual trust is apt to be low. Techniques for building relationships with peers and superiors have already been described in this section of the text. Perhaps the best way to build relationships with followers is to spend time listening to what they have to say. Because many leaders tend to be action oriented and get paid to solve (rather than listen to) problems, some leaders overlook the importance of spending time with followers. Yet leaders who take the time to build relationships with followers are much more likely to understand their followers' perspectives of organizational issues, intrinsic motivators, values, level of competence for different tasks, or career aspirations. Leaders armed with this knowledge may be better able to influence and get work done through others. More on building relationships with followers can be found in the "Coaching" section of Part V.

Expertise × Trust

Leaders vary tremendously in their levels of both expertise and trust, and these differences have distinct implications for leaders wanting to improve their credibility. Take leaders who fall into the first quadrant of Figure CR.1. These individuals have a high level of trust and a high level of expertise; they would likely be seen by others as highly credible. Individuals falling into the second quadrant might include leaders who have spent little time with followers, who do not follow through with commitments, or who are new to the organization and have had little time to build relationships with co-workers. In all three cases, leaders wanting to improve their

Advanced Leadership Skills   **529**

FIGURE CR.1
The credibility matrix.

Source: G. J. Curphy, *Credibility: Building Your Reputation throughout the Organization* (Minneapolis: Personnel Decisions International, 1997).

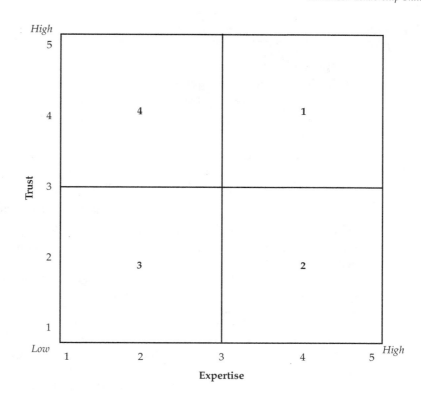

credibility should include building relationships with co-workers as key development objectives. Leaders falling into the third quadrant may be new college hires or people joining the company from an entirely different industry. It is unlikely that either type of leader would have the technical competence, organizational or industry knowledge, or time to build relationships with co-workers. These leaders may be in touch with their values and have a personal mission statement, but they will need to share their statement with others and act in a manner consistent with this statement in order to build their credibility. Other development objectives could include building expertise and strong relationships with others. Leaders falling into the fourth quadrant might include those promoted from among peers or transferring from another department within the company. Both sets of leaders may be in touch with their values, have a leadership credo, share strong relationships with co-workers, and have organizational and industry knowledge, but the former may need to develop leadership knowledge or skills and the latter technical competence if they wish to increase their credibility. Finally, it is important to note that leadership credos and development plans also have credibility implications because leaders who do not strive to live up to their ideals or fail to follow through with their developmental commitments are likely to be seen as less trustworthy than those who do.

Coaching

People who are coaches will be the norm. Other people won't get promoted.

Jack Welch, General Electric CEO

A key success factor in most organizations today is having leaders and followers with the right knowledge and skills. More and more, companies are looking at "bench strength" as a competitive advantage moving into the next century. There are essentially two ways to acquire bench strength; employers can either buy (i.e., hire) the talent they need, or they can build their existing talent through development and coaching programs. Given that many employers face a labor shortage in certain critical positions, many are looking to build their own internal talent (Tichy & Cohen, 1997). Much of this talent is being developed through informal coaching. As we noted in Chapter 8, most leaders engage in some form of informal coaching. But how good of a coach are they? The authors' conversations with a multitude of leaders indicate that almost every single one was unsure what to do as a coach. Some thought it involved directing their employees on how to do tasks. Others thought it involved counseling employees on personal problems. One stated that his only example of coaching came from his high school football coach, and he wouldn't want to wish that on anyone.

Two thought leaders in this area are Peterson and Hicks (1996), who described coaching as the "process of equipping people with the tools, knowledge, and opportunities they need to develop themselves and become more successful" (p. 14). According to Peterson and Hicks, good coaches orchestrate rather than dictate development. Good coaches help followers clarify career goals, identify and prioritize development needs, create and stick to development plans, and create environments that support learning and coaching. To some extent, many of the steps to coaching have been described under some of the other skills in Part V. Thus, coaching is really a blend of several different leadership skills. Being a good coach means having well-developed skills, determining where a follower is in the coaching process, and intervening as appropriate. The five steps of coaching provide leaders with both a good road map and a diagnostic model for improving the bench strength of their followers.

Peterson and Hicks (1996) pointed out that this model works particularly well for high performers—individuals who tend to benefit the most from, but are often overlooked by, leaders when coaching. We noted in Chapter 9 that high performers produce 20–50 percent more than average employees (Hunter, Schmidt, & Judiesch, 1990), so coaching can have a considerable impact on the bottom line if it is targeted at high performers. Further support for the idea that top performers may benefit the most from coaching comes from athletics. If you watched any of the Sydney Olympics in 2000, then you would have seen that many of the world's top athletes had at least one and sometimes two or three coaches. If these world-class athletes feel that coaching can enhance their performance, then it is likely that good coaches can also enhance the performance of any organization's top employees. Although the five-step model also works with poorly performing employees, more appropriate interventions might also include diagnosing performance problems, goal setting, providing rewards and constructive feedback, and punishing these individuals, particularly if informal coaching is not achieving desired results.

Forging a Partnership

The first step in informal coaching involves establishing a relationship built on mutual trust and respect with a follower. If a follower does not trust or respect her leader, then it will be very unlikely that she will pay much attention to his ideas for her development. There are several things leaders can do to forge a partnership with coachees. First, it will be much easier for leaders with high credibility to build strong partnerships with followers than for leaders with low credibility. Therefore, leaders need to determine where they are on the credibility matrix (Figure CR.1), and they may need to take appropriate developmental steps to improve their credibility before their coaching suggestions will have much impact. These developmental steps may include building technical and organizational knowledge as well as building strong relationships with the individuals they want to coach. Having an understanding of the context in which the employee operates can be as important as the relationship the leader shares with the employee. In the "Credibility" section, we noted that leaders will also need to spend time listening to their coachees; they need to understand coachees' career aspirations, values, intrinsic motivators, view of the organization, and current work situation. Good coaches can put themselves in their coachees' shoes, and can understand how coachees may view issues or opportunities differently from themselves. While forging a partnership, leaders can also provide coachees with realistic career advice, as sometimes coachees have unrealistic estimations of their skills and opportunities. For example, a new graduate from a top MBA program might want to be a partner at a consulting firm after two years with the company, but company policy may dictate that this decision will not be made until she has been with the firm for at least eight years. Her coach should inform her of this policy, and then work with her to map out a series of shorter-term career objectives that would help her become a partner in eight years. If coaches do not know what drives their coachees' behaviors, then another step to forging a partnership is to start asking a lot of questions. This is an excellent opportunity for leaders to practice their listening skills so as to better understand their coachees' career aspirations and intrinsic motivators.

Inspiring Commitment: Conducting a GAPS Analysis

This step in the coaching process is very similar to the GAPS analysis and the gaps-of-the-GAPS analysis, discussed in "Development Planning." The only difference is that these two analyses are now done from the coachee's perspective. Figure CH.1

FIGURE CH.1

A GAPS analysis for an employee.

Source: D. B. Peterson, and M. D. Hicks, *Leader as Coach* (Minneapolis: Personnel Decisions International, 1996); and G. J. Curphy, *The Leadership Development Process Manual* (Minneapolis: Personnel Decisions International, 1998).

Goals: What does the employee want to do?	**Abilities:** What can the employee do now?
Step 1: Career objectives: —To become an Engineering Supervisor	*Step 2:* What strengths does the employee have for his or her career objectives? — Understand operational side of the business — Good planning skills — Good job function definition skills — Set clear individual and team goals *Step 3:* What development needs will he or she have to overcome? — Multidirection communication; may need to improve listening skills — May need to improve conflict resolution skills
Standards: What do you or the organization expect?	**Perceptions:** How do others see the employee?
Step 5: Expectations: • *Boss:* To be promoted, will need to: — Get along better with peers — Develop stronger listening skills	*Step 4:* PPRP and feedback from others: • *Boss* — Good technician — Develops good plans and holds people accountable — More interested in own rather than others' ideas • *Peers* — Can be counted on to get the job done — Can be too set in ways; too argumentative • *Direct Reports* — Has clear goals — Understands technical side of business — Doesn't value our ideas and opinions

might help to clarify this difference in perspective. Thus, in the Goals quadrant of the GAPS analysis the leader should write down the coachee's career objectives, and in the Perceptions quadrant the leader would write down how the coachee's behavior is impacting others. It is entirely possible that the leader may not be able to complete all of the quadrants of the GAPS for a coachee. If so, then the leader will need to gather more information before going any further. This information gathering may include discussing career goals and abilities with the coachee, reviewing the coachee's 360-degree feedback results, asking peers about how the coachee comes across or impacts others, or asking human resources about the educational or experience standards relevant to the coachee's career goals. One way to gather additional information is to have both the leader and the coach complete a GAPS analysis independently, and then get together and discuss areas of agreement and disagreement. This can help ensure that the best information is available for the GAPS analysis and also help to build the partnership between the leader and

Advanced Leadership Skills   **533**

TABLE CH.1
Development
Plan Checklist

Source: G. J.
Curphy, *The
Leadership
Development Process
Manual*
(Minneapolis:
Personnel Decisions
International, 1998).

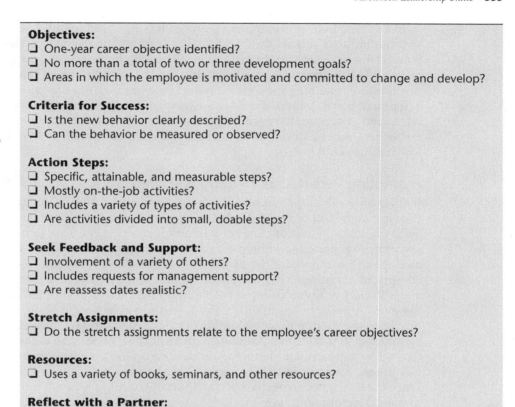

Objectives:
❏ One-year career objective identified?
❏ No more than a total of two or three development goals?
❏ Areas in which the employee is motivated and committed to change and develop?

Criteria for Success:
❏ Is the new behavior clearly described?
❏ Can the behavior be measured or observed?

Action Steps:
❏ Specific, attainable, and measurable steps?
❏ Mostly on-the-job activities?
❏ Includes a variety of types of activities?
❏ Are activities divided into small, doable steps?

Seek Feedback and Support:
❏ Involvement of a variety of others?
❏ Includes requests for management support?
❏ Are reassess dates realistic?

Stretch Assignments:
❏ Do the stretch assignments relate to the employee's career objectives?

Resources:
❏ Uses a variety of books, seminars, and other resources?

Reflect with a Partner:
❏ Includes periodic reviews of learnings?

coachee. During this discussion the leader and coachee should also do a gaps-of-the-GAPS analysis to identify and prioritize development needs. Usually leaders will get more commitment to development needs if coachees feel they had an important role in determining these needs, and a gaps-of-the-GAPS discussion is a way to build buy-in. This discussion can also help ensure that development needs are aligned with career goals.

Growing Skills: Creating Development and Coaching Plans

Once the coachee's development needs are identified and prioritized, coachees will need to build development plans to overcome targeted needs. These plans are identical to those described in the "Development Planning" section. Leaders generally do not build development plans for their coachees. Instead, they may want to go over a sample (or their own) development plan and coach their coachees on the seven steps in building a plan. They can then either jointly build a plan or have the coachee individually build a plan for the leader to review. Providing coachees with an important role in development planning should increase their level of commitment to the plan. Once a draft development plan is created, the leader and coach can then use the development planning checklist in Table CH.1 to review the plan.

In addition to the development plan, leaders will need to build a coaching plan that outlines the actions they will take to support their coachees' development. Some of these actions might include meeting with the coachees on a regular basis to provide developmental feedback, identifying developmental resources or opportunities, or helping the coachee reflect on what they have learned. As with development plans, leaders should share their coaching plans so that coachees know what kind of support they will be getting. This will also publicly commit the leaders to the coachees' development, which will make it more likely that they will follow through with the coaching plan.

Promoting Persistence: Helping Followers Stick to Their Plans

Just because development and coaching plans are in place is no guarantee that development will occur. Sometimes coachees build development plans with great enthusiasm, but then never take any further action. This step in the coaching process is designed to help coachees "manage the mundane." An example of managing the mundane might be illustrative. One of the authors successfully completed a triathlon. The most difficult part of this accomplishment was not the event itself, but rather doing all of the training needed to successfully complete the event. Similarly, the inability to stick to a diet or keep a New Year's resolution is primarily due to an inability to manage the mundane; people are initially committed to these goals but have a difficult time sticking to them. The same is true with development planning. Conducting a GAPS analysis and creating a development plan are relatively easy; sticking to the plan is much more difficult. From the leader's perspective, a large part of coaching is helping followers stick to their development plan.

Several development-planning steps were specifically designed to promote persistence. For example, ensuring alignment between career and development objectives, getting feedback from multiple sources on a regular basis, and reflecting with a partner can help keep coachees focused on their development. If the leader is a coachee's developmental partner, then reflection sessions can help followers persist with their development. If leaders are not designated as partners in the development plan, then they should commit to meeting regularly with the coachees to discuss progress, what the leaders can do to support development, developmental opportunities, developmental feedback, and so forth.

Leaders can also help to promote persistence by capitalizing on coachable moments. Say a coachee was working on listening skills, and the leader and coach were in a staff meeting together. If the leader provides feedback to the coachee about her listening skills immediately after the staff meeting, then the leader has capitalized on a coachable moment. To capitalize on a coachable moment, leaders must know the followers' developmental objectives, be in situations where they can observe followers practicing their objectives, and then provide immediate feedback on their observations. Few coaches capitalize on coachable moments, but they can go a long way toward promoting persistence in coachees. It is important to note that capitalizing on coachable moments should take little time, often less than two minutes. In the example above, the leader could provide feedback to the coachee during their walk back to the office after the staff meeting.

Transferring Skills: Creating a Learning Environment

To build bench strength, leaders need to create a learning environment so that personal development becomes an ongoing process rather than a one-time event. As Tichy and Cohen (1997) aptly point out, the most successful organizations are those that emphasize the learning and teaching process—they focus on constantly creating leaders throughout the company. In reality, leaders have quite a bit of control over the kind of learning environments they want to create for their followers, and there are several interventions they can take to ensure that development becomes an ongoing process. Perhaps the most important intervention is for leaders to role-model development. In that regard, if leaders are not getting regular feedback from followers, then they are probably not doing a good job of role-modeling development. By regularly soliciting feedback from followers, leaders are also likely to create a feedback-rich work environment. Once feedback becomes a group norm, people will be much more willing to help build team member skills, which in turn can have a catalytic effect on group performance. It is important to note that the leader will play a large role in this group norm, because if the leader is feedback averse, it will be difficult to see how this norm will be adopted by followers.

Leaders can also create learning environments by regularly reviewing their followers' development. Perhaps the easiest way to do this is by making leaders and followers development partners; then both parties can provide regular feedback and on-going support. During these discussions leaders and followers should review and update their development plans to capitalize on new development opportunities or acquire new skills. Leaders and followers can also review coaching plans to see what is and is not working and make the necessary adjustments.

Concluding Comments

Perhaps one of the greatest misperceptions of coaching, and the primary reason why leaders state they do not coach others, is that it takes a lot of time. In reality, nothing could be further from the truth. Leaders are working to build credibility, build relationships with followers, and understand followers' career aspirations and view of the world. Although these do take time, they are also activities leaders should be engaged in even if they are not coaching followers. Doing a GAPS analysis, identifying and prioritizing development needs, helping followers create development plans, and creating coaching plans often takes less than four hours. Although leaders will need to take these steps with all their followers, these four hours can be spread out over a four- to six-week period. As stated earlier, meeting with followers on a regular basis to review development (perhaps monthly) and capitalizing on coachable moments also take little time. Finally, many of the actions outlined in "Create a Learning Environment" either take little time or are extensions of actions outlined earlier. The bottom line is that coaching really can take little additional time; it is really more a function of changing how you spend time with followers so that you can maximize their development.

Another note about the coaching model is that good coaches are equally versatile at all five steps of coaching. Some leaders are very good at forging a partnership, but then fail to carry development to the next level by conducting a GAPS analysis or helping followers build a development plan. Other leaders may help followers build a development plan but do not do anything to promote persistence or create a learning environment. Just as leaders need to develop their technical skills, so might they need to assess and in turn develop certain coaching skills. It is also important to remember that coaching is a very dynamic process—good coaches assess where followers are in the coaching process and intervene appropriately. By regularly assessing where they are with followers, they may determine that the relationship with a particular follower is not as strong as they thought, and this lack of relationship is why followers are not sticking to their development plan. In this case, a good coach would go back to forging a partnership with the follower and, once a trusting relationship had been created, go through another GAPS analysis, and so forth.

Finally, it is important to note that people can and do develop skills on their own. Nevertheless, leaders who commit to the five steps of informal coaching outlined above will both create learning organizations and help to raise development to a new level. Given the competitive advantage of companies that have a well-developed and capable workforce, in the future it will be hard to imagine leadership excellence without coaching. Good leaders are those who create successors, and coaching may be the best way to make this happen.

Empowerment

What Is Empowerment?
The Psychological Components of Empowerment
Six Best Practices of Empowerment

Do what you can, where you are at, with what you have.

Teddy Roosevelt

Inside every old company is a new company waiting to be born.

Alvin Toffler

Empowerment has become a very popular concept over the past 10 years. Many companies have embarked on various types of empowerment programs to improve results, yet the success of these programs has been mixed at best (Howard, 1996). One of the reasons for the mixed results is that empowerment often means different things to different people. This section describes what empowerment is (and is not), as well as some of the psychological constructs underlying empowerment and some of the best practices of empowering others.

What Is Empowerment?

In general, people seem to fall into one of two camps with respect to empowerment. Some people believe empowerment is all about delegation and accountability, a top-down process where senior leaders articulate a vision and specific goals, and hold followers responsible for achieving them. Others believe empowerment is more of a bottom-up approach that focuses on intelligent risk taking, growth, change, trust, and ownership; followers act as entrepreneurs and owners that question rules and make intelligent decisions. Leaders tolerate mistakes and encourage cooperative behavior in this approach to empowerment (Quinn & Spreitzer, 1997). Needless to say, these two conceptualizations of empowerment have very different implications for leaders and followers. And it is precisely this conceptual confusion which has caused empowerment programs to fail in many organizations (Quinn & Spreitzer, 1997). Because of the conceptual confusion surrounding empowerment, companies such as Motorola will not use this term to describe programs that push decision making to lower organizational levels. These companies would rather coin their own terms to describe these programs, thus avoiding the confusion surrounding empowerment.

We define empowerment as having two key components. For leaders to truly empower employees, they must delegate leadership and decision making down to the lowest level possible. Employees are often the closest to the problem and have the most information, and as such can often make the best decisions. A classic example was the UPS employee who ordered an extra 737 aircraft to haul presents that had been forgotten in the last-minute Christmas rush. This decision was clearly beyond the employee's level of authority, but UPS praised his initiative for seeing the problem and making the right decision. The second component of empowerment, and the one most often overlooked, is equipping followers with the resources, knowledge, and skills necessary to make good decisions. All too often companies adopt an empowerment program and push decision making down to the employee level, but employees have no experience creating business plans, submitting budgets, dealing with other departments within the company, or directly dealing with customers or vendors. Not surprisingly, ill-equipped employees often make poor, uninformed decisions, and managers in turn are likely to believe that empowerment was not all it was cracked up to be. The same happens with downsizing, as employees are asked to take on additional responsibilities but are provided with little training or support. As we stated in Chapter 9, this "forced" empowerment may lead to some short-term stock gains but tends to be disastrous in the long run. Thus, empowerment has both delegation and developmental components; delegation without development is often perceived as abandonment, and development without delegation can often be perceived as micromanagement. Leaders wishing to empower followers must determine what followers are capable of doing, enhance and broaden these capabilities, and give followers commensurate increases in authority and accountability.

The Psychological Components of Empowerment

The psychological components of empowerment can be examined at both macro and micro levels. There are three macro psychological components underlying empowerment, and these are motivation, learning, and stress (Howard, 1996). As a concept, empowerment has been around since at least the 1920s, and the vast majority of companies that have implemented empowerment programs have done so to increase employee motivation and, in turn, productivity. As a motivational technique, however, empowerment has not lived up to its promise; empowered workers may not be any more productive than unempowered workers (Howard, 1996). There are several reasons why this may be the case. First, senior leaders tend to see empowerment through rose-colored glasses. They hear about the benefits an empowerment program is having in another company, but do not consider the time, effort, and changes needed to create a truly empowered workforce. Relatedly, many empowerment programs are poorly implemented—the program is announced with great fanfare, but little real guidance, training, or support is provided and managers are quick to pull the plug on the program as soon as followers start making poor decisions. Adopting an effective empowerment program takes training, trust, and time (Offermann, 1996), but companies most likely to implement an empowerment program (as a panacea for their poor financial situation) often lack these three attributes. Third, as described in Chapter 9, worker productivity and job dissatisfaction in the United States are at an all-time high. Many companies are dealing with high levels of employee burnout, and adding additional responsibilities to already overfilled plates is likely to be counterproductive. As reported by Xie and Johns (1995), some empowerment programs create positions that are just too big for a person to handle effectively, and job burnout is usually the result.

Although the motivational benefits of empowerment seem questionable, the learning and stress reduction benefits of empowerment seem more clear-cut. Given that properly designed and implemented empowerment programs include a strong developmental component, one of the key benefits to these programs is that they help employees learn more about their jobs, company, and industry. These knowledge and skill gains increase the intellectual capital of the company and can be a competitive advantage in moving ahead. In addition to the learning benefits, well-designed empowerment programs can actually help to reduce burnout. People can tolerate high levels of stress when they have a high level of control. Given that many employees are putting in longer hours than ever before and work demands are at an all-time high, empowerment can help followers gain some control over their lives and better cope with stress. Although an empowered worker may have the same high work demands as an unempowered worker, the empowered worker will have more choices on how and when to accomplish these demands and as such will suffer from less stress. And because stress is a key component of dysfunctional turnover, giving workers more control over their work demands can reduce turnover and in turn positively impact the company's bottom line.

There are also four micro components of empowerment. These components can be used to determine whether employees are empowered or unempowered, and include self-determination, meaning, competence, and influence (Quinn & Spreitzer, 1997; Spreitzer, 1995). Empowered employees have a sense of self-determination; they can make choices about what they do, how they do it, and when they need to get it done. Empowered employees also have a strong sense of meaning; they be-

FIGURE EM.1
The empowerment continuum.

Empowered Employee ← → **Unempowered Employees**	
• Self-determined	• Other-determined
• Sense of meaning	• Not sure if what they do is important
• High competence	• Low competence
• High influence	• Low influence

lieve what they do is important to them and to the company's success. Empowered employees have a high level of competence in that they know what they are doing and are confident they can get the job done. Finally, empowered employees have an impact on others and believe that they can influence their teams or work units and that co-workers and leaders will listen to their ideas. In summary, empowered employees have latitude to make decisions, are comfortable making these decisions, believe what they do is important, and are seen as influential members of their team. Unempowered employees may have little latitude to make decisions, may feel ill equipped and may not want to make decisions, and may have little impact on their work unit, even if they have good ideas. Most employees probably fall somewhere in between the two extremes of the empowerment continuum, depicted in Figure EM.1. Leaders wanting to create more empowered followers may want to adopt some of the best practices techniques outlined below.

Six Best Practices of Empowerment

Do We Really Want or Need Empowerment?

Perhaps the first question leaders should ask before adopting an empowerment program is whether the company wants or needs empowerment. Leaders may agree that empowerment is important but may have fundamental differences as to the actions leaders need to take to create an empowered organization. Having a clear initial understanding of just what empowerment is will make the implementation of the program that much easier.

Leaders wanting to adopt an empowerment program must also consider how their own jobs and roles will be affected. They may need to fundamentally change their leadership style to better tolerate employee mistakes, play more of a coaching than directing role, and be willing to be challenged on a regular basis. Because empowered employees have access to considerably more information, they will be much more likely to question past or current decisions, and leaders will need to exert more personal power in order to get decisions adopted. Leaders feeling that this role transition is too much of a stretch will not enthusiastically embrace an empowerment program, making companywide adoption of the program difficult.

Creating a Clear Vision, Goals, and Accountabilities

Once a decision is made to develop and implement an empowerment program, top management must ensure that the company's vision, business strategies, and operational goals are clear and are understood by everyone in the company. It is difficult to ask employees to make wise decisions if they do not know where the company is headed. Employees should know what the company and work unit are trying to accomplish and how these accomplishments will be measured, and they should be given regular feedback on progress. In addition, employees will need to understand how their own goals are related to work unit and company goals.

Developing Others

Just because employees have a clear understanding of their work goals does not mean they have the knowledge, skills, and resources necessary to get them accomplished. Leaders will need to determine what employees can currently do, what they need to be able to do, and how they will help employees bridge the gaps between current and future capabilities. Perhaps the best way to do this is for leaders to adopt the five steps described in the "Coaching" section of Part V. A key component of empowerment is trust, and leaders can build trust by taking the actions prescribed in "Forging a Partnership." Leaders can identify and prioritize development needs through a GAPS analysis, and can work to increase knowledge and skills through development plans, coaching plans, and the actions outlined under "Promote Persistence" and "Transferring Skills." The five steps of informal coaching give leaders a road map for improving the bench strength of their followers and systematically equipping them to meet the increased challenges of empowerment. Taking these development steps helps with the competence component of empowerment.

Delegating Decision Making to Followers

Once followers are starting to develop the skills, knowledge, and experience necessary to make wise decisions, leaders must systematically increase the degree of latitude and autonomy employees are given to make decisions. Although this sounds fairly straightforward, in practice it can be fairly difficult. Some of the typical mistakes leaders make in this area are pushing followers into decision making too quickly, holding on to decision-making power too long, or taking decision-making power away from followers during a crisis. Other difficulties include the fact that many leaders associate decision making with leadership and may feel personally threatened by delegating decision-making authority to others. This may be particularly true when organizations have recently gone through a downsizing or when the level of trust between leaders and followers is low. Some followers may also feel reluctant to take on increased decision-making responsibility, as their level of skill may be exposed in ways it never had before (Offermann, 1996). Another complication is that some employees may feel that because they are taking on additional responsibilities, they should be paid more. This is particularly true when empowerment programs are introduced in union environments.

One way to determine how much latitude and authority to provide followers is to use the Situational Leadership® Theory, described in Chapter 12. This model provides a useful heuristic for developing employees and determining when they are ready to take on additional decision-making responsibilities. Another way to effectively delegate decision making to followers is to provide clear boundaries around the decisions they make. For example, employees at the Ritz-Carlton hotels have fixed limits on the amounts employees can spend to satisfy disgruntled guests. As the level of followers' knowledge and experience increases, the scope of the decisions can be increased and their boundaries loosened. Leaders delegating tasks and responsibilities should also follow the tenets of setting goals and delegating described earlier in this section of the text. Because followers will not be very skilled in making wise decisions, leaders will need to be prepared to tolerate followers' mistakes and help them learn from these experiences. The actions outlined under this best practice will help with the self-determination and influence components of empowerment.

Leading by Example

Leaders must be an example of empowerment if they want to successfully empower their employees. An illustration of how a leader could role-model empowerment will be useful. A multimillion-dollar consulting firm, run by one of the authors, was facing an acute labor shortage. Customer requests for additional services created enough work for four new positions. The office had a strong financial track record, and financial analyses provided solid support for the additional positions. Moreover, employee workload was extremely high, and the office was in desperate need of additional help. Armed with these facts, the author submitted job requisitions for the four additional positions to corporate headquarters. But after two months and numerous phone calls to corporate staff, the positions did not seem to be any closer to being approved. The author went ahead and hired the four additional staff, and informed corporate headquarters of his decision once the new personnel were onboard. Although the author took a considerable amount of heat from the COO and the vice president of human resources, the office continued to be financially successful, office morale dramatically improved, and the author sent a clear signal to his staff to seek forgiveness rather than permission.

Quinn and Spreitzer (1997) have claimed that it is nearly impossible for unempowered leaders to empower followers. Although there is some truth to this statement, empowerment needs to start somewhere, and it is all too easy for leaders to say that "they" are not allowing us to empower our followers. All too often "they" are the very same people who are making these statements, and it is their own preconceived notions of leadership and misunderstandings of empowerment that are getting in the way. When this occurs, it is all too easy for leaders to waste time finger-pointing and overlook the areas where they *can* empower followers. In the above example the author was not empowered to make these hiring decisions, yet he went ahead and did it anyway. This could have been a career-ending decision for the author, but he weighed the consequences of failing to hire additional help and thought the benefits were greater than the political costs. There is a certain amount of risk taking to leadership, and good leaders are those who themselves take, and allow their followers to take, intelligent risks. Like UPS and the employee who ordered the additional 737, good leaders reward intelligent risk taking and do not punish decisions that were well thought out but failed.

Empowerment Must Be Systemic to Be Successful

Although individual leaders who take initiative can empower their followers, it will be much easier and more effective if senior leadership embraces empowerment as a key business strategy. When reward and performance appraisal systems, selection systems, work processes, training programs, organizational structure, and information systems are strongly aligned with the organization's definition of empowerment, then all these programs will be very successful. On the other hand, merely introducing an empowerment program but failing to make the necessary adjustments in the organizational systems, processes, and structure will likely be a recipe for failure.

Management   September 14, 2007

3M: Struggle Between Efficiency and Creativity

How CEO George Buckley is managing the yin and yang of discipline and imagination

by Brian Hindo

Not too many years ago, the temple of management was General Electric (GE). Former CEO Jack Welch was the high priest, and his disciples spread the word to executive suites throughout the land. One of his most highly regarded followers, James McNerney, was quickly snatched up by 3M after falling short in the closely watched race to succeed Welch. 3M's board considered McNerney a huge prize, and the company's stock jumped nearly 20% in the days after Dec. 5, 2000, when his selection as CEO was announced. The mere mention of his name made everyone richer.

McNerney was the first outsider to lead the insular St. Paul (Minn.) company in its 100-year history. He had barely stepped off the plane before he announced he would change the DNA of the place. His playbook was vintage GE. McNerney axed 8,000 workers (about 11% of the workforce), intensified the performance-review process, and tightened the purse strings at a company that had become a profligate spender. He also imported GE's vaunted Six Sigma program—a series of management techniques designed to decrease production defects and increase efficiency. Thousands of staffers became trained as Six Sigma "black belts." The plan appeared to work: McNerney jolted 3M's moribund stock back to life and won accolades for bringing discipline to an organization that had become unwieldy, erratic, and sluggish.

Then, four and a half years after arriving, McNerney abruptly left for a bigger opportunity, the top job at Boeing (BA). Now his successors face a challenging question: whether the relentless emphasis on efficiency had made 3M a less creative company. That's a vitally important issue for a company whose very identity is built on innovation. After all, 3M is the birthplace of masking tape, Thinsulate, and the Post-it note. It is the invention machine whose methods were consecrated in the influential 1994 best-seller *Built to Last* by Jim Collins and Jerry I. Porras. But those old hits have become distant memories. It has been a long time since the debut of 3M's last game-changing technology: the multilayered optical films that coat liquid-crystal display screens. At the company that has always prided itself on drawing at least one-third of sales from products released in the past five years, today that fraction has slipped to only one-quarter.

Those results are not coincidental. Efficiency programs such as Six Sigma are designed to identify problems in work processes—and then use rigorous measurement to reduce variation and eliminate defects. When these types of initiatives become ingrained in a company's culture, as they did at 3M, creativity can easily get squelched. After all, a breakthrough innovation is something that challenges existing procedures and norms. "Invention is by its very nature a disorderly process," says current CEO George Buckley, who has dialed back many of McNerney's initiatives. "You can't put a Six Sigma process into that area and say, well, I'm getting behind on invention, so I'm going to schedule myself for three good ideas on Wednesday and two on Friday. That's not how creativity works." McNerney declined to comment for this story.

PROUD CREATIVE CULTURE

The tension that Buckley is trying to manage—between innovation and efficiency—is one that's bedeviling CEOs everywhere. There is no doubt that the application of lean and mean work processes at thousands of companies, often through programs with obscure-sounding names such as ISO 9000 and Total Quality Management, has been one of the most important business trends of past decades. But as once-bloated U.S. manufacturers have shaped up and become profitable global competitors, the onus shifts to growth and innovation, especially in today's idea-based, design-obsessed economy. While process excellence demands precision, consistency, and repetition, innovation calls for variation, failure, and serendipity.

Indeed, the very factors that make Six Sigma effective in one context can make it ineffective in another. Traditionally, it uses rigorous statistical analysis to produce unambiguous data that help produce better quality, lower costs, and more efficiency. That all sounds great when you know what outcomes you'd like to control. But what about when there are few facts to go on—or you don't even know the nature of the problem you're trying to define? "New things look very bad on this scale," says MITSloan School of Management professor Eric von Hippel, who has worked with 3M on innovation projects that he says "took a backseat" once Six Sigma settled in. "The more you hardwire a company on total quality management, [the more] it is going to hurt breakthrough innovation," adds Vijay Govindarajan, a management professor at Dartmouth's Tuck School of Business. "The mindset that is needed, the capabilities that are needed, the metrics that are needed, the whole culture that is needed for discontinuous innovation, are fundamentally different."

The exigencies of Wall Street are another matter. Investors liked McNerney's approach to boosting earnings, which may have sacrificed creativity but made up for it in consistency. Profits grew, on average, 22% a year. In Buckley's first year, sales approached $23 billion and profits totaled $1.4 billion, but two quarterly earnings misses and a languishing stock made it a rocky ride. In 2007, Buckley seems to have satisfied many skeptics on the Street, convincing them he can ignite top-line growth without killing the McNerney-led productivity improvements. Shares are up 12% since January.

Buckley's Street cred was hard-won. He's nowhere near the management rock star his predecessor was. McNerney could play the President on TV. He's tall and athletic, with charisma to spare. Buckley is of average height, with a slight middle-age paunch, an informal demeanor, and a scientist's natural curiosity. In the office he prefers checked shirts and khakis to suits and ties. He's bookish and puckish, in the way of a tenured professor.

Buckley, in short, is just the kind of guy who has traditionally thrived at 3M. It was one of the pillars of the "3M Way" that workers could seek out funding from a number of company sources to get their pet projects off the ground. Official company policy allowed employees to use 15% of their time to pursue independent projects. The company explicitly encouraged risk and tolerated failure. 3M's creative culture foreshadowed the one that is currently celebrated unanimously at Google (GOOG).

Perhaps all of that made it particularly painful for 3M's proud workforce to deal with the hard reality the company faced by the late '90s. Profit and sales growth were wildly erratic. It bungled operations in Asia amid the 1998 financial crisis there. The stock sat out the entire late '90s boom, budging less than 1% from September, 1997, to September, 2000. The flexibility and lack of structure, which had enabled the company's success, had also by then produced a bloated staff and inefficient workflow. So McNerney had plenty of cause to whip things into shape.

GREEN-BELT TRAINING REGIMEN

One of his main tools was Six Sigma, which originated at Motorola (MOT) in 1986 and became a staple of corporate life in the '90s after it was embraced by GE. The term is now so widely and divergently applied that it's hard to pin down what it actually means. At some companies, Six

Sigma is plainly a euphemism for cost-cutting. Others explain it as a tool for analyzing a problem (high shipping costs, for instance) and then using data to solve each component of it. But on a basic level, Six Sigma seeks to remove variability from a process. In that way you avoid errors, or defects, and increase predictability (technically speaking, Six Sigma quality has come to be accepted as no more than 3.4 defects per million).

At 3M, McNerney introduced the two main Six Sigma tools. The first and more traditional version is an acronym known as DMAIC (pronounced "dee-may-ic"), which stands for: define, measure, analyze, improve, control. These five steps are the essence of the Six Sigma approach to problem solving. The other flavor is called Design for Six Sigma, or DFSS, which purports to systematize a new product development process so that something can be made to Six Sigma quality from the start.

Thousands of 3Mers were trained as black belts, an honorific awarded to experts who often act as internal consultants for their companies. Nearly every employee participated in a several-day "green-belt" training regimen, which explained DMAIC and DFSS, familiarized workers with statistics, and showed them how to track data and create charts and tables on a computer program called Minitab. The black belts fanned out and led bigger-scale "black-belt projects," such as increasing production speed 40% by reducing variations and removing wasted steps from manufacturing. They also often oversaw smaller "green-belt projects," such as improving the order fulfillment process. This Six Sigma drive undoubtedly contributed to 3M's astronomical profitability improvements under McNerney; operating margins went from 17% in 2001 to 23% in 2005.

While Six Sigma was invented as a way to improve quality, its main value to corporations now clearly is its ability to save time and money. McNerney arrived at a company that had been criticized for throwing cash at problems. In his first full year, he slashed capital expenditures 22%, from $980 million to $763 million, and 11% more to a trough of $677 million in 2003. As a percentage of sales, capital expenditures dropped from 6.1% in 2001 to just 3.7% in 2003. McNerney also held research and development funding constant from 2001 to 2005, hovering over $1 billion a year. "If you take over a company that's been living on innovation, clearly you can squeeze costs out," says Charles O'Reilly, a Stanford Graduate School of Business management professor. "The question is, what's the long-term damage to the company?"

Under McNerney, the R&D function at 3M was systematized in ways that were unheard of and downright heretical in St. Paul, even though the guidelines would have looked familiar at many other conglomerates. Some employees found the constant analysis stifling. Steven Boyd, a PhD who had worked as a researcher at 3M for 32 years before his job was eliminated in 2004, was one of them. After a couple of months on a research project, he would have to fill in a "red book" with scores of pages worth of charts and tables, analyzing everything from the potential commercial application, to the size of the market, to possible manufacturing concerns.

Traditionally, 3M had been a place where researchers had been given wide latitude to pursue research down whatever alleys they wished. After the arrival of the new boss, the DMAIC process was laid over a phase-review process for innovations—a novelty at 3M. The goal was to speed up and systematize the progress of inventions into the new-product pipeline. The DMAIC questions "are all wonderful considerations, but are they appropriate for somebody who's just trying to...develop some ideas?" asks Boyd. The impact of the Six Sigma regime, according to Boyd and other former 3Mers, was that more predictable, incremental work took precedence over blue-sky research. "You're supposed to be having something that was going to be producing a profit, if not next quarter, it better be the quarter after that," Boyd says.

For a long time, 3M had allowed researchers to spend years testing products. Consider, for example, the Post-it note. Its inventor, Art Fry, a 3M scientist who's now retired, and others fiddled with the idea for several years before the product went into full production in 1980. Early during the Six Sigma effort, after a meeting at which technical employees were briefed on the new process, "we all came to the conclusion that there was no way in the world that anything like a Post-it note would ever emerge from this new system," says Michael Mucci, who worked at 3M for 27 years before his dismissal in 2004. (Mucci has alleged in a class action that 3M engaged in age discrimination; the company says the claims are without merit.)

There has been little formal research on whether the tension between Six Sigma and innovation is inevitable. But the most notable attempt yet, by Wharton School professor Mary Benner and Harvard Business School professor Michael L. Tushman, suggests that Six Sigma will lead to more incremental innovation at the expense of more blue-sky work. The two professors analyzed the types of patents granted to paint and photography companies over a 20-year period, before and after a quality improvement drive. Their work shows that, after the quality push, patents issued based primarily on prior work made up a dramatically larger share of the total, while those not based on prior work dwindled.

Defenders of Six Sigma at 3M claim that a more systematic new-product introduction process allows innovations to get to market faster. But Fry, the Post-it note inventor, disagrees. In fact, he places the blame for 3M's recent lack of innovative sizzle squarely on Six Sigma's application in 3M's research labs. Innovation, he says, is "a numbers game. You have to go through 5,000 to 6,000 raw ideas to find one successful business." Six Sigma would ask, why not eliminate all that waste and just come up with the right idea the first time? That way of thinking, says Fry, can have serious side effects. "What's remarkable is how fast a culture can be torn apart," says Fry, who lives in Maplewood, Minn., just a few minutes south of the corporate campus and pops into the office regularly to help with colleagues' projects. "[McNerney] didn't kill it, because he wasn't here long enough. But if he had been here much longer, I think he could have."

REINVIGORATED WORKFORCE

Buckley, a PhD chemical engineer by training, seems to recognize the cultural ramifications of a process-focused program on an organization whose fate and history is so bound up in inventing new stuff. "You cannot create in that atmosphere of confinement or sameness," Buckley says. "Perhaps one of the mistakes that we made as a company—it's one of the dangers of Six Sigma—is that when you value sameness more than you value creativity, I think you potentially undermine the heart and soul of a company like 3M."

In recent years, the company's reputation as an innovator has been sliding. In 2004, 3M was ranked No. 1 on Boston Consulting Group's Most Innovative Companies list (now the *BusinessWeek*/BCG list). It dropped to No. 2 in 2005, to No. 3 in 2006, and down to No. 7 this year. "People have kind of forgotten about these guys," says Dev Patnaik, managing associate of innovation consultancy Jump Associates. "When was the last time you saw something innovative or experimental coming out of there?"

Buckley has loosened the reins a bit by removing 3M research scientists' obligation to hew to Six Sigma objectives. There was perhaps a one-size-fits-all approach to the application of Six Sigma as the initial implementation got under way, says Dr. Larry Wendling, a vice-president who directs the "R" in 3M's R&D operation. "Since [McNerney] was driving it to the organization, you know, there were metrics established across the organization and quite frankly, some of them did not make as much sense for the lab as they did other parts of the organization," Wendling says. What sort of metrics? Keeping track of how many black-belt and green-belt projects were completed, for one.

In fact, it's not uncommon for Six Sigma to become an end unto itself. That may be appropriate in an operations context—at the end of the year, it's easy enough for a line manager to count up all the money he's saved by doing green-belt projects. But what 3Mers came to realize is that these financially definitive outcomes were much more elusive in the context of a research lab. "In some cases in the lab it made sense, but in other cases, people were going around dreaming up green-belt programs to fill their quota of green-belt programs for that time period," says Wendling. "We were letting, I think, the process get in the way of doing the actual invention."

To help get the creative juices flowing, Buckley is opening the money spigot—hiking spending on R&D, acquisitions, and capital expenditures. The overall R&D budget will grow 20% this year, to $1.5 billion. Even more significant than the increase in money is Buckley's reallocation of those funds. He's funneling cash into what he calls "core" areas of 3M technology, 45 in all, from abrasives to nanotechnology to flexible electronics. That is another departure from McNerney's priorities; he told *BusinessWeek* in 2004 that the 3M product with the most promise was skin-care cream Aldara, the centerpiece to a burgeoning pharmaceuticals business. In January, Buckley sold the pharma business for $2 billion.

Quietly, the McNerney legacy is being revised at 3M. While there is no doubt the former CEO brought some positive change to the company, many workers say they are reinvigorated now that the corporate emphasis has shifted from profitability and process discipline to growth and innovation. Timm Hammond, the director of strategic business development, says "[Buckley] has brought back a spark around creativity." Adds Bob Anderson, a business director in 3M's radio frequency identification division: "We feel like we can dream again."

Hindo is *BusinessWeek*'s Corporate Strategies editor in New York.

11

Conflict Management and Negotiation

Learning Objectives

After studying this chapter, you should be able to:

- **Define** and describe the conflict process.
- **Recognize** symptoms of conflict.
- **Identify** sources of conflict.
- **Differentiate** between functional and dysfunctional conflict.
- **Utilize** conflict styles appropriately.
- **Apply** conflict management strategies.
- **Bargain** and negotiate.

RESTRUCTURING PROMOTES QUALITY AT GM'S SATURN PLANT

When Saturn was first envisioned in 1985 by a seminal group of management and United Autoworkers Union (UAW) representatives at General Motors, the contract called for UAW representatives to be equal partners in making all start-up decisions for Saturn. This included where to put the plant, how it would be set up, and even which advertising agency to retain. At first, both management and union officials found it difficult to jettison the familiar confrontational ways in favor of a spirit of cooperation. But that gradually changed as Saturn engineers traveled around the world looking for world-class approaches to the process of building a car, and UAW production workers went with them.

"There are still conflicts, but they are managed differently than before," says Mike Bennett, the local union president. "It's not adversarial. It's more advocacy in terms of finding a better solution or better options." An example of such conflict came when GM's chairman, Robert Stempel, arrived for a visit and found a demonstration by union people wearing black-and-orange armbands to protest a plan to increase production—because they thought it would compromise quality. The workers thought that adding teams to the production line too quickly would hinder ongoing efforts to work out all the problems and improve the quality of the cars. The union protesters made—and won—their case. Instead of increasing production quickly to 700 cars a day to try to meet the strong demand in the marketplace, GM increased production slowly as kinks in the process were worked out. Today, the line produces 1,000 cars a day—90 percent of capacity.

Plant manager Robert Boruff recalls this incident with awe: "Think about an organization where you've got people coming from 146 GM locations, all of whom have been raised with a bias that the members are first and quality is second. They aren't protesting line speedup. They're not protesting health and safety issues. They just want to ensure the quality of the product. That's not a problem, that's a gift from God."

Source: Adapted from Beverly Geber, "Saturn's Grand Experiment," *Training* (June 1992), pp. 27–35.

Every relationship contains conflict, disagreement, and opposed interests. Conflict has the potential to destroy relationships, put companies out of business, and ruin careers, but these outcomes are not inevitable. Negative consequences usually arise from failure to handle conflict in constructive ways. As demonstrated by the union and management cooperation in the General Motor's Saturn opening vignette, constructive conflict management produces creative solutions to problems, higher-quality relationships, and constructive change. Unless relationships of any type are able to withstand the stress involved in inevitable conflicts, and manage them productively, they are not likely to endure.[1] This chapter provides a game plan for understanding and managing conflict productively in both personal and organizational situations.

What Is Conflict?

conflict
A disagreement between two or more parties who perceive that they have incompatible concerns.

Conflict is a disagreement between two or more parties—for example, individuals, groups, departments, organizations, countries—who perceive that they have incompatible concerns. Conflicts exist whenever an action by one party is perceived as preventing or interfering with the goals, needs, or actions of another party. Conflicts can arise over a multiple of organizational experiences, such as incompatible goals, differences in the interpretation of facts, negative feelings, differences of values and philosophies, or disputes over shared resources.[2] As defined above, conflict sounds pretty negative. But, in some cases, it can actually stimulate creative problem solving and improve the situation for all parties involved.

Functional versus Dysfunctional Conflict

The traditional view of conflict assumed that it was undesirable and led to negative outcomes like aggression, violence, and hostility. This *dysfunctional view* of conflict implied that managers should determine the causes of conflict and eliminate them, and make sure that future conflicts were prevented.

This was the view of the board of directors of Sunbeam-Oster, which fired its CEO, Paul Kazarian, in 1993, three years after he had been hired to save the company from bankruptcy. Most would think that Kazarian took a high risk and failed, but that was not the case. In fact, he saved the company, turning its multimillion-dollar losses into multimillion-dollar profits in one year. His success continued until even the day before he was fired, when quarterly profits were reported to have increased 40 percent. Mr. Kazarian's problem was that he created dysfunctional conflicts for other influential people in the company. Although Kazarian rationalized his approach by saying, "You don't change a company in bankruptcy without making a few waves," others viewed him as creating more work for people who were already working beyond capacity, pitting people against each other, and intimidating managers, employees, and even outside suppliers and customers.[3]

If Kazarian was right however, as his economic results verified, conflict can be viewed as *functional* because of its potential to stimulate creative resolution of problems and corrective actions and to keep people and organizations from slipping into complacency. Perhaps it shouldn't matter if individuals don't like conflict. If it increases performance and is beneficial to the group or organization as a whole, it is functional.

This outcome of the conflict is the criterion for determining if it is functional or dysfunctional, that is, whether it has positive or negative outcomes for the decision-making group (e.g., department, organization, stockholders). Perhaps the most appropriate attitude toward conflict is that it is inevitable and has the potential to be dysfunctional, but if managed constructively, conflict can be functional and enhance performance.

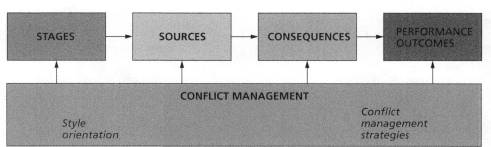

Exhibit 11–1
**The Conflict
Management Process**

Exhibit 11–1 provides an overview of the conflict management process. The first thing a manager needs to do is determine what stage the conflict is in. Then the source of the conflict has to be established. Next the manager can examine the consequences and performance outcomes of the conflict. Finally the manager needs to decide which conflict style orientation and specific strategies to apply to most productively manage the conflict. The following section of this chapter will focus on the first two parts of the conflict management process: the stages and sources of conflict.

The Stages of Conflict

Although a conflict does not exist until one party perceives that another party may negatively affect something that the first party cares about,[4] the development of antecedent conditions (the sources of conflict) marks the start of the process. Afterwards, conflict usually proceeds through the five stages diagrammed in Exhibit 11–2.[5]

Stage 1: Latent Conflict

When two or more parties need each other to achieve desired objectives, there is potential for conflict. Other antecedents of conflict, such as interdependence, different goals, and ambiguity of responsibility, are described in the next section. They don't automatically create conflicts, but when they exist, they make it possible. Latent conflict often arises when a change occurs. Conflict might be caused by a budget cutback, a change in organizational direction, a change in a personal goal, the assignment of a new project to an already overloaded work force, or an expected occurrence (such as a salary increase) that doesn't happen.

Stage 2: Perceived Conflict

This is the point at which members become aware of a problem. Incompatibility of needs is perceived and tension begins as the parties begin to worry about what will happen. At this point, however, no one feels that anything that they care about is actually being overtly threatened.

Stage 3: Felt Conflict

Now the parties become emotionally involved and begin to focus on differences of opinion and opposing interests, sharpening perceived conflict. Internal tensions and frustrations begin to crystallize around specific, defined issues, and people begin to build an emotional commitment to their particular position. What emotions are felt is important because negative ones produce low trust and negative perceptions of the other party's position, which can result in destructive win–lose tactics.[6] More positive feelings, on the other hand, can contribute to a more balanced view of the situation and more collaborative endeavors.[7] In either case, the result is a defining of what the conflict is actually about, which will determine the alternatives available for later resolution.

Exhibit 11–2   **The Stages of Conflict**

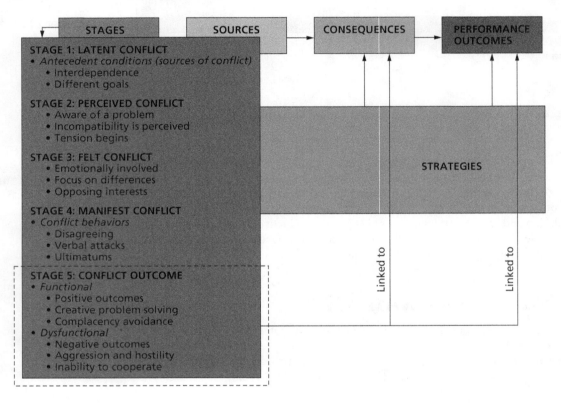

Stage 4: Manifest Conflict

The obvious display of conflict occurs when the opposing parties plan and follow through with acts to achieve their own objectives and frustrate the other. Actions can range from minor disagreeing, questioning, and challenging at one end of the conflict-intensity continuum, to verbal attacks, threats, ultimatums, physical attacks, and even efforts to destroy the other party at the other end.[8]

Stage 5: Conflict Outcome

The interactions of the conflicting parties in the manifest conflict stage result in outcomes that can be functional or dysfunctional for one or both parties. As conflict proceeds through the stages, functional resolution becomes more difficult. The parties become more locked into their positions and more convinced that the conflict is a win–lose situation. It is usually easier to achieve positive collaboration and win–win outcomes when the conflict is recognized early before frustration and other negative sentiments set in.

Sources of Conflict

In order for conflict to occur, certain conditions must exist. These conditions may be outwardly visible, or they may be latent and waiting to surface. Therefore, it is imperative to understand these underlying conditions that can cause conflict. Exhibit 11–3 presents the primary causes of conflict condensed into five general categories: goal incompatibility, structural design, role expectations, degenerative climate, and personal differences.

Exhibit 11–3   **Sources of Conflict**

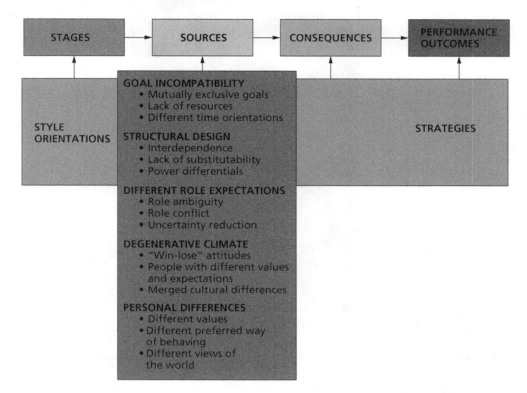

Goal Incompatibility

An ideal situation exists when two parties perceive their goals as mutually enhancing and view each other's behaviors as contributing to the achievement of both sets of goals. In such a case, a high degree of cooperation is likely to result. Design research and marketing departments, for example, will probably enjoy a cooperative relationship because a new line developed by the former will provide the latter with the products it needs to meet its increased sales objectives. Several things can get in the way, however.

MUTUALLY EXCLUSIVE GOALS   When one party's goal achievement is perceived as threatening to another's, the resulting conflict is likely to engender win–lose competition. For example, both design research and marketing departments may interrelate poorly with a production department that has a goal of eliminating new and low-volume production runs. Another classic case of goal conflict often exists between sales departments who want increased volume and market share versus credit departments who want to limit sales to customers with the ability to pay.

INSUFFICIENT SHARED RESOURCES   Most organizations operate with a finite amount of money, personnel, and equipment. As parties compete for their share of the organizational pie, conflict often results. If one party receives more power, higher status, better work assignments, or more material resources, the remaining parties often get less. Dysfunctional conflict results from the win–lose competition that limited resources foster.[9]

DIFFERENT TIME ORIENTATIONS   Another potential source of conflict is the different time spans needed by parties to achieve their goals. Some parties have relatively short time orientations. Production crews, for example, may require hourly feedback about results. Marketing departments often focus on weekly sales volume, while research and

Conflict between groups in a company—many times between employees and upper management—can result in a strike if problem solving isn't effective or initiated quickly enough.

Corbis

finance departments may have to look several years ahead when developing new products or forecasting interest rates and other economic trends.

When parties suboptimize and focus only on accomplishing their own goals, their different time orientations can cause considerable conflict. The marketing department's goal of introducing new products immediately, for example, can conflict with the research department's need for at least six months to design and develop them and production's minimum two-month manufacturing period.

Structural Design

interdependence
The degree to which interactions between parties must be coordinated in order for them to perform adequately.

Differences in goals, resource demands, and time orientations are related to **interdependence**, or the degree to which interactions between parties must be coordinated in order for them to perform adequately. How relationships between parties are structured by the organization determines how they interact to facilitate or hinder each other in accomplishing goals.

INTERDEPENDENCE The relationships between parties can be visualized on a continuum, ranging from complete dependence to complete independence. When one party has the power to determine the performance outcomes and goal achievements of another, the second party is relatively dependent on the first. Two parties are independent only when their respective activities have no impact whatsoever on each other.

Most relationships fall somewhere between complete dependence and independence and are characterized by the need to coordinate certain activities for successful task performance. The more two parties share responsibilities and need to coordinate schedules and to cooperate in decision making, the more interdependent they are. Exhibit 11–4 illustrates three distinct types of interdependent task relationships: pooled, sequential, and reciprocal.[10]

pooled interdependence
Exists when two parties are independent of each other for their own performance outcomes, but each makes a contribution to the overall organization that affects the well-being of both parties.

Pooled interdependence exists when two parties are independent of each other for their own performance outcomes, but each makes a discrete contribution to the overall

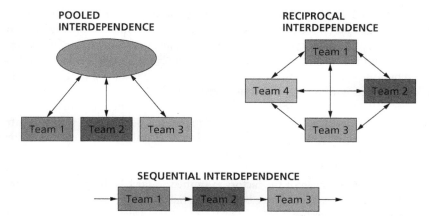

Exhibit 11–4
Types of Task Interdependence

Source: Based on J.D. Thompson, *Organizations in Action* (New York: McGraw-Hill, 1967), pp. 54–56.

organization that affects the well-being of all parties. At Marshall Industries, the electronic components processing company in our video, for example, the finance department and the shipping department handle completely separate functions. They rarely have cause to interact directly with each other, so no direct conflict is likely to occur. Both departments' performances, however, independently contribute to the overall profitability of the company, which affects profit sharing for employees in all departments.

Sequential interdependence occurs when the output of one party provides necessary inputs for another to accomplish its goals. An example of this is when the "pickers" at Marshall Industries pull the specified electronic components out of the warehouse that are needed for the "value-added" department to use in assembling packages for customers. The receiving groups in these situations are dependent on the providing groups for the timing and quality of goods or services needed to do their jobs. This one-way flow of activity can cause considerable anxiety for receiving parties because their goal attainment is dependent on inputs from the supplying party, and they have no real leverage to ensure that their needs are met.

Reciprocal interdependence exists if the outputs of two parties are inputs for each other. In such symbiotic relationships, each party supplies necessary inputs to the other. The Marshall Industries salespeople, for example, relay information to the value-added department so that they can create packages of components that meet customer requirements. If the value-added packages do not satisfy customer demands, salespeople will have a more difficult time securing orders in the future. The potential for conflict between reciprocating groups is great because of the high need for coordination. Success requires effective communication and joint decision making.

Awareness of the nature of interdependence is necessary to manage potential conflict and ensure optimal performance of interacting parties at any level: interpersonal, group, intergroup, and multiorganizational. The complexity of relationships depends on the type of interdependence experienced by two groups. Pooled interdependence is the least complex relationship, while reciprocally interdependent interactions require the most coordination and collaboration.

When groups are dependent on one another for the completion of their tasks, the potential for conflict is high. This is especially true when effective task performance depends on reciprocal interaction. Imagine the potential for disaster if control tower personnel were to experience conflict with flight crew members on aircraft. The potential for conflict also exists among sequentially dependent subgroups. An assembly-line delay in the production of furniture, for example, can cost workers in the finishing department the opportunity to earn their incentive bonus.

sequential interdependence
Occurs when the output of one party provides necessary inputs for another to accomplish its goals.

reciprocal interdependence
Exists if the outputs of two parties are inputs for each other.

LACK OF SUBSTITUTABILITY   The more alternative sources of needed resources and services available to a party, the greater its degree of substitutability. Many organizations require that parties use the services of certain other parties within the organization in order to ensure full utilization of resources. This policy creates a sequential dependency relationship because the supplying party has power over the receiving party. The lack of available alternatives is often perceived as a conflict by the dependent party. This is because differences in goals and time orientations could be dysfunctional for them. Intergroup conflict could occur, for example, when a marketing department wants to introduce a wide variety of new products but is required to work only with the company's own small design research department, which is already stretched to capacity.

POWER DIFFERENTIALS   Each of the factors examined so far has the potential to create differences in influence and dependence between parties, which in turn contribute to differences in power. In December 1995, 8,700 United Auto Workers at Caterpillar, Inc., finally ended a 17-month strike with nothing gained and about $32,000 lost in wages per worker because, as one striker said, "The company's in complete control. We have to accept defeat."[11] It was not until March of 1998 that the UAW ratified a formal contract with Caterpillar. The contract permitted all workers fired during the strike to be hired back.[12]

If party A makes certain decisions that impact on party B's ability to accomplish its goals, party A has power over party B. The more dependent party C is on receiving vital inputs from party D, the more power supplier party D has over receiver party C. The more important party A's function in an interdependent situation, the more all other parties need it, and the more influence party A will command. Since most groups, like most individuals, do not like to be completely dependent on someone else, power differences can cause intergroup conflict, especially when areas critical to goal achievement or satisfaction are involved.

Different Role Expectations[13]

role
A set of related tasks and behaviors that an individual or group is expected to perform.

A **role** is a set of related tasks and behaviors that an individual or group is expected to carry out. A **role set** is all the people who interact with a person or group in a specific role and have expectations about appropriate behavior. A role set for a manager would include his or her supervisor and subordinates plus members of other groups who attempt to influence the manager's behavior. Since all members of a role set depend on the incumbent's performance in some manner, they actively attempt to bring about behavior consistent with their needs. Identifying a role set helps explain who influences a particular person or group to behave in certain ways.

role set
All the people who interact with a person or group in a specific role and have expectations about appropriate behavior.

role ambiguity
Exists when role sets do not make clear their expectations of role holders.

ROLE AMBIGUITY   Role sets need to make clear what they expect from parties who fulfill specified roles. When members of a role set fail to transmit enough information about their expectations, incumbents experience **role ambiguity.** It is difficult to behave acceptably when it is not clear what others expect.

Role ambiguity has several causes. Sometimes those in the role set aren't clear themselves about what should be required, so they don't say anything or the expectations that are communicated are vague. A role holder may, for example, receive feedback to be a "better" group member but fail to glean any specifics as to what "better" actually means. "Better" may apply to standards of productivity, but it could just as easily apply to interpersonal relationships within the group. The resulting uncertainty can have paralyzing effects. Another source of confusion is contradictions between communicated expectations and contrary reactions after a group member complies with the expectations. For example, a group member is told that teamwork is what counts but later is denied a salary increase on the grounds that he or she didn't exhibit "outstanding individual achievements" relative to others.

ROLE CONFLICT   When a party's own expectations and those of other role set members differ, **role conflict** occurs. Japanese managers who join U.S. firms, for example, often face social ostracism from the close-knit community of Japanese expatriates when they adopt behaviors and customs expected in their American organizations that are contrary to Japanese customs.[14] There are four types of role conflict.[15]

INTRASENDER CONFLICT   When prescriptions and proscriptions that come from a single member of the role set are inconsistent or conflicting, intrasender role conflict occurs. If, for example, a team leader is asked by the company's president to add the president's cousin to the staff, but at the same time to follow all equal opportunity guidelines, intrasender conflict may result. The team leader will be legitimately confused about the president's motives, the firm's commitment to equal opportunity, and how he or she should act.

INTERSENDER CONFLICT   When pressures from one member of a party's role set conflict with those from one or more others in the same role set, intersender conflict results. A classic example occurs when a group member is promoted to a formal leadership position and finds it impossible to satisfy all the old peers' expectations as well as the new managerial mandates. A first-line supervisor supervising former peer-group members will surely receive pressures from "old buddies" for favors that conflict with the goals of upper-level management.

INTERROLE CONFLICT   When different roles held by the same party require mutually exclusive behaviors, interrole conflict exists. For example, to meet an impending deadline, a project team's boss may request that everyone work late on a night when a team member has an important social engagement with his or her spouse (a conflict between work and personal roles).

PERSON–ROLE CONFLICT   When your role requires you to do something you don't want to do or feel you shouldn't do, person–role conflict exists. Conflict between a person's needs and values and the demands of a role set is exemplified when an individual is asked by other group members to restrict production. If doing so is contrary to the group member's personal code of ethics, person–role conflict will result.

ROLE OVERLOAD   **Role overload** occurs when role expectations exceed a party's ability to respond effectively. This often occurs when multiple role senders have legitimate expectations for a person's behavior that are all impossible to fulfill within a given time limit. Mid-December, for example, is a time of role overload for many college students, especially those working their way through school. They must prepare for final examinations and typically write term papers for four or five courses simultaneously. It is also the height of the holiday shopping season, so those working in retail stores or associated businesses must cope with their employers' demands to work longer hours. Others may feel the self-imposed pressure to work more hours to meet their own increased financial needs. In addition, relatives and friends expect that students will be available for holiday activities. Unfortunately, these conflicting expectations cause frustration and stress for students that offset the prevailing holiday cheer.

MANAGING ROLE PROBLEMS   Anyone can experience any or all of these role conflicts. Different types of role problems are more likely to occur at different levels of an organization, however. At lower levels of the organization, role conflict is more prevalent. The first-line supervisor, for example, has to deal with conflicting expectations from subordinates, peers, union representatives, and upper management. At higher levels, role ambiguity is more likely to be a problem. A new company president, for instance, must somehow cope with the task of "making the company more profitable" without really knowing what the relevant factors are or how to restructure them. Regardless of their specific source, role difficulties frequently cause dysfunctional conflict.[16]

role conflict
Exists when the behavioral expectations of the role holder and/or those of others in the role set do not agree.

role overload
Occurs when role expectations exceed a party's ability to respond effectively.

The pressures and negative consequences of role conflicts can be reduced in several ways. Both role ambiguity and conflict can be reduced by identifying who legitimate role-set members are, reducing interdependencies, and establishing more explicit role expectations. The role difficulties of a working single parent cannot be reduced appreciably, for example, but the roles of many organization members can be streamlined by clarifying role expectations from above and delegating specific tasks downward. A legal secretary who works for three attorneys, one senior and two junior associates, can ask for clear guidelines as to how to prioritize her tasks. There is a paradox to what we have just recommended, however: Some role clarification can actually create dysfunctional conflicts. Uncertainty is the difference between what is actually known and what needs to be known in order to make correct decisions and perform adequately. Eliminating uncertainty requires establishing task clarity, that is, making sure that the responsibilities of parties are clearly stated and understood. It is fairly easy to eliminate task uncertainty for groups in routine jobs such as manufacturing by establishing policies, standard operating procedures, and rules. Groups responsible for nonroutine tasks, such as developing new products or marketing strategies, however, experience much higher levels of uncertainty and require customized responses.

Some groups are assigned the responsibility of reducing uncertainty for other groups by making decisions or creating rules and procedures that establish operating standards for them. A good example is when an accounting department provides regulations that control how sales representatives must handle expense accounts. Intergroup conflict often results from power differences created when the group assigned to reduce uncertainty imposes rules or procedures perceived to interfere with another group's goal accomplishment.

Degenerative Climate

As discussed in Chapter 4, the organization's culture influences the general nature of employee relationships. In Chapter 9, we demonstrated how some cultures encourage a **degenerative interaction climate** where *"win–lose" attitudes* set the stage for dysfunctional conflict relationships to flourish. Degenerative climates are easy to establish and difficult to overcome. All it would take to destroy a cooperative overall organizational climate, for example, would be an accounting department that flaunts its power by reporting all expense-account errors to higher management and disclosing publicly the names of those "caught" violating the established procedures.

Another way that climate can create dysfunctional conflict is in cases where people with different values and expectations established from experiences in previous organizational cultures must interact together. Many production workers, for example, have little formal education and are concerned with the pragmatic aspects of specific tasks in highly structured environments. Scientists in research and development groups, on the other hand, may have many years of formal education and spend most of their relatively unstructured work hours engaged in esoteric, future-oriented activities. These differences may make it virtually impossible for such groups to understand one another's values, expectations, and priorities. See the Eye on Ethics box to see how the actions of a new CEO at Sunbeam created a degenerative corporate climate, which, in turn, caused his removal from the CEO position.

Another example of culture clash occurred when General Electric acquired Kidder, Peabody & Company. There were big merged cultural differences between GE's organization men, with their generous pension plans, and the entrepreneurial prima donnas of Kidder, who chafed at any management controls and made so much money they didn't need a pension plan. The differences in previous cultures caused the Kidder and GE Capital groups to dislike each other intensely. The Kidder group referred to the GE people as "credit clerks," and the GE Capital group thought the Kidder people were overpaid, arro-

degenerative interaction climate An organizational climate that encourages dysfunctional conflict.

Cutting the Fat or Cutting Too Deep?

Eye on Ethics

In 1996, Sunbeam decided it was time for a massive change, and change is what Sunbeam received. The corporation announced that Al Dunlap would be the new CEO. "Chainsaw," as he is known in the corporate world, got the nickname for his management style: hacking, slicing, and dicing up corporations, removing anything and anyone that might be considered "corporate fat." His strategies had been successful in the past. In just 603 days as CEO of Scott Paper, he had "chainsawed" his way through the company, cutting costs everywhere and selling the company for $6.5 billion more than it had been worth when he had arrived. It is estimated that he personally earned around $100 million (mainly in stock options) for his efforts. Sunbeam needed changes, but would Al "Chainsaw" Dunlap be the answer? Wall Street seemed to think so. Before he even took office, the stock price surged 50 percent in one day on the announcement alone.

Chainsaw began his role as CEO at Sunbeam as he began his prior endeavors: cutting, cutting, and more cutting. In his first meeting with management, firings took place at point blank range. A couple of breaths later, the company's work force was slashed in half (some 6,000 jobs gone) and the number of production and warehouse sites was cut from 43 to 13. At the same time, he demanded that at least 30 new products be rolled out per year, which required product development time to be cut from 2.5 years to 6 months.

Although Wall Street applauded and the stock price continued to rise, what did this all mean in the long term for Sunbeam? His "in your face" management style was difficult for many Sunbeam employees to handle. He was known for pounding his fists on tables and even throwing office furniture during meetings. Job requirements were reduced to: "Make the goddamn number or else!"

This environment was extremely degenerative to some. Deidra DenDanto, a young 26-year-old woman that had recently joined the company from Arthur Andersen did not like the accounting practices used to "make the numbers." Her recommendations to management appeared to land on deaf ears, and she began to feel that her internal audit team was just a token team with no real purpose. She addressed these concerns in a memo to management: "It is with much disappointment that internal audit must again bring to management's attention the lack of prudent, ethical behavior being engaged in by this organization in order to 'make numbers' for the company." Not wanting to undermine her boss, she presented it to him before sending it. Her boss convinced her not to send the memo, saying she was misinterpreting some practices and should wait and see what happened. However, the environment never changed and she left Sunbeam.

As tensions grew and Wall Street began to doubt the real successes of Sunbeam, the company started to unravel. Rich Goudis, the investor relations chief, and several other key executives and managers resigned because the pressure drove them to the breaking point. By June 1998, the board had had enough. The five members met secretly and decided Chainsaw had to go.

Sources: "CHAINSAW: He Anointed Himself America's Best CEO. But AL DUNLAP Drove Sunbeam into the Ground," *Business Week* (October 18, 1999) p. 128; "Chainsaw Al to the Rescue?," *Forbes* (August 26, 1996), p. 42; "Al Dunlap Revs His Chainsaw," *Business Week* (November 25, 1996), p. 37.

gant, and undertalented. Consequently, just about everything that could go wrong did, including destructive competition and loss of profitable business.[17]

Personal Differences

As we discussed in Chapter 9 on interpersonal relations, there are some people you have an instant affinity to while others you immediately dislike. There is a high potential for conflict between people with different values, different preferred ways of behaving, and different views of the world.

The next section describes in depth the consequences of conflict. As you will see, the consequences of conflict can either be functional or dysfunctional, with team or individual performance increasing or decreasing.

Exhibit 11–5   **The Consequences and Outcomes of Conflict**

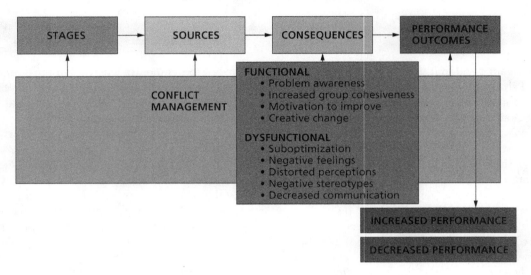

What Are the Consequences and Outcomes of Conflict?

Conflict is inevitable in any organization where individuals and groups must interact to produce complex outputs. Although conflict can often be destructive, at other times it may stimulate creativity, encourage flexibility, and even be satisfying because it provides an interesting environment to work in.[18] As illustrated in Exhibit 11–5, the key is to determine whether the conflict is functional or dysfunctional, and then to manage it appropriately.

Functional Conflict and Performance

If you have grown up in the United States, you are well aware of the value of the kind of competition that stimulates individuals and groups to greater efforts that yield superior results. Spectators pay millions of dollars annually to share the excitement of skilled athletic competitive conflict. In the business world, competition inspires the creation of new products and establishes affordable pricing structures. International competition stimulates nations to advance their technology and develop their resource bases. These examples of **functional conflict** are between competing groups that are not part of the same formal organizational structure. These competing groups do not have to work together to solve common problems or achieve common goals. The reward system provides for one winner and one loser. But in situations where the competing groups or individuals are part of the same organizational structure and must work together to achieve organizational goals, the objective is a win–win, as opposed to a win–lose, outcome.

As we saw in Chapter 10, conflict can improve the quality of decision making in task forces by eliminating groupthink and allowing all points of view to be considered.[19] Janis's analysis of major decisions made by four American presidents demonstrated that constructive conflict resulted in high-quality decisions, whereas decisions where all advisors easily conformed to majority opinion were often disastrous.[20] Research scientists have also been found to be most productive when intellectual conflict exists.[21]

functional conflict
Conflict between groups that stimulates innovations and production.

Conflict is also positively related to productivity in well-established, permanent groups. One study found that high-conflict groups outperformed low-conflict groups by 73 percent.[22] As described in Chapter 10, culturally diverse groups that experience more conflict about different values, perspectives, and approaches generally are more creative and produce higher-quality decisions than do homogeneous groups.[23]

Conflict is inevitable even between individuals or departments that are supposed to cooperate to accomplish organizational goals. To manage conflict so that motivation increases and the quality of work improves, managers need to make sure that interacting parties have cooperative goals and that procedures, attitudes, and skills are in place to productively deal with conflict. A number of benefits can result in a **conflict-positive organization** in which participants perceive conflict as an exciting opportunity for personal and organizational growth:[24]

- Discussing conflict openly can make organizational members more aware and better able to cope with problems.

- Attention is drawn to issues that may interfere with productivity, and organizational practices may be challenged and improved as a result.

- Successfully resolved conflict can strengthen relationships because organizational members understand each other better, release built-up tensions, and learn that relationships are strong enough to work through problems productively.

- Personal development occurs as participants learn about their own conflict styles and increase their competencies in managing interpersonal and interdepartmental problems.

- As a break from standard operating procedures, conflict can be stimulating and fun as participants become involved in solving interesting interdependent problems.

conflict-positive organization
An organization in which participants perceive conflict as an opportunity for personal and organizational growth.

FUNCTIONAL CHANGE *WITHIN* GROUPS   One of the most important places to observe these positive results are within a group experiencing conflict with another group. Four changes typically occur in groups experiencing intergroup conflict: increased cohesion, increased loyalty, increased emphasis on task accomplishment, and acceptance of autocratic leadership.[25]

INCREASED COHESIVENESS   When groups are threatened by other competing groups, members put aside their interpersonal differences and band together against the common enemy, and group membership becomes more attractive. This phenomenon is often seen when nations that traditionally compete economically and politically band together against a common aggressor in wartime. Examples are the Arab nations' cooperation against the common Israeli threat and the European allies' coming together during the world wars.

INCREASED LOYALTY   Group goals take precedence over individual gain or satisfaction as members sacrifice for the common good. Members rigidly adhere to established rules and strictly enforce new ones to eliminate potential conflicts among members that might detract from task accomplishment.

ACCEPTANCE OF AUTOCRATIC LEADERSHIP   In the face of a crisis, group members are more willing to accept the autocratic decisions of a central leader because they are more timely than democratic methods and other members are free to consolidate energy for winning the conflict.

EMPHASIS ON TASK ACCOMPLISHMENT   Personal goals and satisfaction are put aside so that all energy can be concentrated on meeting the challenge put forth by the competing groups. There is a sense of urgency, with no time for goofing off or performing unrelated activities.

FUNCTIONAL CHANGES *BETWEEN* GROUPS   Even dysfunctional intergroup conflict can produce positive consequences if participants learn from the experience and manage conflicts better in the future. Research has demonstrated that conflict can actually promote coordination between departments and contribute to task accomplishment, efficient use of resources, and customer service if the interacting departments have cooperative, but not competitive, goals.[26] Potential positive consequences for relations between groups include:[27]

- Increased problem awareness.
- Decreased tensions after disagreements have been resolved.
- More appropriate readjustments of tasks and resources.
- Establishment of mechanisms for obtaining feedback about intergroup problems.
- Clarification of priorities and tasks.

Dysfunctional Conflict and Performance

dysfunctional conflict
Conflict between groups in the same organization that hinders the achievement of group and organizational goals.

Dysfunctional conflict occurs when the interaction between two or more parties hinders the achievement of individual, group, or organizational goals.[28] Conflict with lose–lose outcomes such as the labor–management dispute at Eastern Airlines in 1989, which contributed to the company's bankruptcy, can be catastrophic.

DYSFUNCTIONAL CHANGES *BETWEEN* GROUPS   Four common intergroup consequences of conflict are hostility, distorted perceptions, negative stereotyping, and decreased communication. All serve to exacerbate negative outcomes in intergroup conflict.[29]

HOSTILITY   Hostility between groups (a "we–they" attitude) often develops, causing each group to see itself as virtuous and the other groups as incompetent or unprincipled enemies. The intense dislike that develops makes reconciliation more difficult.

DISTORTED PERCEPTIONS   Groups in conflict often develop distorted perceptions emphasizing the negative and ignoring the positive traits of competing groups. At the same time, members often develop higher opinions of their own group.

NEGATIVE STEREOTYPES   The resulting negative stereotypes of other groups contribute to decreased and distorted communication, suboptimization, and lack of coordination. Members perceive fewer differences within their own group and greater differences between their group and the "enemy" than really exist, creating even greater conflict between groups and further strengthening cohesiveness within each group.

DECREASED COMMUNICATION   These negative attitudes and stereotypes usually cause communication breakdowns between conflicting groups. Although groups often increase surveillance to detect the plans and weaknesses of competing groups, no real sharing of information takes place, and this void is filled by the distorted perceptions and negative stereotypes already mentioned. Decreased communication is especially dysfunctional where sequential or reciprocal interdependence exists between groups.

DYSFUNCTIONAL CHANGES *WITHIN* GROUPS   Many of the same problems that two individuals experiencing conflict must contend with manifest themselves within groups—lack of trust, decreased cooperation, decreased communication, and so on. Also, in a group, as member satisfaction decreases, so does cohesion and productivity, which can eventually threaten the very survival of a group.[30]

How Can Conflict Be Productively Managed?

The first part of this chapter has shown how conflict can have negative and/or positive consequences for individuals, groups, and organizations. The key variable that determines its outcome is how the conflict is managed. Exhibit 11–6 summarizes conflict style orientations and conflict management methods.

Conflict Management Style Orientations

Parties engaged in a conflict usually have two main concerns: getting what they want for themselves, and maintaining the kind of relationship they want with the other party. When people are primarily concerned for themselves, they are assertive in trying to satisfy their own needs. When they care about the other party and want to maintain a positive relationship, people are cooperative and concerned about making sure the other's needs are satisfied. The different degrees of emphasis that people place on these two basic concerns can be expanded into five specific **conflict management style** orientations: competing, accommodating, avoiding, collaborating, and compromising.[31] These are diagrammed in Exhibit 11–7.[32]

> **conflict management styles**
> The different combinations of assertiveness and cooperation that people emphasize when in a conflict situation.

COMPETING   Competing is assertive and uncooperative behavior, embodied in the parties' pursuit of their own concerns at others' expense. Competing behavior is often used by power-oriented people who will use every technique available to win their point or defend their position.

Competing can be beneficial when quick, decisive action is vital, as in emergencies. It is also useful when unpopular actions, such as discipline or cost cutting, must be implemented. Finally, competing is sometimes necessary to protect against people who take advantage of noncompetitive behavior. If you are too competitive, however, you may find yourself surrounded by yes-men who have learned that it is unwise to disagree with you, which cuts you off from sources of important information.

Exhibit 11–6   **Methods of Managing Conflict**

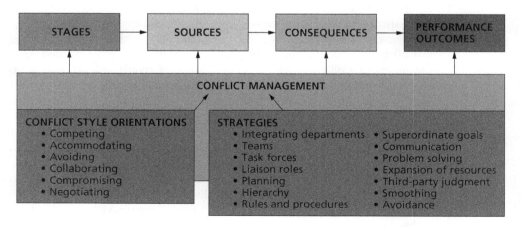

Exhibit 11–7
Interpersonal Conflict Management Styles

Source: Adapted from Thomas I. Ruble and Kenneth W. Thomas, "Support for a Two-Dimensional Model of Conflict Behavior," *Organizational Behavior and Human Performance* 16 (1976), p. 145.

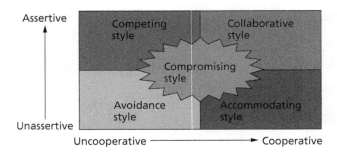

ACCOMMODATING Accommodating is the opposite of competing. It consists of unassertive and cooperative behavior. Accommodating people frequently neglect their own concerns to satisfy the needs of others in order to maintain a positive relationship.

Accommodating is an appropriate strategy when the issue at stake is much more important to the other person. Satisfying another's needs as a goodwill gesture will help maintain a cooperative relationship, building up social credits for use in later conflicts. Accommodating is also appropriate when a manager wishes to develop subordinates by allowing them to experiment and learn from their own mistakes. Too much accommodation, however, can deprive others of your personal contributions and viewpoint.

AVOIDING Avoiding is unassertive and uncooperative behavior. People with this conflict management style pursue neither their own concerns nor those of others. To avoid conflict altogether, a person might diplomatically sidestep an issue, postpone it, or withdraw from the threatening situation.

Avoiding is appropriate when the issue involved is relatively unimportant to you. Also, if you have little power or are in a situation that is very difficult to change, avoiding may be the best choice. Similarly, avoidance may be wise if the potential damage from confronting a conflict outweighs its benefits or you need to let people cool off a little in order to bring tensions back down to a reasonable level. On the other hand, you should not let important decisions be made by default or spend a lot of energy avoiding issues that eventually must be confronted.

COLLABORATING Collaborating is the opposite of avoiding; it consists of both assertive and cooperative behavior. It involves working with the other person to find a solution that fully satisfies both parties. This is a joint problem-solving mode involving communication and creativity on the part of each party to find a mutually beneficial solution.

Collaborating is a necessity when the concerns of both parties are too important to be compromised. Collaborating merges the insights of people with different perspectives. It allows you to test your assumptions and understand others', to gain commitment by incorporating others' concerns, and to work through hard feelings. Not all conflict situations, however, deserve this amount of time and energy. Trivial problems often do not require optimal solutions, and not all personal differences need to be worked through. It also does little good to behave in a collaborative manner if others will not.

COMPROMISING Compromising falls somewhere between assertive and cooperative behaviors. The objective is to find a mutually acceptable middle ground that partially satisfies both parties. This expedient conflict management style splits the difference and makes concessions.

A compromise is appropriate when goals are moderately important but not worth the effort of collaboration or the possible disruption of competition. If a manager is dealing with an opponent of equal power who is strongly committed to a mutually exclusive goal, compromise may be the best hope for leaving both of them in relatively satisfactory positions. Compromise is also wise when a temporary settlement needs to be achieved quickly. It can be a useful safety valve for gracefully getting out of mutually destructive situations. On the other hand, too much compromising might cause you to lose sight of more important principles, values, and long-term objectives. Too much compromise can also create a cynical climate of gamesmanship.

WHAT IS THE MOST APPROPRIATE CONFLICT MANAGEMENT STYLE ORIENTATION

None of these conflict management approaches is better or worse than any other per se. Their effectiveness depends on how appropriate they are for any particular situation. Most people, however, have a "dominant" style that they most often use because it has been successful in the past and they are comfortable with the required behaviors. If their dominant style is not appropriate or does not work, people revert to "backup" styles in attempting to resolve conflicts. This involves stepping out of the comfort zone of your favorite style and adapting to the situation with a more appropriate style. To determine your dominant and backup style hierarchy, complete the Your Turn self-assessment inventory.

If it is important to you to resolve a conflict in a way that enhances your relationship with the other party, collaboration or compromise are far more effective than avoidance or competition. As described in the earlier chapters on communications and interpersonal relations, effective communications and constructive feedback are necessary to support more collaborative efforts and to work through confrontations that may develop.[33] It is also necessary to be flexible and be able to negotiate and bargain with the other party.

CULTURAL AND GENDER DIFFERENCES IN CONFLICT STYLE ORIENTATIONS

Another factor that determines which conflict style orientation is most appropriate is the cultural backgrounds of the participants. If the two parties in a conflict are from similar cultures, a collaborative style orientation is more likely to be attempted. Participants usually share their true concerns more openly, seek each other's opinions, and more fully reveal their bargaining strategy than if the parties were from different cultures.

Participants from different cultures have different conflict style orientations consistent with their cultural value systems.[34] Participants from different cultures perceive the same conflict situation differently and have different goals, values, and priorities. Take, for example, the differences between people from collectivist cultures like Japan, where group goals are valued more than individual goals, and individualistic cultures like the United States, where personal achievement is the predominate value. Consistent with the above model of conflict management style orientations, people from collectivist cultures prefer to collaborate or avoid conflict if both parties cannot be satisfied in order to maintain cohesive relationships. People from individualistic cultures, on the other hand, tend to compete and fall back on compromise if they can't get everything they want. It should be noted that collectivists only collaborate within their own group. When they have a conflict with people outside their group, they can be just as competitive as individualists.[35]

Although other factors may override its influence, gender is another factor that influences conflict style orientations.[36] As discussed in Chapters 8 and 9, women seem to be more concerned than men about maintaining a positive, ongoing relationship between conflicting parties. This leads them to prefer a collaborative style orientation when entering a conflict, and more willingness to compromise, or even accommodate, to preserve the relationship. Men, on the other hand, are usually more competitive and less concerned about the relationship.[37] For more information about how the different gender conflict style orientations mesh in business meetings, read the Dynamics of Diversity box.

Your Turn

What Is Your Conflict Management Style?

Consider conflict situations in which your wishes differed from those of another person or group. Indicate how often you applied each of the following tactics.

		Rarely				Always
1.	I argue to prove my position.	1	2	3	4	(5)
2.	I negotiate for a compromise.	1	2	3	(4)	5
3.	I try to meet others' expectations.	1	2	3	(4)	5
4.	I try to find a mutually acceptable solution.	1	2	3	4	(5)
5.	I firmly pursue my position.	1	2	3	4	(5)
6.	I keep conflicts to myself to avoid hassles.	1	(2)	3	4	5
7.	I hold on to my solution no matter what.	(1)	2	3	4	5
8.	I compromise through give-and-take tactics.	1	2	(3)	4	5
9.	I share information to reach a joint decision.	1	2	3	4	(5)
10.	I keep my differences to myself.	(1)	2	3	4	5
11.	I accommodate the wishes of others.	1	2	3	(4)	5
12.	I try for the best solution for everyone.	1	2	3	(4)	5
13.	I propose middle-ground agreements.	1	2	3	(4)	5
14.	I go along with the suggestions of others.	1	2	(3)	4	5
15.	I avoid hard feelings by not sharing my disagreements.	(1)	2	3	4	5

Scoring: To determine your primary conflict handling style, transfer the number you assigned to each statement on the questionnaire to the scoring key below, and then add the columns. Your conflict handling style is the category with the highest total. See Exhibit 11–7 and the previous discussion for a complete description of these styles.

Competing	Accommodating	Avoiding	Collaborating	Compromising
1. 5	3. 4	6. 2	4. 5	2. 4
5. 5	11. 4	10. 1	9. 5	8. 3
7. 1	14. 3	15. 1	12. 4	13. 4
Total: 11	11	4	14	11

Sources: M. A. Rahim, "A Measure of Styles of Handling Interpersonal Conflict," *Academy of Management Journal* (June 1983), pp. 368–376; and K. W. Thomas and R. H. Kilmann, *Thomas-Kilmann Conflict Mode Instrument* (Sterling Forest, NY: XICOM, Inc., 1977).

Gender Conflicts in the Conference Room

Dynamics of Diversity

Earlier chapters presented some of the differences in behavior between men and women. However, there is no place more visible for these differences to surface than in the corporate conference room. After all, the conference room is the primary place where men and women gather to discuss, argue, express opinions, gain consensus, or simply share ideas. Therefore, it is "ground zero" for potential conflicts.

Research has shown that men and women develop many of their behaviors at an early age. On the playground or ball field, many boys pick up the idea that there are winners and losers, there is a structure usually set via a "team captain," there are rules, and you should brag about your skills. On the other hand, girls have been accustomed through playing jump rope and "swinging on the bars" that everyone gets a turn (rather than defining anyone as a winner or loser) and if you brag about how good you are, you might not be invited back to play.

This differing socialization leads directly into work behaviors as well. Typically, men like to control meetings, and the one with the most information will seize and hang on to the power. Men approach problems with solutions, proving that they are the

"winner," demonstrating their independence, and preserving their status in the hierarchy. In opposition, typically women desire to connect with people more and discuss and explore ideas rather than jump to a quick conclusion. Their use of specific language demonstrates this behavior—"Let's talk about this," or "May I ask a question?" These differences can lead to conflict in the conference room. Recognizing these gender differences is very important because the differing behaviors can directly cause dysfunctional conflict, misunderstandings, and even lead to lawsuits.

Seattle-based Eddie Bauer, where women comprise 69 percent of the work force, addresses potential gender differences directly. The company desires to maintain a teamwork environment that fosters positive and professional relationships. Therefore, Eddie Bauer has strict guidelines for meetings that emphasize personal responsibility and respect for the individual. Every new employee is trained in these guidelines to help diminish gender conflicts, which rarely occur at all today.

Source: Caryn Meyers, "Mars & Venus," *Successful Meetings* (April 1999), pp. 46–50.

Negotiating

Negotiating, or bargaining, is the practical application of the collaborating and compromising approaches to conflict management. **Negotiation** occurs whenever two or more conflicting parties enter into a discussion in an attempt to determine a mutually acceptable exchange rate for their respective goods or services.[38] We know that lawyers and car salesmen spend a lot of time negotiating, but so, too, do managers. They have to negotiate salaries for incoming employees, cut deals with superiors, bargain over budgets, work out differences with associates, and resolve conflicts with subordinates. Negotiating is actually something that just about everyone engages in almost every day, and most of the time without even realizing it. Think back over your past several days. Did you have occasions to do things like clarify the time to meet for dinner, organize a day for a study group to meet, decide on a movie to see with another person?

negotiation
A form of problem solving where two groups with conflicting interests exchange things in order to reach a mutually agreeable resolution.

BARGAINING STRATEGIES   The success of your negotiations depends on the bargaining strategies that you and the other party choose to apply. There are two general approaches to negotiation: *distributive bargaining* and *integrative bargaining*.

DISTRIBUTIVE BARGAINING   You see a used car advertised for sale in the newspaper. It appears to be just what you've been looking for. You go out to see the car. It's great and

distrubutive bargaining
The negotiating process whereby two parties negotiate over the price of an item.

you want it. The owner tells you the asking price. You don't want to pay that much. The two of you then negotiate over the price. The negotiating process you are engaging in is called **distributive bargaining**. Its most identifying feature is that it operates under zero-sum conditions. That is, any gain I make is at your expense, and vice versa. Referring back to the used-car example, every dollar you can get the seller to cut from the car's price is a dollar you save. Conversely, every dollar more he or she can get from you comes at your expense. Thus the essence of distributive bargaining is negotiating over who gets what share of a fixed pie. Appropriate conflict style orientations for distributive bargaining start with compromise, followed by competition and accommodation depending upon the relative importance to you of getting more of what you want versus maintaining a positive relationship with the other party.

Exhibit 11–8 depicts the distributive bargaining strategy, which contains a bargaining zone of mutual acceptance.[39] Let's assume that you and another party represent the two negotiators. Each of you has a *target point* that defines what you would like to achieve. Each of you also has a *resistance point,* which marks the lowest outcome that is acceptable—the point below which you would break off negotiations rather than accept a less-favorable settlement. The area between these resistance points is called the **settlement range**. As long as there is some overlap in the aspiration ranges, there exists a settlement area where each of your aspirations can be met.

settlement range
The area between resistance points where there exists an area where two parties can meet their aspirations.

When engaged in distributive bargaining, your tactics should focus on trying to get your opponent to agree to your specific target point or to get as close to it as possible. Examples of such tactics are persuading your opponent of the impossibility of getting to his or her target point and the advisability of accepting a settlement near yours; arguing that your target is fair, while your opponent's isn't; and attempting to get your opponent to feel emotionally generous toward you and thus accept an outcome close to your target point.

integrative bargaining
The negotiating process whereby the parties assume a win–win solution is possible.

INTEGRATIVE BARGAINING   The collaborative conflict style orientation results in **integrative bargaining**, where the parties assume that it is possible to create a win–win solution. If successful, the result is satisfaction and positive long-term relationships. The following sales–credit negotiation provides an example of integrative bargaining in action.

Assume a sales representative for a women's sportswear manufacturer has just closed a $15,000 order from a small clothing retailer. The sales representative calls in the order

Exhibit 11–8   **Distributive Negotiation Bargaining Zone**

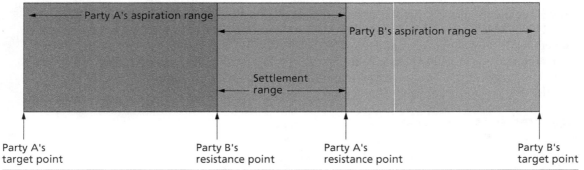

Source: Adapted from Stephen P. Robbins and Phillip L. Hunsaker, *Training in Interpersonal Skills* (Upper Saddle River, NJ: Prentice Hall, 1996), p. 243.

to her firm's credit department. She is told that the firm can't approve credit to this customer because of a past slow-pay record. The next day, the sales representative and the firm's credit supervisor meet to discuss the problem. The sales representative doesn't want to lose the business. Neither does the credit supervisor, but he also doesn't want to get stuck with an uncollectible debt. The two openly review their options. After considerable discussion, they agree on a solution that meets both their needs: The credit supervisor will approve the sale, but the clothing store's owner will provide a bank guarantee that will assure payment if the bill isn't paid within 60 days.

Many experts in negotiation have concluded that integrative bargaining is generally preferable to distributive bargaining. This is because the former builds positive long-term relationships and facilitates working together in the future. It bonds negotiators and allows each to leave the bargaining table feeling that he or she has achieved a victory. Distributive bargaining, on the other hand, leaves one party a loser. It tends to build animosities and deepen divisions between people who have to work together on an ongoing basis.

If this is the case, why isn't there more integrative bargaining in organizations? The answer lies in the conditions necessary for this type of negotiation to succeed. These conditions include openness with information and frankness between parties, sensitivity on the part of each party to the other's needs, the ability to trust one another, and willingness by both parties to maintain flexibility.[40] Unfortunately, many organizational cultures and interpersonal relationships are not characterized by these conditions. In these cases, too much openness and information sharing when trying to collaborate can make you vulnerable because the other party has more information and may use it against you. This can be very costly if the other party does not reciprocate, giving him or her more power to leverage a better deal. So, even if one party begins integrative bargaining by collaborating and attempting to establish trust, if the other party fails to reciprocate, the original collaborating party will usually shift to a distributive win–lose bargaining strategy for self-protection.[41]

Guidelines for Effective Negotiating

During the actual negotiation process, the behaviors of the parties involved are very influential in determining the type and outcome of the negotiation. The most essential behaviors for effective negotiation can be summarized in the following guidelines.[42]

CONSIDER THE OTHER PARTY'S SITUATION   Acquire as much information as you can about your opponent's interests and goals. What are his or her real needs versus wants? What constituencies must he or she appease? What is his or her strategy? This information will help you understand your opponent's behavior, predict his or her responses to your offers, and frame solutions in terms of his or her interests. Additionally, when you can anticipate your opponent's position, you are better equipped to counter his or her arguments with the facts and figures that support your position.

HAVE A PLAN AND CONCRETE STRATEGY   Your chances of obtaining a favorable negotiation outcome increase if you plan and set goals before the action starts.[43] Treat negotiation like a chess match. Expert chess players have a plan and a strategy. They know ahead of time how they will respond to any given situation. How strong is your situation and how important is the issue? Are you willing to split differences to achieve an early solution? If the issue is very important to you, is your position strong enough to let you play hardball and show little or no willingness to compromise? These are questions you should address before you begin bargaining.

BEGIN WITH A POSITIVE OVERTURE Establish rapport and mutual interests before starting the negotiation. Then begin bargaining with a positive overture—perhaps a small concession. Concessions tend to be reciprocated and lead to agreements. A positive climate can be developed by reciprocating your opponent's concessions, also. But keep in mind that although concessions enable parties to move toward the area of agreement, establish good faith, and provide information about the relative importance of various negotiation concerns, the meaning of making concessions does vary from culture to culture. For example, Russians typically view concessions as a sign of weakness while Chinese negotiators generally pull back when the other parties change from initial positions.[44]

ADDRESS PROBLEMS, NOT PERSONALITIES Concentrate on the negotiation issues, not on the personal characteristics of your opponent. When negotiations get tough, avoid the tendency to attack your opponent. If other people feel threatened, they concentrate on defending their self-esteem, as opposed to solving the problem. It's your opponent's ideas or position that you disagree with, not him or her personally. Separate the people from the problem, and don't personalize differences.

MAINTAIN A RATIONAL, GOAL-ORIENTED FRAME OF MIND Use the previous guideline in reverse if your opponent attacks or gets emotional with you. Don't get hooked by emotional outbursts. Let the other person blow off steam without taking it personally while you try to understand the problem or strategy behind the aggression.

PAY LITTLE ATTENTION TO INITIAL OFFERS Treat an initial offer as merely a point of departure. Everyone has to have an initial position. These initial offers tend to be extreme and idealistic. Treat them as such. Focus on the other person's interests and your own goals and principles, while you generate other possibilities.

EMPHASIZE WIN–WIN SOLUTIONS Bargainers often assume that their gain must come at the expense of the other party. As noted with integrative bargaining, that needn't be the case. There are often win–win solutions. But assuming a zero-sum game means missed opportunities for trade-offs that could benefit both sides. So if conditions are supportive, look for an integrative solution. Create additional alternatives, especially low-cost concessions you can make that have high value to the other party. Frame options in terms of your opponent's interests and look for solutions that can allow your opponent, as well as yourself, to declare a victory.

CREATE A CLIMATE OF TRUST Of course, neither side is going to make themselves vulnerable by sharing information in an attempt for a collaborative agreement if they do not trust the other party. Consequently, you want to avoid words and phrases that may irritate the other party or cause mistrust. Skilled negotiators don't make exaggerated statements, make absurd opening offers, or renege on commitments. They listen, ask questions, and try to empathize with the other party, while being patient and avoiding defensiveness if the other party tests them in the beginning.

INSIST ON USING OBJECTIVE CRITERIA Make your negotiated decisions based on principles and results, not emotions or pressure.[45] Agree upon objective criteria that can aid both parties in assessing the reasonableness of the alternatives. Don't succumb to emotional pleas, assertiveness, or stubbornness if the other party's underlying rationale does not meet these criteria.

BE OPEN TO ACCEPTING THIRD-PARTY ASSISTANCE   When stalemates are reached, consider using a neutral third party. The two most common forms of third-party assistance are mediation and arbitration. *Mediators* can help parties come to an agreement, but they don't impose a settlement. Companies like Texaco have used ombuds officers to mediate conflicts in areas such as racial discrimination allegations in attempts to maintain a positive and trusting environment.[46] *Arbitrators* hear both sides of the dispute and then impose a binding solution. They are often utilized in the final stage of union grievance negotiations.

Which approach is best depends upon the specific conflict situation. Mediation provides the greatest potential for employee satisfaction when dealing with minor conflicts because it allows the parties more responsibility in determining the outcome. When the parties are at a definite stalemate, however, arbitration is usually most appropriate because its structured rules and processes provide the best sense of fairness.[47]

ADAPT TO CULTURAL DIFFERENCES   As with conflict style orientations, negotiation practices are heavily influenced by national culture. So if you're negotiating with people from a different cultural background, take into consideration how cultural influences are likely to shape their goals and negotiating tactics. For example, don't expect a Chinese negotiator to quickly jump into bargaining with you if he or she doesn't know you. This is because the Chinese tend to place a strong emphasis on relationships so they prefer not to negotiate with people they don't know well or trust. After bargaining begins, Chinese negotiators' positions on an issue may become rigid if they feel their goals are being compromised. But, nothing should be considered final in negotiations with the Chinese until the terms have been actually realized.[48]

It is also important to take into consideration how cultural influences are likely to shape your own goals and negotiating tactics, and how these come across to negotiators from different cultures. For example, generally Americans play down status distinctions because they value informality and equality. Because of their task orientation, Americans also get frustrated with time delays when another negotiator has to wait for approval from higher-ups in his or her home country before obtaining closure to an agreement. They also get impatient with the small talk and socializing which is necessary in many countries, to allow negotiators to get to know each other, before bargaining begins. Americans also often become angry when their foreign counterparts adhere to different ethical standards (like dishonesty or bribery, or backing out on an agreement).[49]

It is important to adapt to the cultural expectations of negotiators from different countries in order to maintain the rapport and credibility necessary for potential integrative outcomes. It is also important to keep in touch with your own cultural biases and styles so that they are not exploited by savvy negotiators from other countries. Chinese negotiators, for example, have been known to consciously stall the bargaining process and inject long periods of silence when negotiating with Americans to purposely exploit the latter's propensity for impatience.[50]

The advent and growth of the Internet is leading to many new and unforeseen challenges for international negotiators. The lack of face-to-face contact is disturbing for negotiators from countries where building rapport and relationships before establishing agreements is important, but is a welcome relief to task-oriented Americans. On the other hand, there are a host of additional problems that e-commerce has created for international negotiations. This situation is explored in the Technology Transformation box.

Technology Transformation

Negotiating the E-Commerce Cyberspace

Technology enables e-commerce—the electronic distribution of goods and services. Business can essentially be done from anywhere in the world, pushing globalization to its limits. However, the rapid increase in the amount of e-commerce business leads to new international trade questions. Countries are being forced to converge on topics such as:

- What constitutes an electronic signature?
- What taxes apply in which countries?
- Is pornography legal?
- Can drug prescriptions be ordered over the Internet?
- How are Internet crimes enforced?
- How will intellectual property rights be enforced?
- What should be done about Internet sites that give instructions on how to build weapons such as bombs, guns, and hazardous chemicals?

These are just the tip of the iceberg when it comes to international trade negotiations about e-commerce. However, the answers to rules about these questions are as diverse as the countries involved. Different cultures place different values on just about every topic, making international negotiations very difficult. One country might try to prevent Internet pornography, while another country might prevent the sale of American items to "protect the local culture."

Traditionally, U.S. trade negotiators reported to one agency—the government. However, with e-commerce, the roles and responsibilities of negotiators are shifting. Companies are leading the charge into new Internet goods and services; therefore, new pressures for trade issues are coming from companies and public interest groups, not the government. Negotiators now find themselves caught in the middle. Furthermore, the skills necessary to negotiate multilateral agreements on technology are different than skills required for steel negotiations. Negotiators must be well-versed in different high-technology areas while at the same time bridging cultural gaps. And, in the case of e-commerce, these gaps can be significantly wide.

Source: "Horse Trading in Cyberspace: U.S. Trade Policy in the Information Age," *Journal of International Affairs* (Spring 1998), pp. 473–496.

Conflict Management Strategies

It is a truism that parties, be they individuals, groups, organizations, or countries, that cooperate with each other are usually more productive than those that do not.[51] But there are many areas of potential conflict. Conflict erupted at Apple Computer in the early 1980s, for example, even though groups were in independent divisions. The newly created Macintosh division was assigned the task of developing a creative breakthrough product as quickly as possible and was receiving a disproportionate share of the company's publicity and resources. At least this was how the Apple II division, which was bringing in most of the company's profits, saw it. This situation led to jealousy, resentment, and name calling between the two divisions.

Since dysfunctional conflict can have destructive consequences, it is important to detect, reduce, and act to prevent its recurrence. On the other hand, even dysfunctional conflict is useful in that it signals needed changes. Also, functional conflict that serves to improve the quality of decision making and stimulate creative breakthroughs should be judiciously managed to achieve the most beneficial results for the organization.[52] Consequently, the critical issue is not how to eliminate conflict but how to manage it productively to obtain positive change and avoid negative consequences.

Attempts to manage intergroup conflict take the form of win–lose (competing and accommodating), lose–lose (avoiding), win–win (collaborating), or compromise (bargaining) outcomes. Win–lose outcomes are brought about by all-or-nothing competitive

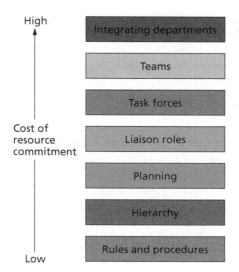

Exhibit 11–9
**Strategies for
Coordinating
Intergroup
Performance**

strategies that encourage one group to win at the expense of the other. Since organizations consist of ongoing relationships, zero-sum strategies create destructive political environments. Avoiding strategies don't solve problems, they leave the problems to fester and erupt later. At best, they allow some temporary productivity until the groups can address the conflict more effectively. Compromise strategies allow both groups to gain a little, but neither to obtain all that its members desire. Since win–win strategies allow both groups to obtain their goals through creative integration of their concerns, the best practice is to try a win–win strategy first. If this does not work, a compromise strategy can provide some benefits to both groups. Organizations with intergroup coordination strategies can often manage conflict productively without it becoming destructive.

Coordination Strategies for Avoiding Intergroup Conflict

Exhibit 11–9 identifies seven of the most frequently used methods for coordinating intergroup performance to avoid dysfunctional conflicts. The seven strategies are listed on a continuum of increasing cost in terms of resource and energy commitment. The strategies are not mutually exclusive. In most organizations, the simpler strategies listed at the low end of the continuum are used in conjunction with the more complex strategies listed at the high end.[53] For example, managers using task forces to coordinate intergroup performance are likely to be using rules and procedures in conjunction with the higher-level task force strategy.

RULES AND PROCEDURES   One of the simplest and least costly ways of avoiding intergroup conflict is to spell out in advance the required activities and behaviors in the form of rules and procedures. Written standards tell interacting parties what to do in specific situations to ensure adequate performance and avoid having to work things through each time. If the typing pool is tied up with the finance department's quarterly report, for example, and if the personnel department knows ahead of time that under such conditions it is free to hire temporary help from an outside agency, no confrontational interaction between personnel and finance will be necessary.

The problem with rules and procedures is that they only help when activities are re-occurring and can be anticipated in advance. When uncertainty and change characterize the task environment, however, rules and procedures alone may not guarantee that no dysfunctional conflict will occur.

HIERARCHY When rules and procedures are not sufficient for coping with intergroup problems, conflict can be passed up the hierarchy to a common superior for resolution. If conflict arises between copywriters and graphic designers in an advertising department, for example, the advertising production manager may intervene as mediator. But if the sales force perceives conflict with the entire advertising operation, the vice president in charge of marketing may have to resolve the issue.

PLANNING In more complex situations, coordinating intergroup activities requires more than rules, procedures, or hierarchies. Planning can be essential to task accomplishments when it is necessary to determine in advance the goals, roles, and responsibilities of all groups that need to cooperate.

A classic example of the need for planning is in building construction. Most interactions can be anticipated and the behaviors of various groups controlled in a programmed fashion. All groups—diggers, concrete pourers, bricklayers, carpenters, plasterers, painters—must know in advance what they are supposed to do and when. Activities are controlled by a master plan that coordinates the efforts of the interacting groups.

LIAISON ROLES When the number of interactions between several groups becomes more frequent or complex, organizations often establish coordinating personnel to handle these ongoing interaction requirements. A **liaison** expedites lateral communication much more effectively than could a cumbersome formal information system alone. Because liaisons are well acquainted with the nature of the work all parties perform, they can cut through the bureaucracy to provide quicker, more effective communication. An example would be an MBA with an undergraduate degree in engineering who acts as a liaison between the engineering and production departments.

TASK FORCES When several groups interact over time in a complex situation, another way of facilitating cooperation is to establish a temporary **task force** made up of one or more individuals from each of the interacting units. This group investigates problems, suggests solutions, and facilitates communication among all groups involved. When the problem or task has been completed, the task group disbands and members return to their respective groups and resume their normal activities. A task force of a new product for a major customer, for example, might consist of individuals from production, research, and marketing, along with the customer's representatives.

TEAMS When several groups must interact in a complex situation over a long period of time, more permanent teams can be formed to manage intergroup activities. Team members maintain their original roles in their functional department in addition to their new ones as coordinating team members. Task teams are established at universities to function as standing committees that periodically make decisions about such things as granting tenure to faculty members or allocating annual budgets. At International Paper Company, the United Paper Workers Union and management agreed to create a team made up of the union president, company president, and three members of each group, whose goal was to enhance cooperation and avoid confrontation. This team has provided benefits such as an agreement that the company would steer clear of attempts to eliminate the union from certain plants in return for the union's willingness to grant cheaper pension formulas.[54]

INTEGRATING DEPARTMENTS When the complexity of information flows between several interacting groups is beyond the capacity of plans, temporary task forces, or permanent teams, an entire integrating department can be established. These are permanent departments with full-time individuals whose only responsibility is the effective coordination of intergroup activities. Since this is a very expensive method, it is usually used

liaison
A party that expedites lateral communication between interacting groups by circumventing formal organizational boundaries.

task force
A temporary group made up of individuals from interacting groups that resolves problems, facilitates cooperation, and promotes integration of efforts.

only if an organization's business requires a lot of ongoing cooperation between groups with conflicting goals or if recurring, nonroutine problems can significantly impact overall organizational success. Integrating departments is the most complex mechanism for managing intergroup coordination. If problems beyond the capabilities of such departments arise, a major organizational redesign is probably called for.

Strategies for Reducing Dysfunctional Conflict

Persistent dysfunctional conflict needs to be confronted.[55] A variety of techniques that can reduce[56,57] dysfunctional conflict are presented in this section. It should be kept in mind, however, that different cultures prefer different approaches to resolving conflicts. Some of these cultural differences are shown in Exhibit 11–10.

SUPERORDINATE GOALS   One of the most effective ways to reduce conflict is to determine an overriding goal that requires the cooperative effort of both conflicting parties. Such a goal must be unattainable by either party alone and of sufficient importance to supersede all their other goals. One fairly common superordinate goal is *survival* of the organization. This usually requires the elimination of suboptimal strategies on the part of conflicting opponents. In the airline industry, for example, several unions have agreed to forgo pay increases and have even accepted temporary pay reductions when the survival of an airline was threatened.

This strategy *eliminates win–lose situations* as participants shift efforts toward cooperation so they all can pull together to maximize organizational effectiveness. Setting up an appraisal system that *rewards total organizational effectiveness* rather than individual or group accomplishments also supports these efforts. Marshall Industries, for example, did this to promote cooperation rather than competition between groups, resulting in the virtual elimination of conflicts and increased profits and stock prices.

A derivative strategy to restore alliances and increase cooperation is focusing on a *common enemy.* At the international level, bickering nations unite against a common adversary in times of war or natural catastrophe. Players on athletic teams that normally compete in a particular league join together to produce an all-star team and challenge another

Exhibit 11–10   **International Conflict Resolution Approaches**

	NORTH AMERICANS	**ARABS**	**RUSSIANS**
Primary negotiating style and process	Factual: Appeals made to logic	Affective: Appeals made to emotions	Axiomatic: Appeals made to ideals
Opponent's arguments countered with . . .	Objective facts	Subjective feelings	Asserted ideals
Making concessions	Small concessions made early to establish a relationship	Concessions made throughout as a part of the bargaining process	Few, if any, small concessions made
Response to opponent's concessions	Usually reciprocate opponent's concessions	Almost always reciprocate opponent's concessions	Opponent's concessions viewed as weakness and almost never reciprocated
Relationship	Short term	Long term	No continuing relationship
Authority	Broad	Broad	Limited
Initial position	Moderate	Extreme	Extreme
Deadline	Very important	Casual	Ignored

Source: Nancy J. Adler and D. M. Hunt, *International Dimensions of Organizational Behavior,* 2nd ed. (Boston: PWS-Kent, 1991), pp. 179–217. Copyright 1991. Reprinted with permission of South-Western College Publishing, a division of Thomson Learning.

400   *Part III: Managing Behavior between People*

World Watch

International Espionage or "Just Doing My Job!"

In the winter of 1997, Richard Bliss faced some cold realities. Before accepting a short overseas assignment, he probably never envisioned that he would end up in a Russian prison and an international espionage battle. Or, did he?

Mr. Bliss, a 29-year-old employee of the San Diego–based telecommunications firm Qualcomm, went to Rostov-on-Don, Russia, to assist Electrosviaz in the implementation of a $5.8 million wireless system. Carrying with him high-tech global positioning (GPS) and computer equipment, he was taken into custody by Russia's Federal Security Service (FSS) and accused of spying. Facing a 20-year prison sentence and the death penalty, the U.S. government moved quickly into negotiations with Russia to free Mr. Bliss. Executive-level pressure from Vice President Al Gore and the State Department permitted Mr. Bliss's release, but not before he spent 11 days in an isolation cell.

Since the end of the cold war, Russia has maintained the image of a pro-Western business environment. Under the leadership of Boris Yeltsin, Russia sought Western help in the building of a telecommunications infrastructure. As Georgi Yurchenko, director of the local Russian mobile phone company Dontelekom put it, "We ask these

Westerners to come here to help us develop our communications, and then we arrest them for doing so. It's absurd."

Why was Mr. Bliss being held? Was he really spying, or were there other reasons for his imprisonment? Could a man that had no military background, no Russian language skills, no college degree, and never set foot outside the United States until this 2-month assignment really be a spy? It is probably more plausible that he was being held for other reasons. Perhaps he or Qualcomm had not paid a local bribe to conduct business there. Or, perhaps Qualcomm had not filed the appropriate documentation. In any case, the Russian government appeared to realize that bigger things were at stake, and that putting U.S. businessmen in prison would probably not attract future Western investment. Mr. Bliss was released in time to return to the United States for the Christmas holidays on the promise he would return to Russia to face the charges. To date, he has not returned nor has Russia pressed the issue.

Sources: "Russia Says an American Accused of Espionage Can Return Home for the Holidays," *The New York Times* (December 24, 1997), sec. A, p. 8; "Russian Spy Case a Puzzler," *The San Diego Union-Tribune* (December 16, 1997) p. C-1; "Figure in 'Spy' Case Settles Lawsuit; He Asked Qualcomm for $1 Million after Being Held in Russia," *The San Diego Union-Tribune* (August 31, 1999), p. C-1.

league. Nothing halts the squabbles of Democrats faster than a reminder that the Republicans are gaining strength. Like all these factions, warring groups will suppress their conflicts and join together to help their organization compete successfully against another. Sometimes, however, they must be reminded that the opposition is out there. See the World Watch box that describes an international negotiation situation where it appears that a superordinate goal might have helped resolve the conflict.

INCREASED COMMUNICATION   In cases where conflicting parties are not competing for scarce resources or trying to achieve inherently opposed goals, devising means to increase communication can do much to correct misunderstandings, reduce negative stereotypes, and develop more positive feelings among the parties. Requiring parties to meet together to solve common problems can reduce stereotypical images, faulty perceptions, and contribute to mutual understanding. NCR Corp. (formerly National Cash Register Company) began tearing down the walls between its engineering and manufacturing groups by putting people from design, purchasing, manufacturing, and field support in adjacent cubicles to allow them to communicate with one another throughout the design and manufacturing process. This process reduced assembly time from 30 minutes to 5 and permitted assembly without special tools. The free flow of information across groups enabled NCR to get better products to market much faster.[58]

Eyewire

There are companies that provide alternative dispute resolution for businesses. These mediators help parties settle disputes without using the courts, thus saving huge amounts of money and relieving the overburdened judicial system.

PROBLEM SOLVING Problem solving is a more structured means of bringing together conflicting parties for a face-to-face confrontation. The purpose of a problem-solving meeting is to identify and solve conflicts through a mutual airing of differences, complaints, and negative feelings. An effort is made to work through differences and bring about a greater understanding of the opposing party's attitudes, perceptions, and position.

The problem-solving approach requires considerable time and commitment, but it can be effective when conflicts stem from misunderstandings or differences in perceptions. Specific problem-solving strategies and techniques can be found in Chapter 12.

EXPANSION OF RESOURCES When the major cause of conflict is limited resources, the likely outcome is a win–lose situation in which one party succeeds at the expense of another. If at all possible, the organization should eliminate this source of conflict by expanding its resource base. Additional investments may pay off handsomely in terms of increased productivity.

THIRD-PARTY JUDGMENT As described in the earlier section on negotiation skills, conflicting parties may appeal to a common boss or an outside judge to serve as a mediator in resolving their dispute. Often this is easier, less time consuming, and less expensive than working through every issue with intergroup problem-solving techniques. At other times, more collaborative approaches have failed, and arbitration is the last resort.

Professional arbitrators are commonly brought in to resolve disputes between unions and management. In November 1993, the highest manager to intervene was President Clinton, who engineered binding federal arbitration to brake a disastrous strike that grounded two-thirds of American Airlines' flights over the busy Thanksgiving season. Another ongoing example is the National Conference of Commissioners on Uniform State Laws statute that lets most fired workers who feel their terminations were unjustified take their cases to a neutral arbitrator who can decide disputes in a few weeks. Compare this to the other common option of expensive and time-consuming lawsuits.[59]

Within organizations, common superiors are often called in to recommend solutions to conflicts between individuals or departments. Managers acting as third-party arbitrators have significant clout because the warring parties agree beforehand to abide by the arbitrator's decision. Depending on the criteria established for successful dispute resolution (e.g., fairness, performance effectiveness), managers may select a variety of intervention strategies ranging from investigation of facts to adversarial (e.g., trial-like) confrontation meetings.[60]

The advantages of arbitration can carry a hidden cost. An arbitrator usually hands down a win–lose decision that is unlikely to receive the loser's full commitment. Like a parental decision on who is "right" when two children fight over a toy, an arbitrated outcome may solve the immediate problem but increase hostility between the conflicting factions. No one is left with an enhanced understanding of what caused the basic conflict or how future clashes can be prevented. When an arbitrator hands down a compromise solution that only partially fulfills the demands of both sides, neither group is totally satisfied with the outcome. Although this may be slightly preferable to a win–lose decision, the sources of conflict are likely to remain.[61]

CHANGING ORGANIZATIONAL STRUCTURE   When the reasons for conflict are scarce resources, status differences, or power imbalances, changes in organizational structure may be the answer.[62] Structural changes include things like rotating group members on a semipermanent basis, creating liaison or coordinator positions, and eliminating special-interest groups that exist within the organization. Marshall Industries, for example, rotates new employees through a variety of assignments in different groups to ease the competitive effects of single-group identification, enhance understanding of interaction in the whole system, and provide a total organization identification. Marshall Industries essentially regrouped people from different departments with different specialties into overlapping, cross-trained teams. This decreased identity with one particular department and increased understanding of the requirements and needs of other groups. In other situations, conflicting parties can be relocated, task responsibilities can be redefined, and hierarchies can be decentralized. Sometimes two conflicting groups can be merged into one. If the conflict clearly centers around personal animosities of two or more strong individuals, the key instigators can be removed.

Restructuring has produced increased quality, productivity, and cooperation for companies such as Corning Glass Works, Ford Motor, and Hewlett-Packard, which are shifting their focus from how individual departments function to how different departments work together. Companies such as Conrail, Dun & Bradstreet Europe, Du Pont, and Royal Bank of Canada have created network groups of department managers with appropriate business skills, personal motivations, resource control, and positions to shape and implement organizational strategy. The free flow of information to all network group members who need it and the emphasis on horizontal collaboration and leadership have clarified joint business goals and helped meet deadlines.[63]

AVOIDANCE   Some groups may be able to ignore dysfunctional situations temporarily by looking the other way or disregarding the threatening actions of others in the hope that the situation will resolve itself. But most conflicts don't fade away; usually, they worsen with time. Although avoidance is ineffective in the long run, certain controlled conditions can be established to lessen the short-term consequences of conflict. Sometimes conflicting parties can be physically separated, or the amount of interaction between them can be limited. Procrastination, disregard for the demands of others, and attempts at peaceful coexistence are all variations of the avoidance process.

Restructuring Promotes Quality at GM's Saturn Plant—A Second Look

General Motors' objective for creating Saturn was to develop a quality compact car that could compete well with Japanese imports from Honda, Toyota, and Nissan. In 1994, the average Saturn dealer in the United States sold almost twice as many cars per month (more than 100) than its Japanese competitors. Part of this success has been due to high quality (lowest defect rates of any U.S. brand) and customer satisfaction (e.g., only Lexus and Infinity were better in the 1994 J.D. Power survey). But the main input for Saturn's success has been attributed to the "gift from God" referred to in the opening vignette: the cooperation between the union and management.

From the start, human factors were always as important as financial ones. Union management collaboration was invaluable as Saturn developed from a vision to a new style of organization where old competitive behaviors were left behind in favor of more cooperative ones. Previously competing groups were united behind the common vision of a team-oriented organization outside the traditional GM hierarchy. To achieve their superordinate goal and compete against the common enemy (i.e., Japanese imports), Saturn developed improved communications, ensured sufficient resources for all, and abolished win–lose climates—for example, they even eliminated reserved parking places and executive dining rooms to establish a sense of common community.[64]

Summary

Organizations are made up of interacting individuals and groups with varying needs, objectives, values, and perspectives that naturally lead to the emergence of conflicts. When conflict occurs, it can either stimulate new positive changes or result in negative consequences. Members of a group in conflict with another group, for example, often experience increased cohesion, loyalty, task concentration, and autocratic leadership. Between themselves, however, the conflicting groups can experience dysfunctional hostility, distorted perceptions, negative stereotypes, and decreased communication.

Conflicts need to be managed appropriately to provide positive outcomes and avoid the negative possibilities. Interpersonal conflict management styles include competing, avoiding, accommodating, collaborating, and compromising. Interacting groups can be coordinated through rules and procedures, hierarchy, planning, liaison roles, task forces, teams, or integrating departments. Strategies for preventing and reducing dysfunctional intergroup conflict include emphasizing the total organization by focusing on superordinate goals or a common enemy, increasing communication, joint problem solving, negotiating, expanding resources, obtaining a mediator, changing organizational structure, smoothing things over, and avoiding potential win–lose conflict situations.

Personal Skills Inventory

It is difficult, if not impossible, to think of a relationship of any type that does not encounter disagreements at one time or another. Unless relationships are able to withstand the stress involved in their inevitable conflicts, and manage them productively, they are not likely to endure.[65] Because of inherent characteristics such as scarce resources, interdependence, different goals, and the need for coordination, conflict is a natural phenomenon in organizational life. Consequently, it's not surprising that some organization researchers have concluded "no skill is more important for organizational effectiveness than the constructive management and resolution of conflict."[66] Following are the essential skills for managing conflict productively in both interpersonal and intergroup situations.

1. **Assess the nature of the conflict.** Conflict is natural to any relationship and it can never be completely eliminated, nor should it be. If not

managed properly, conflict can be dysfunctional and lead to undesirable consequences like hostility, lack of cooperation, violence, destroyed relationships, and even company failure. But, when managed effectively, conflict can stimulate creativity, innovation, change, and build better relationships.

2. **Identify the sources of conflict.** Conflicts can arise for a large variety of reasons, such as incompatible goals, differences in the interpretation of facts, negative feelings, differences of values and philosophies, or disputes over shared resources. The five main sources in organizations to be on the lookout for are goal incompatibility, structural design, role expectations, degenerative climate, and personal differences.

3. **Use the most appropriate style orientation for managing a specific conflict.** Each of us has a preferred style orientation for handling conflicts. Nevertheless it is important to be flexible and vary our conflict management style response according to each specific situation. Know when it is most appropriate to draw upon each of the five conflict style orientations of avoidance, accommodation, forcing, compromise, and collaboration when attempting to resolve dysfunctional conflicts.

4. **Empathize with the other conflict parties.** Your chances of success in managing a conflict will be greatly enhanced if you can view the conflict situation through the eyes of the conflicting parties. Determine who's involved in the conflict, what interests each party represents, and each player's values, personality, feelings, and resources.

5. **Have a plan and concrete strategy.** Your chances of obtaining a favorable outcome increase if you plan and set goals before the action starts.[67] Ask yourself questions such as, how strong your position is, how important the issue is to both yourself and the other party, and if you are willing to negotiate and split differences.

6. **Address problems, not personalities.** Concentrate on the issues, not on the personal characteristics of your opponent. It's your opponent's ideas or position that you disagree with, not him or her personally. Separate the people from the problem, and don't personalize differences.

7. **Maintain a rational, goal-oriented frame of mind.** Don't get hooked by emotional outbursts. Let the other person blow off steam without taking it personally while you try to understand the problem or strategy behind the aggression.

8. **Emphasize win–win solutions.** In conflict situations it initially appears that our gains must come at the expense of the other party. But that needn't be the case, and there are often win–win solutions. But assuming a zero-sum game means missed opportunities for trade-offs that could benefit both sides. So if conditions are supportive, look for an integrative solution.

9. **Create a climate of trust.** Neither side is going to make itself vulnerable by sharing information in an attempt for a collaborative agreement if it does not trust the other party. Consequently, avoid words and phrases that may irritate the other party or cause mistrust. Listen, ask questions, and try to empathize with the other party, while being patient and avoiding defensiveness if the other party is competitive in the beginning.

10. **Adapt to culture differences.** Conflict style orientations and negotiation practices are heavily influenced by national culture. So if you're negotiating with someone from a different cultural background, take into consideration how cultural influences are likely to shape the other person's goals and negotiating tactics.

Questions for Study and Discussion

1. Review the major factors that cause intergroup conflicts. Now, think of a group to which you currently belong. How do these factors influence your behavior and feelings toward other groups with which your group interacts?

2. Describe situations from your personal experience in which conflict was functional and situations where it was dysfunctional.

3. Discuss the mechanisms for resolving conflicts between students and faculty on your campus. Are they effective? Why or why not? What mechanisms do you suggest to better resolve such conflicts?

4. Explain this statement: "An organization can experience too little or too much conflict."

5. Define pooled interdependence, sequential interdependence, and reciprocal interdependence. In which situation is conflict most likely to occur? Why? Which type of interdependence exists between groups with which you are familiar?

6. Suggest the appropriate conflict reduction strategies for a collective bargaining stalemate in which both management and union groups have a record of hostility and noncooperation. Could such

potential conflict be prevented by the design chosen for a new industrial organization? How?

7. What is the predominant intergroup conflict at your school or place of work? What is being done to resolve this conflict? What could be done?

8. What is your dominant conflict management style? How did you develop it? When does it work best for you? When doesn't it work?

Key Concepts

conflict, *p.* 374

interdependence. *p.* 378

pooled interdependence, *p.* 378

sequential interdependence, *p.* 379

reciprocal interdependence, *p.* 379

role, *p.* 380

role set, *p.* 380

role ambiguity, *p.* 380

role conflict, *p.* 381

role overload, *p.* 381

degenerative interaction climate, *p.* 382

functional conflict, *p.* 384

conflict-positive organization, *p.* 385

dysfunctional conflict, *p.* 386

conflict management style, *p.* 387

negotiation, *p.* 391

distributive bargaining, *p.* 392

settlement range, *p.* 392

integrative bargaining, *p.* 392

liaison, *p.* 398

task force, *p.* 399

Personal Skills Exercise
Used Car Negotiation[68]

Directions This is a role play designed to help you develop your compromise approach to conflict resolution through practicing negotiation skills. The class should first break into pairs. Then decide which person will play the role of the seller and which person will play the role of the buyer. You have five minutes to read the situation, your role, and to prepare your targets. Do not read the other person's role. The negotiation should not take longer than 15 minutes. After that, the class will compare outcomes and discuss the various strategies utilized.

Situation You are about to negotiate the purchase/sale of an automobile. The buyer advertised the car in the local newspaper. Before advertising it, the buyer took the car to the local Volkswagon dealer, who has provided the following information.

- 1988 VW Rabbit convertible; standard shift.
- White with red upholstery, tinted glass.
- AM/FM, cassette. 30,450 miles.
- Steel-belted radial tires expected to last to 65,000 miles.
- 35 miles per gallon.

- No rust; dent on passenger door barely noticeable.
- Mechanically perfect except exhaust system, which may or may not last another 10,000 miles (costs $300 to replace).
- "Blue book" retail value, $5,000; wholesale, $4,400.
- Car has spent its entire life in the local area.

Buyer's Role Your car was stolen and wrecked two weeks ago. You do a lot of traveling in your job, so you need a car that is economical and easy to drive. The Rabbit advertised looks like a good deal, and you would like to buy it right away if possible. The insurance company gave you $4,000 for your old car. You have only $700 in savings that you had intended to spend on a trip with an extremely attractive companion—a chance you really don't want to pass up.

Your credit has been stretched for some time, so if you borrow money, it will have to be at an 18 percent interest rate. Furthermore, you need to buy a replacement car quickly, because you have been renting a car for business purposes, and it is costing you a great deal. The Rabbit is the best deal you've seen, and the car is fun to drive. As an alternative, you can immediately buy a used 1989 Ford Escort for $3,800 (the wholesale value), which gets 28 miles per gallon and will depreciate much faster than the Rabbit.

406   *Part III: Managing Behavior between People*

The seller of the Rabbit is a complete stranger to you. Before beginning this negotiation, set the following targets for yourself:

1. The price you would like to pay for the car: _____

2. The price you will initially offer the seller: _____

3. The highest price you will pay for the car: _____

Seller's Role   You have bought a used Mercedes from a dealer. The down payment is $4,700 on the car, with steep monthly payments. You are stretched on credit, so if you can't make the down payment, you will have to borrow at 18 percent. You're going to pick up the Mercedes in two hours, so you want to sell your old car, the Rabbit convertible, before you go.

You advertised the car (which is in particularly good condition) in the newspaper and have had several calls. Your only really good prospect right now is the person with whom you are about to bargain—a stranger. You don't *have* to sell it to this person, but if you don't sell the car right away, you will have to pay high interest charges until you do sell it.

The Mercedes dealer will only give you $4,400 for the Rabbit, since he will have to resell it to a Volkswagen dealer. The local VW dealer is not anxious to buy the car from you since he just received a shipment of new cars; in any case, he probably would not give you more than $4,400 either.

Before beginning this negotiation, set the following targets for yourself:

1. The price you would like to receive for the car: _____

2. The price you will initially request: _____

3. The lowest price you will accept for the car: _____

Team Exercise

Win as Much as You Can[69]

Goals

1. To diagnose and manage a potential conflict situation within an organization competing with another organization.

2. To provide opportunities for practicing negotiation skills.

3. To explore trust building and collaboration in a potential conflict situation.

Time   The total exercise can last from 50 to 75 minutes depending on how much time is allocated for the following activities. Preparation takes from 10 to 15 minutes. The exercise takes 35 minutes for seven rounds. If you drop round 2, six rounds will take about 30 minutes. The debriefing time depends upon how much depth you go into, so it can vary from 10 to 25 minutes.

Directions   Divide the class into two or more organizations. Then divide each organization into four, one- to five-person departments. The four departments in each organization should be far enough apart from each other so that members of each department can communicate without being overheard by other departments.

The exercise consists of seven rounds of decision making in which each department selects either P (profit) or Q (quality) based on its prediction of what the other departments in its organization will do and the payoff schedule. Winnings or losses depend on what is negotiated and what the other departments decide to do.

Process

1. Each player invests $1.00 in his or her company (gives the money to instructor). If any student is uncomfortable risking a dollar, or if it is a very large class, one option is to have each department assign an observer to help the instructor (a) collect and announce decisions; (b) observe internal and intergroup dynamics; (c) handle negotiations; (d) lead department debriefing; and (e) lead class debriefing.

2. Participants study the payoff schedule, the scorecard, and profit distribution matrix. (5 minutes)

3. There is to be no talking between departments, only within departments, except during negotiations.

4. There are opportunities to negotiate with other departments before the rounds with bonuses; that is, after rounds 2, 4, and 6. Departments must direct requests to negotiate to the instructor (or observer), and other departments can agree or refuse. If departments agree to negotiate, one representative from each department meets with one from another department in a private place. Negotiators are not allowed to show their score cards to each other. Departments pick different members to negotiate with each of the other

Chapter 11: Conflict Management and Negotiation   **407**

departments so that all get a chance to negotiate. Actual decisions for the next round can only be made through consensus of department members after they return from negotiations.

5. Departments have 10 minutes to get organized and determine their goals and strategy. Each decision round is three minutes. Each negotiation period is five minutes.

6. *Scoring:* Departments keep their own cumulative scores on their scorecard. The instructor or observer duplicates a scorecard for each organization on the board and keeps total organization scores for each round (i.e., sum of scores for the four departments in each organization).

7. *Payoff Schedule Directions.* At the beginning of each of the seven successive rounds, choose either a P to maximize profit margin or a Q for highest quality. The payoff for each round depends on the pattern of choices made by other departments in your organization. The payoff schedule, scorecard, and profit distribution summary are included on the following Decision Tally Sheet. Scores can be kept on this sheet in the book, but it should be duplicated and passed out to participants separately for easier use.

Profit Distribution   At the end of the seven rounds of play, add up the cumulative organization and department scores. Write these on the board and distribute the total pot as follows:

- The organization with the largest balance gets 40 percent (equally distributed among the four departments).
- The department with the largest balance gets 30 percent (can be either the winning or losing organization).
- The department with the second-largest balance gets 20 percent.
- The department with the third-largest balance gets 10 percent.
- If there is no positive payoff for either organization, there will be no distribution, even if departments have positive balances. The instructor keeps all the money.

Discussion Questions

1. How would you describe the behavior of the departments in your organization?
2. How would you describe your own behavior?
3. Is this real-life behavior?

4. How do you feel about the way you played the game? How do you feel about how the other departments played the game?

5. What did you learn about yourself? About others?

Decision Tally Sheet

Directions   At the beginning of each of the seven successive rounds choose either a P to maximize profit margin, or a Q for highest quality. The "payoff" for each round is dependent upon the pattern of choices made by other departments in your company.

Payoff schedule

4 Ps:	Lose $1.00 each
3 Ps: 1 Q:	Win $1.00 each Lose $3.00
2 Ps: 2 Qs:	Win $2.00 each Lose $2.00 each
1 P: 3 Qs:	Win $3.00 Lose $1.00 each
4 Qs:	Win $1.00 each

Scorecard

Round	Your Choice (Circle)	Group's Pattern of Choices	Your Payoff	Cumulative Balance	
1	P Q	___ Ps ___ Qs			
2	P Q	___ Ps ___ Qs			
3	P Q	___ Ps ___ Qs			Bonus (×3)
4	P Q	___ Ps ___ Qs			
5	P Q	___ Ps ___ Qs			Bonus (×5)
6	P Q	___ Ps ___ Qs			
7	P Q	___ Ps ___ Qs			Bonus (×10)

Profit Distribution

- Company with largest balance gets 40 percent (equally distributed).
- Department with largest balance gets 30 percent.
- Department with second-largest balance gets 20 percent.
- Department with third-largest balance gets 10 percent.
- If no positive payoff for any company, there will be no distribution.

Case

He Said, She Said . . .[70]

Shirley and Abdul both work for a software development company. The manager of the new product division was originally the leader of a project team for which she interviewed and hired Abdul. Shirley, another project team member, also interviewed Abdul but strongly opposed hiring him for the project because she thought he was not competent to do the job.

Seven months after Abdul was hired, the manager left the project to start her own company and recommended that Abdul and Shirley serve as joint project leaders. Shirley agreed reluctantly—with the stipulation that it be made clear she was not working for Abdul. The general manager consented; Shirley and Abdul were to share the project leadership.

Within a month Shirley was angry because Abdul was representing himself to others as the leader of the entire project and giving the impression that Shirley was working for him. Now Shirley and Abdul are meeting with you to see if you can help them resolve the conflict between them.

Shirley says. "Right after the joint leadership arrangement was reached with the general manager, Abdul called a meeting of the project team without even consulting me about the time or content. He just told me when it was being held and said I should be there. At the meeting, Abdul reviewed everyone's duties line by line, including mine, treating me as just another team member working for him. He sends out letters and signs himself as project director, which obviously implies to others that I am working for him."

Abdul says: "Shirley is all hung up with feelings of power and titles. Just because I sign myself as project director doesn't mean that she is working for me. I don't see anything to get excited about. What difference does it make? She is too sensitive about everything. I call a meeting and right away she thinks I'm trying to run everything. Shirley has other things to do—other projects to run—so she doesn't pay too much attention to this one. She mostly lets things slide. But when I take the initiative to set up a meeting, she starts jumping up and down about how I am trying to make her work for me."

Discussion Questions   A variety of strategies can be used to help resolve the conflict between Abdul and Shirley. Explore the concepts on conflict management presented in this chapter. Put yourself in the position of mediator between Abdul and Shirley and consider the following questions:

1. Abdul and Shirley seem to have several conflicts occurring simultaneously. Identify as many of these individual conflicts as possible.

2. Are there any general statements you can make about the overall nature of the conflict between Abdul and Shirley?

3. What are the possible ways to deal with the conflict between Abdul and Shirley (not just the ones that you would recommend, but *all* the options)?

4. Given the choices identified in item three, what is the *best* way for Abdul and Shirley to deal with the conflict between them?

5. Given all the benefits of retrospection, what could or should have been done to avoid this conflict in the first place?

WWW Exercise

Manager's Internet Tools

Web Tips: Conflict Management on the Web   This chapter has focused on conflict and how conflict can be managed. The chapter gives several techniques and ideas on how to manage interpersonal and intergroup conflicts. Since conflict is a serious corporate issue, there are many additional resources for you to use when working with or managing conflict.

World Wide Web Search   Using a search engine, perform a search on the phrase "conflict management." You should come up with several "hits," including companies specializing in conflict management. You should also find pages that list tips for resolving conflict and successful negotiations. What are the similarities and differences between the information you find on the web and the concepts presented in the chapter?

Specific Website   Eddie Bauer was discussed in the Dynamics of Diversity box earlier in this chapter. On the Eddie Bauer site go to the Company Information page and examine the pages under How We Do Business and Corporate Philanthropy (including the Education, Environment, Community Volunteering, and Empowering Women pages). What themes do these pages present, and how would these themes translate into managing internal corporate conflict?

http://www.eddiebauer.com

Video Case
Saturn and AT&T Workers Beat Mexican Plant

Both Saturn and AT&T discovered what researchers have known for some time: Cooperation is better than competition. Both the Saturn auto plant and AT&T workers in the Atlanta Consumer Repair Center have experienced success because of cooperation between management and labor. Most of General Motors' divisions were experiencing record losses and there were several plant closures, with the exception of the Saturn division, located in Tennessee. Saturn employees attend classes on how to break down the traditional barriers between management and workers. The vice president of production and the president of the United Auto Workers (UAW) local have learned to work together to solve problems. Instead of a combative relationship between union and management, the UAW local president reports that he "does 200% more managing than in the old world" of GM. Ninety-eight percent of the union leader's job involves helping to manage the business "with the voice of the worker in the process."

AT&T also benefited from cooperation between union and management. The AT&T Consumer Repair Center was given 18 months to cut costs or be shut down. The problem was that this AT&T plant could not compete with the cheaper labor in Mexico. The plant manager realized that "there was no chance of success if we maintained an adversarial relationship with the union." Working together, managers and production employees sped up production, reduced inventory, and minimized defects, making the plant more cost effective.

Organizations that have the right organizational culture and provide administrative support and training, as do Saturn and AT&T, provide the best regenerative environment in which win–win relationships can thrive. Sat-

urn's management provides a trusting and supportive culture. As Saturn's vice president of production reports, "Potential has always been in the work force, but you have to create the environment for that potential to come out." One member of the Saturn dashboard team says, "Team members are willing to do whatever it takes to get the job accomplished." The dashboard production team even hires its own members, a factor that can lead to increased team cohesiveness. The team also boasts a 99 percent attendance ratio, which would never have been the case at a GM plant with a traditional management style and adversarial culture. Saturn workers are entrusted with making important decisions and are even empowered to stop the production line if there is a problem.

These examples show that for management and union groups to increase productivity, a regenerative, win–win climate must be supported from the top. The cooperation at top levels of management trickles down to production teams who respond with trust in management, commitment, and a strong sense of responsibility. As proof, the AT&T Consumer Repair Center became so efficient despite workers' $16 an hour wages, it took work away from the Mexican plants, where workers made only about $1 an hour!

Discussion Questions

1. What are some positive effects of mutual trust between management and workers as shown by Saturn and AT&T?

2. What strategies for reducing dysfunctional intergroup conflict were applied at AT&T?

3. What conflict management style prevailed at both Saturn and AT&T to produce successful outcomes in both situations? What style do you think was used in the past, with what consequences?

Chapter **Three**

Developing Communication Skills

Learning Objectives

After studying this chapter, you will able to:

1. Define communication.
2. Describe the interpersonal communication process.
3. Describe problems that could arise from conflicting or inappropriate assumptions made in interpersonal communication.
4. Define semantics, and explain its role in interpersonal communication.
5. Define perception.
6. Explain how emotions may affect communication.
7. Explain the concept of feedback in communication.
8. Explain active listening.
9. Describe the grapevine.
10. Define and briefly discuss the e-mail process.
11. Define the Internet and intranets.
12. Discuss two factors that complicate communications in international business activities.

Chapter Preview

Eraser Man seemed like a harmless gimmick to promote lean manufacturing throughout the global operations of Columbia, Maryland-based W. R. Grace & Co. The pink eraser mascot was supposed to convey a simple message: Eradicate or "erase" waste. But when the $2.8 billion specialty chemicals manufacturer introduced Eraser Man during a focus-group session in China, the company's Asian staff was perplexed and perhaps a little miffed. That's because in China, erase actually means invisible.

"They said, 'do you really want this program to be invisible?'" recalls Michael Piergrossi, W. R. Grace's vice president of human resources. "Of course, the answer is no."

Also at issue was the color pink. "Pink is just not an acceptable color in China; it's feminine. No self-respecting man would want to be associated with a program that's marked by the color pink," Piergrossi explained.

Grace's cultural gaffe wasn't unique. In fact, it's becoming all too common for manufacturers as they go global. Fortunately for Grace, the mistake was easily corrected. (Eraser Man is now tan instead of pink and employees in China are asked to "simplify" or "reduce" rather than erase). But other manufacturers worldwide can face much more serious consequences when they don't prepare for the varying customs and workplace practices of their foreign operations. The potential fallout includes trust issues between employees at home and abroad, along with safety and quality standards that don't quite match up with those within domestic operations.

Source: Adapted from Jonathan Katz, "Worlds of Difference," *Industry Week,* December 2007, p. 39.

Analyzing Management Skills

Most people have heard the statement: Actions speak louder than words. What does this statement mean? Do you agree or disagree with the statement?

Applying Management Skills

Go on the Internet and find an example of communications within an organization. Be prepared to describe what you find.

communication
The act of exchanging information.

Communication is the act of exchanging information. It can be used to inform, command, instruct, assess, influence, and persuade other people. Communication skills are important in all aspects of life, including business.

Managers use communication every day. In fact, they spend as much as three-quarters of their time communicating (see Figure 3.1). Good managers develop effective communication skills. They use these skills to absorb information, motivate employees, and deal effectively with customers and co-workers. Good communication can significantly affect a manager's success.

COMMUNICATION AS A MANAGEMENT SKILL

Communicating effectively is an important management skill for several reasons:

- *Managers must give direction to the people who work for them.* Managers who fail to give clear guidance often find that employees perform their jobs poorly because they do not understand what is expected of them.
- *Managers must be able to motivate people.* Good managers use their ability to communicate to get other people excited about their jobs.

FIGURE 3.1
Communicating in the Business World

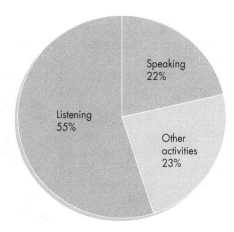

Speaking
22%

Listening
55%

Other
activities
23%

- *Managers must be able to convince customers that they should do business with them.* Effective communication is the key to convincing a customer to purchase a product or service. Without good communication skills, managers will find it difficult to attract customers, even if their companies' products or services meet the customer's needs.
- *Managers must be able to absorb the ideas of others.* Business managers interact with many people, including co-workers, customers, and suppliers. To be effective, they must be able to understand and accept other people's viewpoints.
- *Managers must be able to persuade other people.* Managers often have ideas that others oppose. To persuade other people to accept their ideas, managers must be able to communicate effectively.

INTERPERSONAL COMMUNICATION

Effective communication between individuals, especially between a manager and subordinates, is critical to achieving organizational objectives and, as a result, to managing people effectively. Estimates vary, but it is generally agreed that since managers spend much of their time with their subordinates, effective communication is critical to the wise and effective use of their time.

interpersonal communication
An interactive process between individuals that involves sending and receiving verbal and nonverbal messages.

Interpersonal communication is an interactive process between individuals that involves sending and receiving verbal and nonverbal messages. The basic purpose of interpersonal communication is to transmit information so that the sender of the message is understood and understands the receiver. Figure 3.2 diagrams this dynamic and interactive process. An event or a condition generates information. The desire to share the information, or inform another person about it, creates the need to communicate. The sender then creates a message and communicates it both verbally and nonverbally. The receiver, in turn, perceives and interprets the message and (hopefully) creates a reply message as a response to it. This reply message may generate a response by the sender of the initial message, and the process continues in this fashion.

Often, however, many factors interfere and cause this process to fail. Some causes of interpersonal communication failure are conflicting or inappropriate assumptions, different interpretations of the meanings of words (semantics), differences in perception, emotions either preceding or during communication, poor listening habits, inadequate communication skills, insufficient feedback, and differences in the interpretations of nonverbal communications. Management Illustration 3.1 shows the consequences of communication breakdown.

FIGURE 3.2
Interpersonal Communication Process

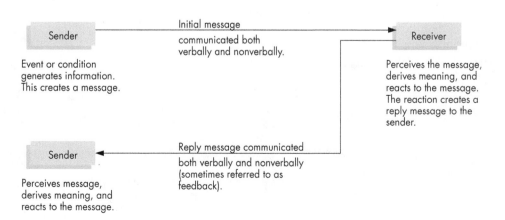

Management Illustration

3.1

COMMUNICATION BREAKDOWN

A communication error was blamed for a near collision at Los Angeles International Airport. The incident occurred when two airliners came within 8,000 feet of each other on a Los Angeles International Airport runway after an air traffic controller miscommunicated with the pilots, the FAA said.

The runway incursion on December 26 involved an American Airlines plane arriving from Mexico and a Mexicana Airlines plane preparing for takeoff. The arriving plane had just landed on the outer runway and was about to cross the inner runway where an Airbus A319 was about to take off for Morelia, Mexico.

The traffic controller told the American Airlines pilot to stop before crossing the inner runway. The pilot apparently misheard the direction and read back that he would go ahead and cross the runway. The controller did not catch the pilot's statement and cleared the Mexicana flight for takeoff before realizing that the American Airlines jetliner was about to roll onto the runway.

Source: Adapted from Jack Gillum, "TIA Tower-Plane Problems Cited," *Tribune Business News,* January 1, 2008, Wire Feed.

Conflicting or Inappropriate Assumptions

Have you ever thought you were being understood when you were really not? This is a common mistake made by couples, teachers, superiors, and parents. If one assumes that communication is flowing as intended, one tends to move on with the dialogue without allowing feedback to indicate whether clarity of expression and communication has been achieved. Good managers always seek verbal or nonverbal feedback, before continuing the communication process. Remember that interpretation of meaning can always be a problem when assumptions are involved. Messages such as "Stop," "Do this right now," and "Please don't" never seem to have the same meanings to children that the adult sender intended. Sound communication usually flows from ensuring that the sender and the receiver see and understand assumptions in the same way.

Semantics

semantics
The science or study of the meanings of words and symbols.

Semantics is the science or study of the meanings of words and symbols. Words themselves have no real meaning. They have meaning only in terms of people's reactions to them. A word may mean very different things to different people, depending on how it is used. In addition, a word may be interpreted differently based on the facial expressions, hand gestures, and voice inflections used.

The problems involved in semantics are of two general types. Some words and phrases invite multiple interpretations. For example, Figure 3.3 shows different interpretations of the word *fix*. Another problem is that groups of people in specific situations often develop their own technical language, which outsiders may or may not understand. For example,

FIGURE 3.3
Interpretations of the Word *Fix*

An Englishman visits America and is completely awed by the many ways we use the word *fix*. For example,

1. His host asks him how he'd like his drink fixed. He meant *mixed*.
2. As he prepares to leave, he discovers he has a flat tire and calls a repairperson, who says he'll fix it immediately. He means *repair*.
3. On the way home, he is given a ticket for speeding. He calls his host, who says, "Don't worry, I'll fix it." He means *nullify*.
4. At the office the next day, he comments on the cost of living in America, and one of his colleagues says, "It's hard to make ends meet on a fixed income." She means *steady* or *unchanging*.
5. He has an argument with a co-worker. The latter says, "I'll fix you." He means *seek revenge*.
6. A cohort remarks that she is in a fix. She means *condition* or *situation*.

Management Illustration

3.2

CROSS-BORDER TRUCKING

It all comes down to the word "establish." In the latest battle over cross-border trucking, the U.S. Department of Transportation, the Teamsters Union, and Congress are at loggerheads over whether to allow trucks from Mexico to cross freely into the United States.

The transportation department has decided to continue its pilot program despite a law against it that Congress passed in December. DOT's argument is that the law prohibits the government from spending any money to "establish" the program—but it began the program in September and simply is continuing it.

The law says: "None of the funds made available under this act may be used to establish a cross-border motor carrier demonstration program to allow Mexico-domiciled motor carriers to operate beyond the commercial zones along the international border between the United States and Mexico."

Semantics aside, the fact that Mexican trucks still are rolling into the United States has rankled the Teamsters Union, which filed a letter in the 9th Circuit Court of Appeals in San Francisco claiming: "The Bush administration broke yet another law in continuing to allow long-haul trucks from Mexico to use U.S. highways." "The lawlessness, recklessness, and sheer arrogance of the Bush administration just blows my mind," Teamsters General President Jim Hoffa said in a statement.

Source: Adapted from Meena Thiruvengadam, *McClatchy-Tribune Business News*, January 10, 2008, Wire Feed.

physicians, government workers, and military employees are often guilty of using acronyms and abbreviations that only they understand.

Words are the most common form of interpersonal communication. Because of the real possibility of misinterpretation, words must be carefully chosen and clearly defined for effective communication. Management Illustration 3.2 illustrates a problem in semantics.

Perception

perception

The mental and sensory processes an individual uses in interpreting information received.

Perception deals with the mental and sensory processes an individual uses in interpreting information she or he receives. Since each individual's perception is unique, people often perceive the same situation in different ways.

Perception begins when the sense organs receive a stimulus. The stimulus is the information received, whether it is conveyed in writing, verbally, nonverbally, or in another way. The sense organs respond to, shape, and organize the information received. When this information reaches the brain, it is further organized and interpreted, resulting in perception. Different people perceive the same information differently because no two people have the same personal experiences, memories, likes, and dislikes. In addition, the phenomenon of selective perception often distorts the intended message: People tend to listen to only part of the message, blocking out the rest for any number of reasons.

Examine Figure 3.4 on page 50 and answer the following questions:

1. In Figure 3.4(a), describe in writing the physical characteristics and age of the woman you see. After writing the physical characteristics and age, turn to page 59 and see how accurate you are.
2. In Figure 3.4(b), which shape is larger?
3. In Figure 3.4(c), which line—AX, CX, CB, or XD—is the longest?

Obviously, if differences exist in how physical objects are perceived, the potential for differences in perception in interpersonal communication is even greater. Differences in perception can occur between younger and older employees, college graduates and noncollege graduates, and supervisors and subordinates. A manager should never assume that his or her actions and words will be perceived exactly as they were intended. In fact, it is probably safer to assume that they will *not* be perceived as they were intended. Feedback is the most effective method for reducing differences in perception.

50 Part One *Foundations*

FIGURE 3.4
Illustrations of Perceptual Distortions

Sources: (a) Edwin G. Boring, "New Ambiguous Figure." *American Journal of Psychology,* July 1930, p. 444. Also see Robert Leeper, "A Study of a Neglected Portion of the Field of Learning—the Development of Sensory Organization," *Journal of Genetic Psychology,* March 1935, p. 62. Originally drawn by cartoonist W. E. Hill and published in *Puck,* November 8, 1915. (b) and (c) Gregory A. Kimble and Normal Gamezy, *General Psychology* (New York: Ronald Press, 1963), pp. 324–25.

a.

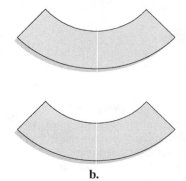
b.

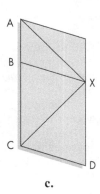
c.

Emotions Either Preceding or During Communication

Just as perception affects our cognitive processes during communication, emotions affect our disposition to send and receive the communication. Anger, joy, fear, sorrow, disgust, or panic (to mention only a few emotions) can all affect the way we send or receive messages. Emotional disposition is like the stage on which the communication piece plays its part: The stage can be perfectly prepared or in total disarray. The setting for the communication piece is obviously important. Communications during periods of high emotion usually have difficulty succeeding. Therefore, managers with good communication skills strive to manage the emotional as well as the physical communication environment.

LEARNING TO COMMUNICATE

Managers communicate in writing and verbally. Before they can master either form of communication, they must be able to identify the audience, develop good listening skills, and understand the importance of feedback and nonverbal communication.

Understanding the Audience

Managers communicate with many different kinds of people. Hotel managers, for example, communicate with hotel guests, food and beverage employees, housekeepers, maintenance people, architects, travel agents, and many other types of people. They also may deal with senior management from the hotel's corporate office. Each of these groups of people represents a different audience.

To communicate effectively, managers need to determine their audience. Specifically, they need to be able to answer the following questions:

1. What does the audience already know?
2. What does it want to know?
3. What is its capacity for absorbing information?
4. What does it hope to gain by listening? Is it hoping to be motivated? Informed? Convinced?
5. Is the audience friendly or hostile?

Hotel managers communicate with the hotel's housekeeping staff about complaints by guests. In doing so, they must inform the staff of the problem and motivate them to work harder to prevent complaints in the future. They would not need to provide background material on the nature of the housekeeper's role. The audience already understands what that role includes.

If a lawsuit is filed against a hotel, managers of the hotel must inform senior management about the situation. In communicating with the hotel's senior management, they would describe what was being done to deal with the situation. They would also provide detailed background information that would allow the corporate officers to fully understand the situation.

Developing Good Listening Skills

One of the most important skills a manager can develop is the ability to listen (see Figure 3.5). Good listening skills enable managers to absorb the information they need, recognize problems, and understand other people's viewpoints.

Managers need to learn to listen actively. **Active listening** involves absorbing what another person is saying and responding to the person's concerns (see Figure 3.6). Learning to listen actively is the key to becoming a good communicator.

Most people do not listen actively. Tests indicate that immediately after listening to a 10-minute oral presentation, the average listener has heard, comprehended, accurately evaluated, and retained about half of what was said. Within 48 hours, the effectiveness level drops to just 25 percent. By the end of a week, listeners recall only about 10 percent or less of what they heard.

Managers need to work at being active listeners. Many people daydream or think about an unrelated topic when someone else is talking. Some people become angry by a speaker's remarks and fail to fully absorb what the person is saying. Others become impatient and interrupt, preferring to talk rather than listen.

Learning to listen actively involves the following steps:

1. *Identify the speaker's purpose.* What is the speaker trying to achieve? Why is the speaker speaking?

2. *Identify the speaker's main ideas.* Which of the points are the key points? Which points need to be addressed by the listener?

3. *Note the speaker's tone as well as his or her body language.* Is the speaker angry? Nervous? Confident?

4. *Respond to the speaker with appropriate comments, questions, and body language.* Use facial expressions and body language to express the emotions you want to express. Establish eye contact, sit up straight, and lean toward the speaker to show interest. Ask a question or make a comment from time to time to show that you are listening attentively.

Feedback

Effective communication is a two-way process. Information must flow back and forth between sender and receiver. The flow from the receiver to the sender is called **feedback**. It informs the sender whether the receiver has received the correct message; it also lets the

In the restaurant industry, managers need to be able to communicate with many different audiences: from the customer to the hostess, from the bartender to the server, from the chef to the food company and on down the line. Managers need to identify their audience in order to communicate with them effectively.

active listening
Absorbing what another person is saying and responding to the person's concerns.

feedback
The flow of information from the receiver to the sender.

FIGURE 3.5
Are You a Good Listener?

- Are you open to what other people say to you, or do you make up your mind about things before you hear other people's views?
- Do you become bored when other people speak?
- Do you interrupt people when they are speaking?
- Do you daydream at meetings?
- Are you hesitant to ask clarifying questions?

FIGURE 3.6
Using Active
Listening

---

1. **Listening**

   Knowing how to listen is an important part of dealing with customers. Using active listening skills helps managers understand why customers are dissatisfied.

2. **Responding**

   The way managers respond to complaints can be just as important as the way they solve the customer's problem. Businesspeople should always be courteous and friendly when dealing with customers. They should demonstrate interest in determining what went wrong and figuring out what they can do to solve the problem.

3. **Making Sure the Customers Are Satisfied**

   Managers need to determine whether they have satisfied the customers' needs. To do so, they must interpret the feedback they receive from the customers.

---

receiver know if he or she has received the correct message. For example, asking a person if she or he understands a message often puts the person on the defensive and can result in limited feedback. Instead of asking if a person understands a message, it is much better to request that the receiver explain what he or she has heard.

In an experiment designed to show the importance of feedback in the communication process, one person was asked to verbally describe to a group of people the layout of the rectangles shown in Figure 3.7. The group members were required to draw the layout based on the verbal description. The experiment was conducted in two ways. First, the group was not allowed to ask questions while the layout was being described, and the person describing the layout was hidden from view so the group could not see the person's facial expressions or other nonverbal communications. Thus, no feedback was present. In the second trial, the group was allowed to ask questions as the layout was being described, and the speaker was openly facing the group. Thus, feedback was present. The results showed the layout was described more quickly to the group when no feedback was allowed. However, feedback greatly improved the accuracy and the group's degree of confidence in the accuracy of their drawings.

Understanding the Importance of Nonverbal Communication

paralanguage
A form of nonverbal communication that includes the pitch, tempo, loudness, and hesitations in the verbal communication.

People have a great capacity to convey meaning through nonverbal means of expression. One form of nonverbal communication, called **paralanguage,** includes the pitch, tempo, loudness, and hesitations in the verbal communication. People also use a variety of gestures in nonverbal communication. In America, for example, one can raise an eyebrow to indicate disapproval, interest, concern, or attention. In Japan, however, that raised eyebrow would be considered an obscene gesture.

FIGURE 3.7
Rectangles in
Communication
Experiment

Source: From Harold J. Leavitt, *Managerial Psychology,* 1972. Reprinted with permission of The University of Chicago Press.

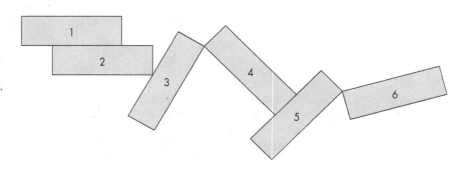

Management Illustration 3.3

WHAT'S THAT ABOUT COMMUNICATIONS?

The newly hired traveling salesman wrote his first sales report to the home office. It stunned the brass in the sales department. Obviously, the new "hope" was a blithering illiterate, for here's what he had written:

> I have seen this outfit which they ain't never bought a dimes worth of nothing from us, and I sole them a couple hundred thousand dollars of guds. I am now going to Chicawgo.

But before the illiterate itinerant could be given the heave-ho by the sales manager, along came another letter.

> I cum hear and sole them haff a millyon.

Fearful if he did, and fearful if he didn't fire the illiterate peddler, the sales manager decided to dump the problem in the lap of the president.

The following morning, the members of the ivory tower were flabbergasted to see the two letters posted on the bulletin board and this letter from the president tacked above:

> We've been spending two much time trying two spel instead of trying to sel. Lets wach those sails. I want ever boddy should read these letters from Gooch who is on the rode doing a grate job for us, and you should go out and do like he done.

Source: unknown.

People also communicate nonverbally by how close they stand to each other. Body posture and eye contact also communicate messages. For example, lack of eye contact can communicate indifference or shyness.

In summary, nonverbal communication is an important supplement to verbal communication and sometimes can even change the meaning of verbal communication. Nonverbal communication is an effective way to communicate emotions. When combined with verbal communication, it gives managers powerful tools for transmitting information to employees.

WRITTEN COMMUNICATION

Managers communicate in writing every day. They send e-mails, write letters, and draft reports. To communicate effectively, managers must be able to write clearly, concisely, and persuasively. Management Illustration 3.3 gives a humorous example of a person who communicated effectively, but whose writing skills were lacking.

Before actually writing a business document, managers need to think about what they want to achieve. They must identify the purpose of the document, the audience, and the main point they want to convey. Using a form like that shown in Figure 3.8 can help them work through this stage of the writing process.

FIGURE 3.8
Identifying the Purpose, Audience, and Main Point of a Document

Purpose

- Why am I writing this document?
- What action do I want the reader to take after reading it?

Audience

- Who will read this document?
- How much does the reader already know about the topic?
- How will the reader use the document?
- Are there any special sensitivities of which I should be aware?

Main Message

- What is the main message I want to convey in this document?
- How will I support that message?

FIGURE 3.9 **Suggestions for Improving Written Communication Skills**

Tips	Examples	
	Weak Writing	**Strong Writing**
Use language that is easy to understand. Avoid using jargon or bureaucratic language.	Interfacing with foreign counterparts is likely to continue in the future at an accelerated pace.	We plan to work closely with foreign partners.
Use short, simple sentences.	After three years of declining sales, corporate management decided to adopt a quality-improvement program, which was instituted in all production units last month, with plans for expansion throughout the company by early April.	Sales fell for three consecutive years. In response, corporate management put a quality-improvement program in place in all production units. By April, it hopes to expand the program throughout the company.
Use restrained, moderate language that is not overly emotional.	Sales were terrible this year!	Sales were weaker than management had expected.
Avoid the passive voice in favor of the active voice.	The decision was made to create two new brochures.	The marketing department decided to create two new brochures.
Use gender-neutral language. Avoid sexist language.	Every man in this company does his best to increase company profits.	Everyone in our company does his or her best to increase company profits.

Principles of Good Writing

Many business managers have difficulty writing well. To improve their writing, managers can apply several basic principles:

1. *Write as simply and clearly as possible.* Avoid writing in a way that is difficult to understand.

2. *Be sure that the content and tone of the document are appropriate for the audience.* Do not waste readers' time communicating information they already know. However, do not assume they are as familiar with the topic as you are. Always use a polite tone, especially when writing to customers.

3. *Proofread the document.* If you are using a computer, use the spell-check function. If you are not using a computer, use a dictionary to check the spelling of words you do not know. Always read the document for incorrect grammar or usage.

Figure 3.9 offers suggestions for improving written communication skills.

ORAL COMMUNICATION

Not all business communication is done in writing. In fact, most business communication is done orally.

Some oral communication is formal and takes place at meetings or interviews. Most oral communication is informal. It takes place in offices and hallways, next to the water fountain, in the cafeteria, and over the telephone.

The Importance of Oral Communication

Communicating well verbally is important for managers. Successful managers use their oral communication skills to give clear instructions, motivate their staffs, and persuade other people.

FIGURE 3.10   **Techniques for Speaking Effectively**

Technique	Example
Enumeration (listing key points)	Our department is looking for people with excellent technical ability, outstanding communication skills, and the desire to contribute to a team.
Generalization followed by examples	We continue to demonstrate our commitment to staff education. Last year we sent almost half of our employees to seminars and training sessions. This year, we expect to include up to 75 percent of all employees in staff education.
Cause and effect	We increased our sales force by 25 percent in the Northeast region in 2001. As a result, sales rose by more than $2 million.
Comparison and contrast	Our newest portable computer is as light as our competitors' and has as much computing power. However, it is $400 less expensive than our competitors' products.

Being able to communicate effectively also is important because it can set the tone within a department or company. In some departments, managers say "good morning" to as many co-workers as they can. They invite their employees to discuss problems with them. In other departments, managers isolate themselves from lower-level employees and make no effort to communicate. These small differences can have a big effect on employee morale.

Developing Oral Communication Skills

All businesspeople need to be able to speak effectively (see Figure 3.10). Whether they are talking to a colleague or presenting a keynote address before thousands of people, they need to follow the same rules of thumb:

1. *Make emotional contact with listeners by addressing them by name where possible.* When talking face-to-face, establish eye contact.
2. *Avoid speaking in a monotone.* Use your voice to emphasize important words within a sentence.
3. *Be enthusiastic and project a positive outlook.* Focus on what is going right, rather than what is going wrong.
4. *Avoid interrupting others.* Even if you know what the other person is going to say, avoid cutting other people off or finishing their sentences for them.
5. *Always be courteous.* Avoid getting angry when other people are talking, even if you disagree with what they are saying.
6. *Avoid empty sounds or words, such as "uh," "um," "like," and "you know."* Sprinkling your speech with empty fillers will make you sound unprofessional.

CHOOSING THE BEST METHOD OF COMMUNICATION

Managers need to master both written and verbal communication skills. They also need to understand when to use each kind of skill. In general, verbal communication is most appropriate for sensitive communications. Written communication is most appropriate for communicating routine information, such as changes in company policies or staff. Choosing the best method of communication will help you relay information in an appropriate and professional manner. Figure 3.11 summarizes the most appropriate method of communication for specific situations.

56   Part One   *Foundations*

FIGURE 3.11
Choosing the Best
Method of
Communication

Method of Communication	Most Appropriate Method of Communication
Oral Communication Alone	• Reprimanding employees • Resolving disputes within the company
Written Communication Alone	• Communicating information requiring future action • Communicating information of a general nature
Oral Communication Followed by Written Communication	• Communicating information requiring immediate action • Communicating directives or orders • Communicating information about an important policy change • Communicating with one's immediate superior about a work-related problem • Praising an employee for outstanding performance

COMMUNICATING WITHIN THE ORGANIZATION

In order to be an effective manager, the importance of the grapevine and e-mail must be understood.

The Grapevine

grapevine
Informal channels of communication within an organization

Many informal paths of communication also exist in organizations. These informal channels are generally referred to as the **grapevine.** During the Civil War, intelligence telegraph lines hung loosely from tree to tree and looked like grapevines. Messages sent over these lines were often garbled; thus, any rumor was said to be from the grapevine. Grapevines develop within organizations when employees share common hobbies, home towns, lunch breaks, family ties, and social relationships. The grapevine always exists within the formal organizational structure. However, it does not follow the organizational hierarchy; it may go from secretary to vice president or from engineer to clerk. The grapevine is not limited to nonmanagement personnel; it also operates among managers and professional personnel.

The grapevine generally has a poor reputation because it is regarded as the primary source of distorted messages and rumors. However, management must recognize that the grapevine is often accurate. Management must also recognize that information in the grapevine travels more rapidly than information in the formal channels of communication. Finally, management must recognize the resilience of the grapevine. No matter how much effort is spent improving the formal channels of communication, grapevines will always exist.

Because the grapevine is inevitable, management should use it to complement formal channels of communication. In utilizing the grapevine, honesty is always the best policy. Rumors and distorted messages will persist, but honest disclaimers by management will stop the spread of inaccurate information.[1]

One of the problems with communicating by "the grapevine" is that information tends to get distorted as it travels to each person and can lead to gossip and rumors.

E-mail

Especially valuable to communication in today's organizations is the use of electronic mail systems, or e-mail, provided by networked and online systems. The e-mail system provides for high-speed exchange of written messages through the use of computerized text processing and computer-oriented communication networks. The primary advantages of this system are that it saves time, eliminates wasted effort (such as unanswered or repeat phone calls), provides written records (if necessary) of communications without the formality of memos, and enables communication among individuals who might not communicate otherwise.

The Internet

Internet
A global collection of independently operating, but interconnected, computers.

The **Internet** is a global collection of independently operating, but interconnected, computers.[2] Frequently referred to as the *information superhighway,* the Internet is actually a network of computer networks. Think of the Internet as analogous to the interstate highway system; just as the interstate system connects to different cities via many different routes, the Internet connects computers around the world via a number of different electronic pathways.

The real value of the Internet to managers is the information that it makes available. Through the Internet, managers can access massive amounts of information by accessing computers around the world that are linked together through the Internet. E-mail uses the Internet.

Intranets

intranet
A private, corporate, computer network that uses Internet products and technologies to provide multimedia applications within organizations.

An **intranet** is a private, corporate, computer network that uses Internet products and technologies to provide multimedia applications within organizations. An intranet connects people to people and people to information and knowledge within the organization; it serves as an "information hub" for the entire organization. Most organizations set up intranets primarily for employees, but they can extend to business partners and even customers with appropriate security clearance. Research has found that the biggest applications for intranets today are internal communications, followed by knowledge sharing and management information systems.[3]

COMMUNICATION IN INTERNATIONAL BUSINESS ACTIVITIES

Communication in international business activities becomes more complicated in both the verbal and nonverbal communication processes. In verbal communication, the obvious problem of dealing with different languages exists. More than 3,000 languages are spoken, and about 100 of these are official languages of nations. English is the leading international language, and its leadership continues to grow. However, as anyone who has studied a modern language knows, verbally communicating with a person in another language complicates the communication process.

The nonverbal communication process is even more complicated. Cultural differences play a significant role in nonverbal communication. For example, in the United States, people tend to place themselves about three feet apart when standing and talking. However, in the Middle East, individuals are likely to stand only a foot or so apart while conversing. This closeness obviously could intimidate an American manager.

There are no simple answers to the problems in communicating in international business activities. However, there are two things the manager should do: (1) learn the culture of the people with whom he or she communicates and (2) write and speak clearly and simply. Most people will have learned English in school and will not understand jargon or slang. As expansion into international business continues, these simple rules will become

Management Illustration   3.4

CULTURAL DIFFERENCES

For North Americans, body language in India can be challenging to understand. Indians say yes and shake their head from side to side, which Westerners misinterpret as no. For no, Indians toss their heads back, similar to the American gesture for yes.

The handshake is used to communicate in many cultures. However, hand contact between men and women is unacceptable in the Islamic world. While carrying on a conversation in Italy, a flailing of the hands and arms would probably go unnoticed. In Japan, however, it may be considered threatening. Furthermore, in the Middle East eating food with the left hand is considered to be unclean.

Source: Various sources.

increasingly important. Management Illustration 3.4 describes several methods of communicating in the international setting.

Summary

1. *Define communication.* Communication is the act of transmitting information.

2. *Describe the interpersonal communication process.* Interpersonal communication occurs between individuals. It is an interactive process that involves a person's effort to attain meaning and respond to it. It involves sending and receiving verbal and nonverbal messages.

3. *Describe problems that could arise from conflicting or inappropriate assumptions made in interpersonal communication.* Misunderstandings can occur when a speaker thinks he or she was being clear or was understood. Questions that go unanswered, points that are misunderstood, and meanings that are misinterpreted are examples of potential problems.

4. *Define semantics, and explain its role in interpersonal communication.* Semantics is the science or study of the meanings of words and symbols. Because of the possibility of misinterpretation, words must be carefully chosen and clearly defined to enable effective communication.

5. *Define perception.* Perception deals with the mental and sensory processes an individual uses in interpreting information received.

6. *Explain how emotions may affect communication.* Emotions affect one's disposition to send and receive communication. Anger, joy, fear, sorrow, disgust, or panic can all affect the way one sends and receives messages. Communications during periods of high emotion are often subject to distortion.

7. *Explain the concept of feedback in communication.* Feedback is the flow of information from the receiver to the sender. For communication to be effective, information must flow back and forth between sender and receiver.

8. *Explain active listening.* Active listening involves absorbing what another person is saying and responding to the person's concerns.

9. *Describe the grapevine.* The grapevine consists of the informal channels of communication that develop within the organization as a result of common hobbies, home towns, lunch breaks, family ties, and social relationships among employees.

10. *Define and briefly discuss the e-mail process.* The electronic mail, or e-mail, system provides for high-speed exchange of written messages through the use of computerized text processing and computer-oriented communication networks.

11. *Define the Internet and intranets.* The Internet is a global collection of independently operating, but interconnected, computers. An intranet is a private, corporate, computer network that uses Internet products and technologies to provide multimedia applications within organizations.

12. *Discuss two factors that complicate communications in international business activities.* Communicating in a foreign language complicates the communication process. Cultural differences exhibited through nonverbal communications are also complicating factors.

Solutions to Perception Questions for Figure 3.4

1. About 60 percent of the people viewing the picture in Figure 3.4(a) for the first time see a young, attractive, and apparently wealthy woman. About 40 percent see an old, ugly, and apparently poor woman. The figure below clarifies the profiles of the two women.

a. Profile of Young
   Woman
b. Profile of Old
   Woman

Source: Robert Leeper, "A Study of a Neglected Portion of the Field of Learning—the Development of Sensory Organization," *Journal of Genetic Psychology,* March 1935, p. 62.

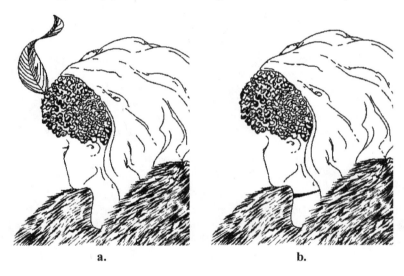

a.   b.

2. Shapes are same size.
3. AK, CK, CB, and XD are same length.

**Review
Questions**

1. What is communication?
2. Define interpersonal communication.
3. Give an illustration of a conflicting assumption.
4. What is semantics?
5. What is perception, and what role does it play in communication?
6. How should one deal with emotions in communication?
7. What is feedback, and how does it affect the communication process?
8. What is active listening?
9. Explain the importance of nonverbal communication in interpersonal communication.
10. Describe the following organizational communication systems:
    a. E-mail communication system
    b. Grapevine
11. Define the Internet and intranets.
12. Describe two factors that complicate communications in international business.

Skill-Building Questions

1. Describe some ways the grapevine can be used effectively in organizations.
2. Explain why many managers frequently raise the following question: "Why didn't you do what I told you to do?"
3. Discuss the following statement: Meanings are in people, not words.
4. "Watch what we do, not what we say." Is this a good practice in organizations? Explain.
5. Poor communication of the organization's objectives is often given as the reason for low organizational performance. Do you think this is usually a valid explanation? Why or why not?

SKILL-BUILDING EXERCISE 3.1 **Writing Skills**

You have been asked by GP&R to write a report describing your company's operations. Here are some facts: There are five project managers, 10 engineers, 14 surveyors, 20 supervisors, 150 heavy equipment operators, 55 laborers, and 33 traffic directors. Equipment includes 24 dump trucks, 25 steam rollers, 38 front-end loaders, 47 backhoes, 39 graders, 35 bulldozers, 27 steam shovels, and six asphalt layers.

You are currently under contract to widen two state highways from two to four lanes; one is 22 miles and the other is 39 miles. You just bid on a job to resurface 113 miles of two-lane state routes. Eighty-eight percent of the equipment is operable at any given time, and your equipment is valued at around $34 million. Payroll is about $300,000 per week. Depending on the size of the job, there are 1–2 project managers, 2–3 engineers, and 4–7 supervisors at the job site.

Write a report explaining your operations to GP&R using the facts given. Feel free to embellish in necessary.

SKILL-BUILDING EXERCISE 3.2 **What's Your Communication Style?**

Carefully read each statement and its four endings. Grade these by assigning a 4 to the ending that most describes you, a 3 to the next ending most like you, a 2 to the next ending most like you, and a 1 to the ending least like you. Once you have assigned a number, you may not use that number again in the set of four endings. For example, you may not assign a grade of 4 to both 1*a* and 1*b*.

1. I am most likely to impress my co-workers as
   a. Down to earth, practical, and to the point.   a ____
   b. Emotional, sensitive to my own and others' feelings.   b ____
   c. Cool, logical, patient.   c ____
   d. Intellectual and somewhat aloof.   d ____

2. When I am assigned a project, I am most concerned that the project will be
   a. Practical, with definite results that will justify my time and energy on it.   a ____
   b. Stimulating, involving lively interaction with others.   b ____
   c. Systematically or logically developed.   c ____
   d. Breaking ground and advancing knowledge.   d ____

3. In reacting to individuals whom I meet socially, I am likely to consider whether
   a. They are assertive and decisive.   a ____
   b. They are caring.   b ____
   c. They seem thorough and exact.   c ____
   d. They seem highly intelligent.   d ____

4. When confronted by others with a different opinion, I find it most useful to
   a. Pinpoint the key differences, and develop compromises so that speedy decisions can be made.   a ____
   b. Put myself in the others' shoes, and try to understand their point of view.   b ____
   c. Keep calm and present my material clearly, simply, and logically.   c ____
   d. Create new proposals.   d ____

5. Under pressure, I suspect I may come through to others as being
   - a. Too concerned with wanting immediate action, and pushing for immediate decisions.   a ____
   - b. Too emotional and occasionally carried away by my feelings.   b ____
   - c. Highly unemotional, impersonal, too analytical and critical.   c ____
   - d. Snobbish, condescending, intellectually superior.   d ____
6. When lecturing to a group, I would like to leave the impression of being
   - a. A practical and resourceful person who can show the audience how to, for example, streamline a procedure.   a ____
   - b. A lively and persuasive individual who is in touch with the audience's emotions and moods.   b ____
   - c. A systematic thinker who can analyze the group's problems.   c ____
   - d. A highly innovative individual.   d ____

Now transcribe the numbers that you wrote beside each ending to the appropriate spaces below. Total the columns for questions 1–3 and for questions 4–6. The initials at the bottom of the columns—S, F, T, and I—stand for the different communication styles: senser, feeler, thinker, and intuitor. The column with the highest total for questions 1–3 is your communication style under relaxed conditions, and the column with the highest total for questions 4–6 is your style under stress conditions. Once you have defined your particular style, check the table at the end of the exercise for the positive and negative traits associated with it. Note that you may have the positive traits without the negative ones or vice versa.

	a	b	c	d			a	b	c	d
1.	____	____	____	____		4.	____	____	____	____
2.	____	____	____	____		5.	____	____	____	____
3.	____	____	____	____		6.	____	____	____	____
Total	**S**	**F**	**T**	**I**		**Total**	**S**	**F**	**T**	**I**

Source: Phyllis Kuhn, "Sharpening Your Communication Skills," *Medical Laboratory Observer*, March 1987. Used with permission from Medical Laboratory Observer. Copyright © 1987 by Nelson Publishing, Inc., www.mlo-online.com.

Some Traits Linked to Each Communication Style

Positive	**Negative**
Intuitor	
Creative	Fantasy-bound
Idealistic	Impractical
Intellectual	Too theoretical
Feeler	
Caring	Wishy-washy
Conscientious	Guilt-ridden
Persuasive	Manipulative
Thinker	
Exact, precise	Nitpicker
Deliberate	Rigid
Weighs all alternatives	Indecisive
Senser	
Decisive	Impulsive
Assertive	Aggressive
Enjoys producing quick results	Lacks trust in others' ability
Technically skillful	Self-involved, status seeking

SKILL-BUILDING EXERCISE 3.3
Effective Listening

Are you an effective listener? Ask a peer that you communicate with regularly and who you know will answer honestly to respond yes or no to these 10 questions. Do not answer the questions yourself. We often view ourselves as great listeners when, in fact, others know that we are not.

1. During the past two weeks, can you recall an incident where you thought I was not listening to you?
2. When you are talking to me, do you feel relaxed at least 90 percent of the time?
3. When you are talking to me, do I maintain eye contact with you most of the time?
4. Do I get defensive when you tell me things with which I disagree?
5. When talking to me, do I often ask questions to clarify what you are saying?
6. In a conversation, do I sometimes overreact to information?
7. Do I ever jump in and finish what you are saying?
8. Do I often change my opinion after talking something over with you?
9. When you are trying to communicate something to me, do I often do too much of the talking?
10. When you are talking to me, do I often play with a pen, pencil, my keys, or something else on my desk?

Use your peer's answers to grade your listening skills. If you received 9 or 10 correct answers, you are an excellent listener; seven or eight correct answers indicates a good listener; five or six correct answers means you possess average listening skills; and less than five correct answers is reflective of a poor listener. The answers most often given for effective listeners are (1) no, (2) yes, (3) yes, (4) no, (5) yes, (6) no, (7) no, (8) yes, (9) no, (10) no.

Source: From Tom D. Lewis and Gerald Graham, "7 Tips for Effective Listening." This excerpt was reprinted with permission from the August 2003 issue of *Internal Auditor,* published by The Institute of Internal Auditors, Inc., www.theiia.org.

SKILL-BUILDING EXERCISE 3.4

We Americans supposedly speak the English language. However, anyone who has ever visited England knows that the English often use different words and phrases than we do. Can you identify what the English words or phrases in Part A below would be if spoken by an American?

A. English phrases

_____ chemist	_____ half five	_____ porter
_____ phone engaged	_____ mind your step	_____ tin
_____ ring-up	_____ a bit dear	_____ lift
_____ round up	_____ way out	_____ queue
_____ wines and spirits	_____ bonnet	_____ lorry .
_____ chipped potatoes	_____ stall	_____ rates
_____ give way	_____ flat	_____ braces
_____ to let	_____ kiosk	_____ gangway
_____ ta!	_____ ironmonger	_____ underground
_____ it's mommy's go	_____ pillar box	

B. American equivalents

a. elevator	*e.* can	*i.* taxes
b. mailbox	*f.* subway	*j.* suspenders
c. orchestra seat	*g.* hood	*k.* aisle
d. line	*h.* newsstand	*l.* apartment

m. janitor	*s.* too expensive	*x.* french fries
n. hardware dealer	*t.* watch your step	*y.* yield
o. truck	*u.* call	*z.* for rent
p. exit	*v.* go halfway around	*aa.* bid adieu
q. drugstore	circle and straight up	*bb.* it's mommy's turn
r. busy	*w.* liquor store	*cc.* five-thirty

SKILL-BUILDING EXERCISE 3.5
Perception Test

Take a maximum of 10 minutes to complete the following test.

1. In 1963, if you went to bed at 8 o'clock PM and set the alarm to get up at 9 o'clock the next morning, how many hours of sleep would you get?
2. If you have only one match and enter a room in which there is a kerosene lamp, an oil stove, and a wood-burning stove, which would you light first?
3. Some months have 30 days; some have 31. How many have 28 days?
4. If a doctor gave you three pills and told you to take one every half-hour, how long would they last?
5. A man builds a house with four sides, and it is rectangular in shape. Each side has a southern exposure. A big bear comes wandering by. What color is the bear?
6. I have in my hand two U.S. coins that total 55 cents in value. One is not a nickel. Please bear that in mind. What are the two coins?
7. Divide 30 by ½ and add 10. What is the answer?
8. Take two apples from three apples, and what do you have?
9. An archaeologist found some gold coins dated 34 B.C. How old are they?
10. How many animals of each species did Moses take aboard the ark with him?

SKILL-BUILDING EXERCISE 3.6
Sexist/Nonsexist Language

As part of communicating that an organization is truly committed to supporting a highly qualified and diverse workforce, managers should take every opportunity to demonstrate the use of nonsexist language.

1. Try to identify a nonsexist word to use in place of each of the following words that may carry a sexist connotation:

Man-hours	Layout man	Foreman
Watchman	Man-made	Draftsman
Girl Friday	Salesman	Policeman
Repairman	Spokesman	Freshman

2. List additional words or terms that you think might carry a sexist connotation.

Case Incident 3.1

Can You Manage This?

Bill Sterling had been reviewing the financial reports for the last quarter. Bill was president of the Advantage Company, makers of high-quality sports apparel. He was unhappy with the cost of materials for a popular line of shorts, shirts, and pants, and thought the company was paying too much for the cotton-knit fabric. He then called Debby Wood, vice president of manufacturing, and told her to cut fabric costs. She in turn called Eddie Perez, the purchasing supervisor, and said, "Mr. Sterling is upset about the cost of the cotton knit you're using and wants it brought down! Do what you need to do. You've let this get out of hand."

Eddie was a bit perplexed. Didn't they know the cost of cotton knit had risen from $1.77 to $2.20 per yard? But he had been instructed to cut costs, so he found a supplier who could sell the fabric for $1.85 per yard and ordered 120 yards, about enough for two weeks of sewing. When the cotton knit arrived, Eddie could tell that the fabric was a lower quality than they had been using, but it could be used.

The next month Heather Schotsky, the assembly supervisor, asked Eddie about the cotton knit they were using. It stretched out during the sewing process, making the garments look baggy. Eddie explained that Mr. Sterling had sent word to cut the fabric cost. "This was the best cotton knit I could find at the lower cost," said Eddie.

When Bill Sterling reviewed the next quarter's financial reports, he found that sales had dropped for their popular Gear Down line of shirts, shorts, and pants. To find out why, he called Keesha Freeman, the marketing director.

"Sears, the Sports Authority, and Belk have all cut back on orders, Bill," Keesha said. "They're saying the garments they've received lately just aren't selling. Customers complain they look baggy, and the fabric feels thinner than before. I talked to Debby, and she said you told her to cut fabric costs. So she told Eddie to do so."

Bill immediately called Debby and reversed his decision to cut fabric costs. He said, "Tell Eddie to start purchasing the better quality fabric." When Debby finally talked to Eddie, he asked her what to do with the lower grade fabric.

"That's your problem, Eddie. You shouldn't have ordered so much," Debby replied. Bill Sterling had really scolded her, and she was still angry about it.

Fortunately, Eddie found another company willing to buy the fabric for $1.45 per yard. He sold it to make room for the new shipment of cotton knit he just ordered.

Three days later Debby called Eddie into her office to find out why he sold the lower grade fabric. "Who told you it was OK to sell that fabric?"

"No one. I thought you said it was my decision. I needed to make room for the new fabric and this was the best price I could get," Eddie answered.

"With decisions like that, this company could end up in the tank. Maybe we could've used that fabric for another line," said Debbie. "Don't let this happen again."

Questions

1. Explain the communications problem?
2. Was the problem handled well?

Case Incident 3.2

Tardy Tom

On September 30, 2007, a large national automobile-leasing firm in Columbus, Ohio, hired Tom Holland as a mechanic. Tom, the only mechanic employed by the firm in Columbus, was to do routine preventive maintenance on the cars. When he first began his job, he was scheduled to punch in on the time clock at 7 AM On October 30, 2007, Tom's supervisor, Russ Brown called him to his office and said, "Tom I've noticed during October that you've been late for work seven times. What can I do to help you get here on time?"

Tom replied, "It would be awfully nice if I could start work at 8 AM instead of 7 AM."

Russ then stated, "Tom I'm very pleased with your overall work performance, so it's OK with me if your workday begins at 8 AM."

During the month of November 2007, Tom was late eight times. Another conversation occurred similar to the one at the end of October. As a result of it, Tom's starting time was changed to 9 AM.

On January 11, 2008, Russ Brown posted the following notice on the bulletin board:

Any employee late for work more than two times in any one particular pay period is subject to termination.

On January 20, 2008, Russ called Tom into his office and gave him a letter that read, "During this pay period, you have been late for work more than two times. If this behavior continues, you are subject to termination." Tom signed the letter to acknowledge that he had received it.

During February 2008, Tom was late eight times and between March 1 and March 11, five times. On March 11, 2008, Russ notified Tom that he had been fired for his tardiness.

On March 12, 2008, Tom came in with his union representative and demanded that he get his job back. Tom alleged that there was another employee in the company who had been late as many times as he had, or more. Tom further charged that Russ was punching the time clock for this employee because Russ was having an affair with her. The union representative stated that three other people in the company had agreed to testify, under oath, to these facts. The union representative then said, "Russ, rules are for everyone. You can't let one person break a rule and penalize someone else for breaking the same rule. Therefore, Tom should have his job back."

Questions

1. Was the manager communicating a message to Tom?
2. Should Tom get his job back?
3. What would you do if you were an arbitrator in this dispute?

References and Additional Readings

1. For additional information, see Mandy Thatcher, "The Grapevine: Communication Tool or Thorn in Your Side?" *Strategic Communication Management,* August 2003, pp. 30–34.

2. For more information on the Internet, see *"The Oxford Dictionary of the Internet"* by Rachel Singer Gordon, *Library Journal,* December 2001, p. 12.

3. For more information see Darlene Fichter, "Making Your Intranet Live Up to Its Potential," *Online,* January/February 2006, pp. 51–53.

Leadership and Lifelong Learning

Leading Change in the Twenty-First Century Organization

Excerpted from

Leading Change

By

John P. Kotter

Harvard Business Press
Boston, Massachusetts

ISBN-13: 978-1-4221-4734-4
4733BC

CHAPTER 12

Leadership and Lifelong Learning

➤ THE KEY TO CREATING AND sustaining the kind of successful twenty-first-century organization described in chapter 11 is leadership—not only at the top of the hierarchy, with a capital *L*, but also in a more modest sense (*l*) throughout the enterprise. This means that over the next few decades we will see both a new form of organization emerge to cope with faster-moving and more competitive environments and a new kind of employee, at least in successful firms.

The twenty-first-century employee will need to know more about both leadership and management than did his or her twentieth-century counterpart. The twenty-first-century manager will need to know much about leadership. With these skills, the type of "learning organization" discussed in chapter 11 can be built and

1

Implications for the Twenty-first Century

maintained. Without these skills, dynamic adaptive enterprises are not possible.

For those raised on traditional notions about leadership, this idea makes no sense. In the most commonly known historical model, leadership is the province of the chosen few. Within that framework, the concept of masses of people helping to provide the leadership needed to drive the eight-stage change process is at best foolhardy. Even if you think you reject the old model, if you have lived on planet earth during the twentieth century this highly elitist notion is likely buried somewhere in your head and may affect your actions in ways invisible to you.

The single biggest error in the traditional model is related to its assumptions about the origins of leadership. Stated simply, the historically dominant concept takes leadership skills as a divine gift of birth, a gift granted to a small number of people. Although I, too, once believed this, I have found that the traditional idea simply does not fit well with what I have observed in nearly thirty years of studying organizations and the people who run them. In particular, the older model is nearly oblivious to the power and the potential of lifelong learning.

A PROTOTYPE OF THE TWENTY-FIRST-CENTURY EXECUTIVE

I first met Manny in 1986. At that time, he was an alert, friendly, and ambitious forty-year-old manager. He had already done well in his career, but nothing about him seemed exceptional. No one in his firm, at least as much as I could tell, called him "a leader." I found him to be a little cautious and somewhat political, like many people raised in twentieth-century bureaucracies. I would have expected him to remain in a senior staff job for a few decades and to make a useful but far from outstanding contribution to his corporation.

The second time I met Manny was in 1995. In only a short conversation, I could sense a depth and sophistication that had been unapparent before. In talking with others at his company, again and again I heard a similar assessment. "Isn't it amazing how much Manny has grown," they told me. "Yes," I said, "it's amazing."

Today Manny is running a business that will generate about $600 million in after-tax profits. That business is rapidly globalizing with all the attendant hazards and opportunities. As I write this, he is leading his group through a major transformation designed to position the organization for a promising future. All from a man who did not look like a leader, much less a great leader, at age forty.

A few people like Manny have always been around. Instead of slowing down and peaking at age thirty-five or forty-five, they keep learning at a rate we normally associate only with children and young adults. These exceptions to the norm help us see that nothing inherent in human DNA prevents growth later in life. The biography that I'm now completing of Japanese industrialist Konosuke Matsushita, one of the twentieth century's most remarkable business leaders, shows this tendency in an extreme form. Descriptions of Matsushita early in life tell us of a hardworking but sickly young man. Nowhere are terms such as *brilliant, dynamic, visionary,* or *charismatic* used to describe him then, much less *leader*. Yet he grew to be an entrepreneur during his twenties, a business leader in his thirties and forties, and a major-league organizational transformer in his fifties. As a result, he helped his firm rebound after the horrors of World War II, absorb new technology, expand globally, and renew itself again and again so as to succeed beyond anyone's dreams. He then took on additional successful careers as a writer in his sixties, a philanthropist in his seventies, and an educator in his eighties.

In the twenty-first century, I think we will see more of these remarkable leaders who develop their skills through lifelong learning, because that pattern of growth is increasingly being rewarded by a rapidly changing environment. In a static world, we can learn virtually everything we need to know in life by the time we are fifteen, and few of us are called on to provide leadership. In an ever changing world, we can never learn it all, even

3

Implications for the Twenty-first Century

4

if we keep growing into our nineties, and the development of leadership skills becomes relevant to an ever-increasing number of people.

As the rate of change increases, the willingness and ability to keep developing become central to career success for individuals and to economic success for organizations. People like Manny or Matsushita often do not begin the race with the most money or intelligence, but they win nevertheless because they outgrow their rivals. They develop the capacity to handle a complex and changing business environment. They grow to become unusually competent in advancing organizational transformation. They learn to be leaders.

THE VALUE OF COMPETITIVE CAPACITY

The importance of lifelong learning in an increasingly changing business environment and its relationship to leadership was demonstrated rather dramatically in a twenty-year study of 115 students from the Harvard Business School class of 1974. In attempting to explain why most were doing well in their careers despite the challenging economic climate that took shape at about the time they graduated, I found that two elements stood out: competitive drive and lifelong learning. These factors seemed to give people an edge by creating an unusually strong competitive capacity (see exhibit 1 on the facing page). Competitive drive helped create lifelong learning, which kept increasing skill and knowledge levels, especially leadership skills, which in turn produced a prodigious ability to deal with an increasingly difficult and fast-moving global economy. Like Manny, people with high standards and a strong willingness to learn became measurably stronger and more able leaders at age fifty than they had been at age forty.

Marcel DePaul was typical of this group. He grew up in a middle-class family and attended a good but not outstanding university in Michigan. He was admitted to the MBA program based less on test scores than on an impressive track record both in

Leadership and Lifelong Learning

EXHIBIT 1

5

The Relationship of Lifelong Learning, Leadership Skills, and the Capacity to Succeed in the Future

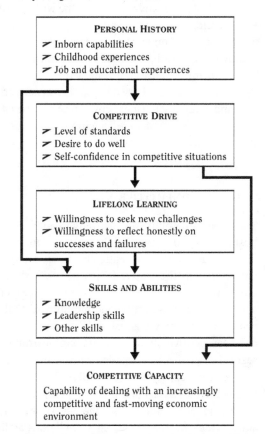

and out of high school. By age thirty-five, he was doing well in his career, but no one was predicting great accomplishments. As a staff officer in a large, European-based manufacturing firm, he had a good but not great reputation. When I interviewed him in

Implications for the Twenty-first Century

1982, the word *leader* never occurred to me. A dozen years later, the story had changed greatly.

By 1994, Marcel was the head of his own company, had hundreds of employees, and was very wealthy. He had invented a product and a market and had built an organization to capitalize on both. Within his world, he was known as a "visionary." One person with whom I talked went on and on about Marcel's "charisma." All this from a guy that didn't much impress me in 1982.

In attempting to explain Marcel's success, I think we are all inclined to look for lucky breaks, and good fortune certainly can be found in his case. But one can also see a difficult business environment that served up plenty of bad luck and hardship. What is striking about Marcel's story is how the bad times didn't wear him down but instead served as a source of learning and growth.

When hit with an unexpected downturn, he would often become angry or morose, but he would never give up or let defensiveness paralyze him. He reflected on good times and bad, and tried to learn from both. Confronting his mistakes, he minimized the arrogant attitudes that often accompany success. With a relatively humble view of himself, he watched more closely and listened more carefully than did most others. As he learned, he relentlessly tested new ideas, even if that meant pushing himself out of his zone of comfort or taking some personal risks.

Listening with an open mind, trying new things, reflecting honestly on successes and failures—none of this requires a high IQ, an MBA degree, or a privileged background. Yet remarkably few people behave in these ways today, especially after age thirty-five and especially when they are already doing well in their careers. But by using these relatively simple techniques, Marcel, Manny, Matsushita, and people like them keep growing while others level off or decline. As a result, they become more and more comfortable with change, they actualize whatever leadership potential they possess, and they help their firms adapt to a rapidly shifting global economy.

Leadership and Lifelong Learning

THE POWER OF COMPOUNDED GROWTH

If you study the Marcels, Mannys, and Matsushitas of the world, you find that the secret to their capacity to develop leadership and other skills is closely related to the power of compounded growth.

Consider this simple example. Between age thirty and fifty, Fran "grows" at the rate of 6 percent—that is, every year she expands her career-relevant skills and knowledge by 6 percent. Her twin sister, Janice, has exactly the same intelligence, skills, and information at age thirty, but during the next twenty years she grows at only 1 percent per year. Perhaps Janice becomes smug and complacent after early successes. Or maybe Fran has some experience that sets a fire underneath her. The question here is, how much difference will this relatively small learning differential make by age fifty?

Given the facts about Fran and Janice, it's clear that the former will be able to do more at age fifty than the latter. But most of us underestimate how much more capable Fran will become. The confusion surrounds the effect of compounding. Just as we often don't realize the difference over twenty years between a bank account earning 7 percent versus 4 percent, we regularly underestimate the effects of learning differentials.

For Fran and Janice, the difference between a 6 percent and a 1 percent growth rate over twenty years is huge. If they each have 100 units of career-related capability at age thirty, twenty years later, Janice will have 122 units, while Fran will have 321. Peers at age thirty, the two will be in totally different leagues at age fifty.

If the world of the twenty-first century were going to be stable, regulated, and prosperous, sort of like the 1950s and 1960s in the United States, then differential growth rates would be of only modest relevance. In that world, while Fran would likely be considered more accomplished than her sister, both would do just fine. Stability, regulation, and prosperity would reduce competition along with the need for growth, leadership skills, and transformation. But that's not what the future holds.

Implications for the Twenty-first Century

8

Just as organizations are going to be forced to learn, change, and constantly reinvent themselves in the twenty-first century, so will increasing numbers of individuals. Lifelong learning and the leadership skills that can be developed through it were relevant to only a small percentage of the population until recently. That percentage will undoubtedly grow over the next few decades.

HABITS OF THE LIFELONG LEARNER

So how do the Frans and Mannys do it? Not with rocket science. The habits they develop are relatively simple (as summarized in exhibit 2 on the facing page).

Lifelong learners take risks. Much more than others, these men and women push themselves out of their comfort zones and try new ideas. While most of us become set in our ways, they keep experimenting.

Risk taking inevitably produces both bigger successes and bigger failures. Much more than most of us, lifelong learners humbly and honestly reflect on their experiences to educate themselves. They don't sweep failure under the rug or examine it from a defensive position that undermines their ability to make rational conclusions.

Lifelong learners actively solicit opinions and ideas from others. They don't make the assumption that they know it all or that most other people have little to contribute. Just the opposite, they believe that with the right approach, they can learn from anyone under almost any circumstance.

Much more than the average person, lifelong learners also listen carefully, and they do so with an open mind. They don't assume that listening will produce big ideas or important information very often. Quite the contrary. But they know that careful listening will help give them accurate feedback on the effect of their actions. And without honest feedback, learning becomes almost impossible.

Leadership and Lifelong Learning

EXHIBIT 2   9
Mental Habits That Support Lifelong Learning

➤ *Risk taking:* Willingness to push oneself out of comfort zones

➤ *Humble self-reflection:* Honest assessment of successes and failures, especially the latter

➤ *Solicitation of opinions:* Aggressive collection of information and ideas from others

➤ *Careful listening:* Propensity to listen to others

➤ *Openness to new ideas:* Willingness to view life with an open mind

---

Q: But these habits are so simple. Why don't more of us develop them?

A: Because in the short term, it's more painful.

Risk taking brings failure as well as success. Honest reflection, listening, solicitation of opinions, and openness bring bad news and negative feedback as well as interesting ideas. In the short term, life is generally more pleasant without failure and negative feedback.

Lifelong learners overcome a natural human tendency to shy away from or abandon habits that produce short-term pain. By surviving difficult experiences, they build up a certain immunity to hardship. With clarity of thought, they come to realize the importance of both these habits and lifelong learning. But most of all, their goals and aspirations facilitate the development of humility, openness, willingness to take risks, and the capacity to listen.

The very best lifelong learners and leaders I've known seem to have high standards, ambitious goals, and a real sense of mission in their lives. Such goals and aspirations spur them on, put their accomplishments in a humbling perspective, and help them

10

endure the short-term pain associated with growth. Sometimes this sense of mission is developed early in life, sometimes later in adulthood, often a combination of the two. Whatever the case, their aspirations help keep them from sliding into a comfortable, safe routine characterized by little sensible risk taking, a relatively closed mind, a minimum of reaching out, and little listening.

Just as a challenging vision can help an organization to adapt to shifting conditions, nothing seems to support the habits that promote personal growth more than ambitious, humanistic goals.

TWENTY-FIRST-CENTURY CAREERS

The more volatile economic environment, along with the need for more leadership and lifelong learning, is also producing careers that look quite different from those typical of the twentieth century.

Most of the successful white-collar workers in the past hundred years found reputable companies to work for early in their lives and then moved up narrow functional hierarchies while learning the art of management. Most successful blue-collar workers found companies with good unions, learned how to do a certain job, and then stayed in that position for decades. In the twenty-first century, neither of these career paths will provide many people with a good life because neither encourages sufficient lifelong learning, especially for leadership skills.

The problem for the blue-collar worker is more obvious. Union rules have often discouraged personal growth. Narrow job classifications, for example, weren't designed to reduce learning, but that has been one of the consequences. In a stable environment, we could live with those kinds of rules. In a rapidly changing globalized marketplace, we probably cannot.

The old white-collar career path did help people learn, but only in narrow functional grooves. One had to absorb more and more knowledge about accounting (or engineering or marketing), but little else. To progress beyond a certain level, one had to learn about management, but not much about leadership.

Successful twenty-first-century careers will be more dynamic. Already we are seeing less linear movement up a single hierarchy. Already we are seeing fewer people doing one job the same way for long periods of time. The greater uncertainty and volatility tend to be uncomfortable for people at first. But most of us seem to get used to it. And the benefits can certainly be significant.

People who learn to master more volatile career paths also usually become more comfortable with change generally and thus better able to play more useful roles in organizational transformations. They more easily develop whatever leadership potential they have. With more leadership, they are in a better position to help their employers advance the transformation process so as to significantly improve meaningful results while minimizing the painful effects of change.

That Necessary Leap into the Future

For a lot of reasons, many people are still embracing the twentieth-century career and growth model. Sometimes complacency is the problem. They have been successful, so why change? Sometimes they have no clear vision of the twenty-first century, and so they don't know how they should change. But often fear is a key issue. They see jobs seeming to disappear all around them. They hear horror stories about people who have been downsized or reengineered out of work. They worry about health insurance and the cost of college for their children. So they don't think about growth. They don't think about personal renewal. They don't think about developing whatever leadership potential they have. Instead they cling defensively to what they currently have. In effect, they embrace the past, not the future.

A strategy of embracing the past will probably become increasingly ineffective over the next few decades. Better for most of us to start learning now how to cope with change, to

Implications for the Twenty-first Century

develop whatever leadership potential we have, and to help our organizations in the transformation process. Better for most of us, despite the risks, to leap into the future. And to do so sooner rather than later.

As an observer of life in organizations, I think I can say with some authority that people who are making an effort to embrace the future are a happier lot than those who are clinging to the past. That is not to say that learning how to become a part of the twenty-first-century enterprise is easy. But people who are attempting to grow, to become more comfortable with change, to develop leadership skills—these men and women are typically driven by a sense that they are doing what is right for themselves, their families, and their organizations. That sense of purpose spurs them on and inspires them during rough periods.

And those people at the top of enterprises today who encourage others to leap into the future, who help them overcome natural fears, and who thus expand the leadership capacity in their organizations—these people provide a profoundly important service for the entire human community.

We need more of those people. And we will get them.